Abolitionist Politics and the Coming of the Civil War

ABOLITIONIST POLITICS
AND THE COMING OF THE
CIVIL WAR

James Brewer Stewart

UNIVERSITY OF MASSACHUSETTS PRESS

Amherst

Copyright © 2008 by University of Massachusetts Press
All rights reserved
Printed in the United States of America

LC 2007032380
ISBN 978-1-55849-635-4 (paper); 634-7 (library cloth)

Designed by Sally Nichols
Set in ITC Galliard
Printed and bound by The Maple-Vail Book Manufacturing Group

Library of Congress Cataloging-in-Publication Data
Stewart, James Brewer.
Abolitionist politics and the coming of the Civil War / James Brewer Stewart.
p.   cm.
Includes bibliographical references and index.
ISBN 978-1-55849-635-4 (paper : alk. paper)—ISBN 978-1-55849-634-7
(library cloth : alk. paper)
1. Antislavery movements—United States—History—
18th century.   2. Antislavery movements—United States—History—
19th century.   3. Abolitionists—United States—Biography.
4. Political activists—United States—Biography.
5. Abolitionists—United States—Political activity—History.
6. Radicalism—United States—History.   7. Equality—
United States—History.   8. United States—Politics and
government—1776–1783.   9. United States—Politics and
government—1783–1865.   10. United States—History—
Civil War, 1861–1865—Causes.   I. Title.
E441.S895 2008
973.7'114—dc22   2007032380

British Library Cataloguing in Publication data are available.

To my extraordinary friends who study the abolitionists.
You all know who you are,
and you all have my deepest gratitude.

Contents

Preface

Before the Civil War, slaveholders made themselves into the most powerful, most deeply rooted, and best organized private interest group within
the United States. There should be no surprise in this. Investment in
slavery, in all of its financial manifestations, was exceeded only by investment in real estate. The U.S. Constitution was studded with guarantees
of slavery's perpetuation. Proslavery presidents, senators, and congressional representatives consistently put forward slavery's interests. The vast
majority of white Americans, Northern and Southern alike, accepted the
institution of slavery, believing strongly that "inferior" African Americans were fitted perfectly to their bondage. As most saw it, the very foundation of white Americans' liberty depended on the ongoing subjugation
of the nation's blacks, the nominally free as well as the enslaved.

This volume seeks to evaluate the extent to which a small group of
radical activists, the abolitionist movement, played pivotal roles in turning American politics against this formidable system. To pose the problem another way, it examines what influence the abolitionist movement
might have had in creating the unfolding political crises that led to civil
war. Or, to restate the matter in most general terms, it attempts to assess
the extent to which a small number of deeply committed reformers made
a truly important difference when demanding that their nation face up to
its most excruciating moral problem.

These are all challenging subjects, not easily addressed either indi-
vidually or all at once. Such is particularly true for a book like this one,
designed as it is not only for specialists but also for undergraduates and
graduate students. For these reasons, the essays presented here respond
to these challenging subjects by examining several much more accessible
and specific questions about who the abolitionists were and what their
work involved.

These questions are: What were the abolitionists actually up against when seeking to overthrow slavery and white supremacy? What motivated and sustained them during their long and difficult struggles? What larger historical contexts (religious, social, economic, cultural, and political) influenced their choices and determined their behavior? What roles did extraordinary leaders play in shaping the movement? What were the contributions of abolitionism's unheralded "foot-soldiers"? What political agency did this handful of activists finally exercise on the nation's governing systems, that is, on its elections, on debates in Congress, on state and local politics, and on political culture? What factors ultimately determined, for better or worse, the abolitionists' impact on American politics and the realization of their equalitarian goals?

Each of these questions is a historical perennial. Generations of scholars have wrestled with all of them. What makes this volume distinctive, I hope, is that it brings them all into a common focus to explain in a comprehensive way why the abolitionists' crusade truly mattered.

Hence, this is, above all, a book about meanings. It offers a series of flesh and blood insights into what the movement meant to its leaders, supporters, and most vocal opponents; what it meant to the powerful men who governed the nation and led its political parties; what it meant to the great mass of voters, those (almost entirely white) men whose ballots determined the fates of those politicians; what it meant to those in the North, free African Americans, Native Americans, and women in particular, who found themselves excluded from formal politics; what, in short, the abolitionist movement meant to the deeply and multiply conflicted generation that witnessed the coming of the Civil War.

To promise "flesh and blood insights" is to promise a great deal. In my opinion, satisfying this promise requires seeing deeply into individuals' lives and into relationships between those lives and the changing politics of the nation. For this reason, this volume emphasizes biography. Readers will quickly notice this feature as they read along, and I hope that it magnifies the book's focus, accessibility, and interest. Certain key figures, specifically Wendell Phillips, Hosea Easton, William Lloyd Garrison, Benjamin Roberts, and Joshua R. Giddings, people whose lives I have come to know particularly well, reappear in multiple contexts, their lives (public and private) juxtaposed against the ongoing struggles of abolitionists and the changing political scene. In this way, the book sustains a human interest element that I hope its readers will find enriching. No less important, this biographical emphasis makes possible my attempt to explain abolitionism in "flesh and blood" terms.

A final prefatory note. I have been persuaded to abandon my practice of using quotation marks around the terms "black," "white," and "race" in most cases. My instinct to use them has something to do with the familiar academic assessment that "race is a social construction," a "signifier" rather than a fact. More important, however, I wanted to acknowledge the problem of addressing a wide range of belief on the topic, with some people regarding race as a self-evident fact and others, conscious of their "mixed" backgrounds, resisting the dialectic of black versus white. I hope readers will keep these crucial distinctions in mind as they proceed through the volume.

Acknowledgments

Clark Dougan and John Stauffer made this book possible. Deborah Smith made it considerably better. My warmest thanks go to each of them.

Abolitionist Politics and the Coming of the Civil War

Narratives

Few historical narratives are as complex or as open to conflicting interpretation as those recounting the coming of the Civil War. Though agreeing on the major events is easy enough, disagreement inevitably arises when one asks how these events should be interpreted when determining who and what was responsible for causing that war. This introductory essay narrates the history of the political crisis over slavery from perspectives that members of the abolitionist movement themselves might have recognized as according with their own. It aims to refresh readers about national events that led to the breakup of the Union while offering a broad introductory understanding of the history of the abolitionist movement itself.

From Moral Suasion to Political Confrontation
American Abolitionists and the Problem of Resistance, 1831–1861

In January 1863, as warfare raged between North and South, the great abolitionist orator Wendell Phillips addressed an enormous audience of over ten thousand in Brooklyn, New York. Just days earlier, President Abraham Lincoln, in his Emancipation Proclamation, had defined the destruction of slavery as the North's new and overriding war aim. This decision, Phillips assured his listeners, marked the grand culmination "of a great fight, going on the world over, and which began ages ago . . . between free institutions and caste institutions, Freedom and Democracy against institutions of privilege and class."[1] A serious student of the past, Phillips acknowledged the fact that behind the Emancipation Proclamation lay a long history of opposition to slavery by not only African Americans, free and enslaved, but also by ever-increasing numbers of whites. In Haiti, Cuba, Jamaica, Brazil, and Surinam, slave insurrection helped to catalyze emancipation. Abolition in the United States, by contrast, had its prelude in civil war among whites, not in black insurrection, a result impossible to imagine had not growing numbers of Anglo-Americans before 1861 chosen to resist the institution of slavery directly and to oppose what they feared was its growing dominion over the nation's

Originally published as "From Moral Suasion to Political Confrontation: American Abolitionists and the Problem of Resistance," in David W. Blight, ed., *Passages to Freedom: The Underground Railroad in History and Memory* (Washington, DC: Smithsonian Press, 2004), 67–94. Reprinted with permission.

1. For the biographical treatment of Phillips that informs this essay at numerous points, see James Brewer Stewart, *Wendell Phillips, Liberty's Hero* (Baton Rouge: Louisiana State University Press, 1986; repr. 1998). For the quotation, see Wendell Phillips, "The War for the Union," in *Speeches, Lectures, and Letters* (Boston: Higginson and Lee, 1863), 438–39.

government and civic life. No clearer example of this crucial development can be found than Wendell Phillips himself. For this reason his career provides a useful starting point for considering the development of militant resistance within the abolitionist movement and its influence in pushing Northerners closer, first, to Civil War, and then to abolishing slavery.

This compelling Boston orator burst on to the national stage in 1837 when vociferously denouncing a mob of proslavery rioters in Alton, Illinois, that had murdered the abolitionist editor Elijah Lovejoy. Thereafter, Phillips developed a rich abolitionist career in which he all but covered the spectrum of resistance, legal and extra-legal. On a day-to-day basis, he claimed the role of agitator by making speeches, publishing articles, and petitioning legislatures, all forms of resistance protected by the Constitution's Bill of Rights. At various junctures he relied on these protections to urge defiance of proslavery law and government, to engage in peaceful civil disobedience, and even to give rhetorical encouragement of the use of violence. More specifically, he customarily defied legally sanctioned white supremacy by seating himself in railway cars reserved for "colored only," agitated in favor of desegregating Massachusetts's public facilities (schools in particular), and demanded that citizens organize vigilante actions in the free states to protect against the recapture of fugitive slaves.[2]

All of these actions were the logical consequences of his most fundamental conviction of all—that slavery itself was so heinous a crime in the eyes of God and so fundamental a violation of all principles of American freedom that it ought, by every measure of justice, to be destroyed in the twinkling of an eye. Like all fully committed abolitionists, black and white, Phillips demanded "immediate abolition." By the 1840s and 1850s, he had followed this logic to justify still more militant forms of resistance. Now he announced that moral Americans must deny the legitimacy of the nation's proslavery Constitution, welcome slave revolts in the South, openly defy federal law enforcement officers to prevent the

---

2. Stewart, *Wendell Phillips*; also see Richard Hofstadter, "Wendell Phillips: Patrician as Agitator," in *The American Political Tradition and the Men Who Made It* (New York: Alfred Knopf, 1948), 137–63.

recapture of fugitives, and celebrate the insurrectionist John Brown for his 1859 raid on Harpers Ferry, Virginia.[3]

Most important of all, when Phillips voiced his insurgency the American public paid closest attention, and as the decades passed, increasing numbers of Northerners felt compelled to agree with him. From the mid-1840s onward, Phillips achieved wide renown as an extraordinary orator who presented the most radical abolitionist opinions in a way that audiences always found compelling, even enchanting. "You heard him . . . an hour, two hours, three hours," listeners typically recalled, "and had no consciousness of the passage of time. . . . He steals upon the audience and surprises them into enthusiasm." The fullest testimony to Phillips's preeminence as "abolition's golden trumpet," however, came from slavery's defenders, who feared him as "an infernal machine set to music," an exponent of racial upheaval and political chaos so eloquent in his espousals of resistance that he simply overpowered his listeners' better judgment. "For the present generation, he is a most dangerous agitator," one such critic observed, because he possessed an unerring ability "to take premises we all grant to be true and to weave them into an enchantment of logic from which there is no escape."[4]

But explaining Phillips's remarkable impact involves more than appreciating his oratory. More important, his unusual public appeal documents a broadening agreement among white Northerners about the necessity of resisting slavery. As Phillips's reputation grew, so did both his espousals of resistance and his audiences' receptivity to his ever more militant message. Between 1831, when white "immediate" abolitionists first began mobilizing, and 1860, after that most violent resistor of all, John Brown, had been hanged, powerful insurgent impulses increasingly permeated the abolitionist movement. Much to the advantage of Wendell Phillips as a public speaker, they also radiated ever more powerfully into the broader political culture of the North, a fact that angry slaveholders fully appreciated when voting to secede from the Federal Union. This

---

3. Stewart, *Wendell Phillips*, 117–76.

4. Descriptions of Phillips's oratory are found in ibid., 177–95. Quotations are found in the *Ohio State Journal*, reprinted in *Liberator*, April 5, 1861; also see *Liberator*, December 15, 1850, and February 19, 1855.

essay, therefore, examines the roots of white abolitionists' postures of resistance, the evolving forms that this resistance took, and the reasons why increasing numbers of white Northerners joined with abolitionists like Phillips to register defiance to the slave South.[5]

When launching their movement against slavery in the early 1830s, the first white exponents of "immediate abolitionism" presented themselves as apostles of Christian reconciliation, not as agents of insurgent resistance. Most of these early crusaders drew their inspiration from a wave of Protestant religious revivalism, the Second Great Awakening, which swept the nation in the 1820s. Led by powerful evangelical ministers such as Charles Grandison Finney and Lyman Beecher, this religious outpouring emphasized the individual's free will choice to renounce sin, strive for personal holiness, and then, once "saved," bring God's truth to the "unredeemed" and to combat the evils that sin inevitably perpetuated—drunkenness, impiety, sexual license, and exploitation of the defenseless. In the ears of young white abolitionists-to-be—Congregational revivalists such as Arthur and Lewis Tappan, Theodore Dwight Weld, and Elizur Wright Jr., Baptists such as William Lloyd Garrison, and radical Quakers such as Lucretia Mott and John Greenleaf Whittier—these doctrines confirmed that slavery was the most God-defying of all sins and the most corrosive behavior of all to harmony among his people.[6]

In what other system did exploitation of the defenseless occur more brazenly? Where was sexual wantonness more rampant than in the debauchery by masters of their female slaves? Where was impiety more deliberately fostered than in masters' refusals to permit their slaves to read the Scriptures? Where was brutality more evident than in the master's heavy use of whips, or his willingness to dismember the slaves'

5. Vast amounts have been written about the development of antislavery ideology in the free states and secessionist ideology in the South in the 1840s and 1850s. Two fine introductions are Eric Foner, *Free Soil, Free Labor, Free Men: The Ideology of the Republican Party before the Civil War* (New York: Oxford University Press, 1970); and William J. Cooper Jr., *The South and the Politics of Slavery, 1828–1856* (Baton Rouge: Louisiana State University Press, 1978).

6. The fullest recent treatment of the development of immediatist religious sensibility is Robert B. Abzug, *Cosmos Crumbling: American Reform and the Religious Imagination* (New York: Oxford University Press, 1994). See also Bertram Wyatt-Brown, *Lewis Tappan and the Evangelical War against Slavery* (Cleveland, OH: Press of Case Western Reserve, 1969), 78–125; and Ronald Walters, *The Antislavery Appeal: Abolitionism after 1830* (Baltimore: Johns Hopkins University Press, 1978).

ties of family? The solution to all these terrible questions was the truth of "immediate emancipation," pressed urgently upon the slumbering consciences of American citizens, slaveholders and nonslaveholders alike, by means of peaceful exhortations of Christian morality.[7]

Calling this strategy "moral suasion," these neophyte abolitionists believed that theirs was a message of healing and reconciliation to be delivered by Christian peacemakers, not by divisive insurgents. Their goal was not simply to resist slavery but actually to obliterate it, rapidly and forever. Their method was to touch the (presumably) guilty and therefore receptive consciences of slaveholders with appeals for "immediate emancipation," inspire masters voluntarily to release their slaves and thereby lead the nation into a redemptive new era of Christian reconciliation and moral harmony. Guided by such visions, they quite naturally insisted that "immediate emancipation" would do away with racial conflict by ending the bitter enmity between masters and slaves and relieve dangerous political tensions already inflaming North against South. "Our object is to save life, not destroy it," William Lloyd Garrison stressed in 1831. "Make the slave free and every inducement to revolt is taken away, every possibility ended for servile as well as civil war." Moreover, they felt certain that the practice of "immediatism" would enrich daily living for everyone by expanding adherence to time-honored values to which morally upright citizens already held fast. As Garrison sharply questioned, "Are we then fanatics because we cry 'Do not rob! Do not murder!'?" And finally, immediate abolitionists saw themselves as harmonizers, not insurgents, because the vast majority of them forswore violent resistance. The American Anti-Slavery Society's founding declaration, published in 1833 made this requirement clear when its signers pledged to reject "the use of all carnal weapons" and to adhere to Christian principles that forbade "the doing of evil that good may come." "Immediatists," in short, saw themselves not as resisting slavery by responding to it reactively but instead as uprooting it by spiritually revolutionizing the corrupted values of its practitioners and supporters.[8]

---

7. For the historical contexts that gave rise to these feelings of empathy, see Elizabeth B. Clark, " 'The Sacred Rights of the Weak': Pain, Sympathy, and the Culture of Individual Rights in Antebellum America," *Journal of American History* 82 (1995): 463–93.

8. Garrison quoted in *Liberator*, August 7, 1832, February 2, 1833, and December 14, 1833.

By adopting Christian pacifism and regarding themselves as revolutionary peacemakers, these earliest white immediatists woefully underestimated the power of the forces opposing them. Well before they launched their crusade, slavery had secured formidable dominance in the nation's economy and political culture. To challenge so deeply entrenched and powerful an institution eventually meant adopting postures of intransigence for which these abolitionists were, initially, wholly unprepared. A review of slavery's actual position within the nation's political economy and culture suggests why.

From the 1830s until the onset of the Civil War, enslaved humans constituted the nation's second largest form of capital investment, exceeded only by investment in land itself. After 1810, when Eli Whitney's gin had opened vast new opportunities for planters to adapt slave labor to an important new commodity, cotton had quickly replaced rice and tobacco as the South's most lucrative product. Slavery's geographical center shifted rapidly southwestward from Virginia and Maryland into the newly admitted states of Mississippi, Alabama, Louisiana, Missouri, and Arkansas. Multiplying slave populations mirrored this expanding geography. In 1790, the nation's enslaved had numbered six hundred thousand. By 1830, they counted for close to two million and were concentrated increasingly in these newly developing western lands. To hasten this process, masters developed a far-flung interstate slave trade by uprooting enslaved families in the upper South and selling their scattered members to eager buyers on the "cotton frontier." Meantime, in New England, wealthy industrial entrepreneurs with names such as Lowell, Appleton, and Lawrence linked southwestern cotton and slavery to their own region's emerging leadership in the industrial revolution. Throughout the 1830s, they established water-powered textile mills across New England that transformed raw cotton into fabric that clothed ever-increasing millions of Americans, thereby uniting North with South in ever-tightening bonds of commerce, investment, and credit.[9]

---

9. For deeper explanations of these trends, see John Ashworth, *Slavery, Capitalism, and Politics in the Antebellum Republic*, vol. 1, *Commerce and Compromise, 1820–1850* (New York: Cambridge University Press, 1995); Walter Johnson, *Soul by Soul: Life Inside the Antebellum Slave Mart* (New York: Cambridge University Press, 1999); and Thomas O'Connor, *The Lords of the Loom: The Cotton Whigs and the Coming of the Civil War* (New York: Alfred Knopf, 1968).

In politics as in the economy, slaveholding interests predominated as the nation expanded its boundaries and consolidated its systems of government. Back in 1787, the framers of the U.S. Constitution had provided slavery with legal legitimacy and significant political advantage that became increasingly obvious during the antebellum years. Article Four confirmed masters' rights to recover runaways, and the Tenth Amendment forbade the federal government to interfere with slavery on the state level. The former provision insured the legal sanctity of slaves as property and the latter gave slaveholders ample constitutional support for adding new slave states to the Federal Union. Most crucially, the Constitution guaranteed slaveholders political power that far exceeded their actual numbers when providing, in Article One, that in addition to the free population, three-fifths of the slave population also be counted for purposes of taxation and representation in the House of Representatives. This imposing advantage for Southern planters took on still greater importance in the 1830s when politicians assembled a national two-party system based on universal white manhood suffrage.[10]

The men who perfected this expansive new approach to politics competed as Whigs and Democrats. Influential among them were representatives of the same elite groups that underwrote slavery's southwestern expansion and fostered the economic transformation so closely related to slavery—Northern industrialization. Rousing unprecedented numbers of voters by organizing speakers, parades and rallies, barbecues, and partisan newspapers, their two parties offered contrasting approaches to fiscal policy, banking, tariffs, the opening of western lands, and support for roads and canals. Concerning slavery, however, their differences were superficial. Led by the slaveholding war hero Andrew Jackson and organized by talented party operatives in both sections, Democrats across the nation stood foursquare behind the institution. Whigs both North and South sometimes phrased their support in more measured accents when embracing the leadership of the Kentucky planter–politician Henry Clay and Daniel Webster, New England's powerful spokesman for

---

10. A full, recent discussion of the Constitution's relationship to slavery is Paul Finkelman, *Slavery and the Founders: Race and Liberty in the Age of Jefferson* (London M. E. Sharp, 1996). For the broader implications of slavery's relationship to federal governance, see Leonard L. Richards, *The Slave Power: The Free North and Southern Domination* (Baton Rouge: Louisiana State University Press, 2000).

industrialization. Strategies for victory required both parties to mobilize a white majority of voters that encompassed both regions. This, in turn, led politicians to suppress sectionally divisive disagreements over slavery and to appeal forcefully to powerful new ideologies of white supremacy that circulated freely in both North and South. As the 1830s opened and abolitionists launched their crusade, deepening racial prejudice even more than slavery's entrenched positions in politics and the economy secured it as the nation's most formidable institution.[11]

In the South, of course, it had long been established that heavily enforced white supremacy constituted the cornerstone of a free, "white" society. By contrast, the racial tensions that developed in the 1820s in the North were of a much newer sort. As urban life in the North rapidly grew more complicated during this decade, feelings of white supremacy and conflict between people of differing colors grew increasingly chronic as well. In Northern cities, industrialization fostered a rapid transition from artisan work to wage labor, which, in turn, attracted waves of immigrants from all over the British Isles, particularly from Ireland. When encountering the traumas of adjustment to unfamiliar circumstances, these newly arrived workers saw in the "blackness" of their African American neighbors unwelcome competition in a tightening labor market and, even more important, a mirror of their diminishing ability to shape their own futures as "independent" men. Irish Catholics in particular feared personal "enslavement" to the Protestant "bosses" who paid their wages. Acting on these anxieties, they claimed to be "white" just like all other presumably "free" citizens and then asserted this "whiteness" through acts of aggression against free blacks. On the opposite end of the social spectrum, elite white ministers, lawyers, and businessmen noted these growing frictions and increasingly convinced themselves that free blacks constituted an ever more turbulent, dangerous people. Such blacks should be encouraged to "return" to Africa under the auspices of the

---

11. See John M. McFaul, "Expedience vs. Morality: Jacksonian Politics and Slavery," *Journal of American History* 62 (1975): 24–39; Michael F. Holt, *The Political Crisis of the 1850s* (New York: Norton, 1978), 17–33; and Leonard L. Richards, "Jacksonians and Slavery," in Lewis Perry and Michael Fellman, eds., *Antislavery Reconsidered: New Perspectives on the Abolitionists* (Baton Rouge: Louisiana State University Press, 1978), 99–118.

American Colonization Society, a "benevolent" movement favored by prominent Northerners.

Free blacks, for their part, refused to abandon their hard-fought struggles, dating from the American Revolution, to claim full citizenship and build "respectable" communities around their churches, schools, and voluntary associations. In their view, invitations to resettle in Africa were gross insults and ominous signs that whites were planning their forced deportation. Threats by these white elitists as well as by white rabble required sternest responses.[12]

These volatile racial tensions turned the 1820s into a decade of white racial tyranny. Lower-class whites felt a mounting impunity to harass, abuse, vandalize, and even murder. Typical were the Philadelphia rioters in 1824 who hurled garbage and paving stones when driving away their dark-skinned fellow citizens from the Fourth of July ceremonies in which everyone had, until then, participated amicably. Particularly horrifying was the Cincinnati "race riot" of 1829. Armed mobs returned for three successive nights to terrorize black neighborhoods, leaving homes and churches in rubble, several dead, and more than six hundred in stupefied exile, some permanently to Lower Canada. While less disastrous incidents disrupted other major cities such as New York, Boston, and Hartford, racial bigotry overtook state legislatures in the North as politicians methodically stripped free blacks of their citizenship. Legislators in Ohio, Indiana, and Illinois opened the franchise to all white men while simultaneously enacting "black codes" that all but eliminated the political rights of free blacks. Pennsylvania, New York, and Connecticut likewise approved universal white manhood suffrage while requiring blacks to "qualify" as voters by satisfying all-but-impossible property requirements. Newspapers, bar rooms, and theaters suddenly teemed with viciously racist cartoons and satires. White Americans in the North

---

12. See David Roediger, *The Wages of Whiteness: Race and the Making of the America Working Class* (New York: Verso Press, 1997); Joanne Pope Melish, *Disowning Slavery: Gradual Emancipation and Race in New England* (Ithaca: Cornell University Press, 1998); Richard S. Newman, *The Transformation of Abolitionism: Fighting Slavery in the Early Republic* (Chapel Hill: University of North Carolina Press, 2002); Patrick Rael, *Black Identity and Black Protest in the Antebellum North* (Chapel Hill: University of North Carolina Press, 2002); and James Oliver Horton and Lois Horton, *In Hope of Liberty: Culture, Community, and Protest among Northern Free Blacks, 1700–1860* (New York: Oxford University Press, 1997).

no less than in the South had now made color the primary criterion for living unchallenged or in oppression on "free" American soil.[13]

With the nation's most powerful institutions so tightly aligned in support of slavery and white supremacy, it is clear that young white abolitionists were profoundly self-deceived when characterizing their work as "the destruction of error by the potency of truth—the overthrow of prejudice by the power of love—the abolition of slavery by the spirit of repentance." When so contending, they were deeply sincere and grievously wrong. To crusade for slavery's rapid obliteration was, in truth, to stimulate not "the power of love" and "repentance" but instead the opposition of an overwhelming number of powerful enemies—the entire political system, the nation's most potent economic interests, the society's most influential elites, and a popular political culture in the North more deeply suffused with racial bigotry than at any previous time in the nation's history. Three headline events that opened the 1830s ominously suggested what the future actually held for these young idealists.[14]

The first, the Nullification Crisis in South Carolina (1828–1832), revealed just how enraged by "immediate abolitionism" slaveholders were likely to become. Well before the start of the abolitionists' crusade, extremist planters in this state were already mobilizing armies and threatening secession to protect slavery from "meddling outsiders" and the power of the federal government. The second, involving the militant pamphleteer David Walker, highlighted just how desperate race relations across the nation had actually become. Walker published his *Appeal to the Colored Citizens of the World*, in Boston in 1829 and 1830, and immediately it became a landmark expression of African American political ideology. With angry accents and uncompromising ideas, Walker excoriated whites for their bigotry and free blacks for their apathy, calling, in extreme circumstances, for slaves to rise in violence. As Walker made all too clear, white oppression was driving black leaders in the free states to desperation even as angry planters closed ranks around their "peculiar

---

13. In addition to titles in the previous note, see Leon Litwack, *North of Slavery: The Negro in the Free States, 1790–1860* (New York: Oxford University Press, 1965).

14. For the fullest statement of white supremacy's multiplying influences on political culture in the early republic, see Alexander Saxton, *The Rise and Fall of the White Republic* (New York: Verso Press, 1978).

institution." Then in late 1831, in Southampton County, Virginia, the insurrectionist Nat Turner led a bloody uprising that accounted for the lives of fifty-five whites and a far greater number of blacks. Yet when responding to all this turmoil, the newly committed immediatist Samuel E. Sewell saw only portents of redemption, offering the prediction in that "the whole system of slavery will fall to pieces with a rapidity that will astonish." Garrison even went so far as to prognosticate that "the day is not far off when black skin will be not simply endurable, but even popular!"[15] To these "Bible believing" abolitionists, sectional crisis and racial upheaval did not portend disaster but instead gave reassurance that a God who hated slavery was making his anger manifest.

For all its obviousness, this enormous naiveté was actually one of the abolitionists' greatest initial strengths. Their fervent belief that God would make all things right as slavery rapidly was swept aside drove them as nothing else could have to shoulder otherwise unthinkable tasks and endure otherwise unimaginable risks. Thus, for a full six years, from 1831 through 1837, abolitionists made themselves into whirlwinds of agitation. Fully intent on uprooting, not simply resisting, the institution of slavery, they energetically canvassed the free states, creating hundreds of antislavery societies, dozens of newspapers, blizzards of pamphlets and broadsides, and innumerable local controversies over the "sin of slavery." Working closely with long-established groups of free African American activists in the Northern cities, they also struck directly at what they termed "color phobia" by founding schools, churches, and voluntary associations in which people of all ancestries and both genders associated freely. In the same spirit, abolitionists met as "promiscuous assemblies" (as detractors called them) with men mixing publicly with women and light-skinned people with dark. By 1835, abolitionists had exploited the U.S. Postal Service to flood slaveholders' mailboxes with warnings of impending damnation and pleas to repent and emancipate. The next year they launched the "Great Petition Campaign," sending to the U.S.

---

15. For nullification, see William W. Freenling, *Prelude to Civil War: The Nullification Crisis in South Carolina, 1816–1836* (New York: Oxford University Press, 1969). For Walker, see Peter Hinks, *To Awaken My Afflicted Brethren: David Walker and the Problem of Antebellum Slave Resistance* (University Park: Pennsylvania State University Press, 1997); and Samuel E. Sewall to Samuel J. May, July 7, 1831, Antislavery Collection, Boston Public Library. For Garrison quotation, see *Liberator*, April 16, 1832.

House of Representatives a tidal wave of citizen requests that Congress legislate against the interests of slavery.[16]

Judged by the urgency of the issues they raised and the controversies they provoked, the abolitionists' initial impact vastly exceeded their modest numbers. (Never were fully engaged immediatists any more than a minuscule portion of the North's population.) Judged by their self-professed goals and expectations, however, these first campaigns led them straight to a disaster that changed their movement forever. Elected officials from President Andrew Jackson on down, civic leaders of every variety, ministers from nearly all denominations, and masses of ordinary people in both North and South responded to "immediatism" with a harrowing barrage of repression. In response, white abolitionists had no choice but to redirect their movement from a crusade for rapid emancipation to a long-term resistance struggle against the intractable tyranny of slavery and white supremacy.

In the slave states, mobs urged on by elected officials invaded post offices and burned abolitionist mailings while state legislatures voted cash bounties for the capture of leading abolitionists. White Southerners suspected of "abolitionist sympathies" faced harassment, indictment, and sometimes the whip or the tar-bucket as public criticism of slavery all but ended throughout the Lower South. Meanwhile, in Washington, D.C., Whigs and Democrats joined in 1836 to pass a "gag rule" that prohibited all discussion of abolitionists' petitions to the House of Representatives, a truly unprecedented restriction of citizens' freedom of political expression. In elections across the nation these same two parties competed for votes by stressing antiabolitionism and white supremacy as central to their beliefs. This sudden emergence of intensely competitive two-party politics based on mass participation and universal white manhood suffrage was thus inextricably tied to campaigns to suppress the abolitionist movement and visit still further woe on people of dark complexion.[17]

---

16. For an overview of these activities, see James Brewer Stewart, *Holy Warriors: The Abolitionists and American Slavery* (New York: Hill and Wang, 1996), 51–74.

17. Valuable accounts of these developments include Leonard L. Richards, *"Gentlemen of Property and Standing": Antiabolitionist Mobs in Jacksonian America* (New York: Oxford University Press, 1970); William Lee Miller, *Arguing about Slavery: The Great Battle in the United States Congress* (New York:

While politicians legislated against "immediatism" and campaigned for white men's votes, mayhem erupted in cities and towns throughout the free states. Utica, Boston, Philadelphia, Rochester, Pittsburgh, and Syracuse witnessed unruly gangs that disrupted abolitionists' meetings and threatened black citizens with rocks, garbage, fists, and firebrands. Similar conflicts erupted in dozens of small towns and crossroads villages as well. When the immediatist Prudence Crandall tried to establish an academy for young women of color in one such hamlet, Canterbury, Connecticut, in 1831 and 1832, her neighbors tried to burn her schoolhouse and ultimately succeeded in driving her from the state. Soon thereafter, the state legislature made schools such as Crandall's illegal and passed laws restricting abolitionists' rights to move freely within the state. In Dover, New Hampshire, the local residents used a brace of oxen to destroy a building that abolitionists had purchased to house a school open to black students as well as to whites, while in 1831, in New Haven, Connecticut, simply the proposal by abolitionists to develop a manual-labor school for young black men provoked stern condemnation from Yale University's administrators, an attack on a home owned by Arthur Tappan, and two days of racial warfare in the city's black neighborhoods. On and on the mayhem went. For abolitionists whatever their color, disillusionment compounded as the damage mounted.[18]

In Hartford, in 1836, for example, the Reverend Hosea Easton surveyed the smoking rubble of what had been the First Congregational Church, his African American congregation's treasured symbol of spirituality and community achievement. In this instance, white marauders did not even bother to use "abolitionism" as their pretext when deploying arson against free people of color. In New York City in 1834 and (again) in Cincinnati in 1836, sheriffs and constabularies looked on unconcerned as buildings in black neighborhoods burned, pillagers looted, and people of color either hid or fled. Unlike in the riots of the 1820s, however, these marauders sought out white abolitionists as well as blacks. In New York

---

Oxford University Press, 1996); and Leonard L. Richards, *The Life and Times of John Quincy Adams* (New York: Oxford University Press, 1986).

18. See Richards, *"Gentlemen of Property and Standing"*; and James Brewer Stewart, "The Emergence of Racial Modernity and the Rise of the White North," *Journal of the Early Republic* 18 (Summer 1998): 202–11.

City the targets were Arthur and Lewis Tappan, millionaire merchants and militant white immediatists who underwrote a broad medley of abolitionist projects and associations. In Cincinnati, the victim was James G. Birney, editor of the immediatist newspaper, the *Philanthropist*. Mobs there repeatedly sacked his office and hurled his printing press into the Ohio River. A practitioner of "non-resistance," Birney himself escaped unharmed though his offices did not, and neither, predictably, did the dwellings and businesses of Cincinnati's African Americans.[19]

Another embattled abolitionist, however, the editor Elijah Lovejoy, scorned "non-resistance" as mobs in Alton, Illinois, repeatedly destroyed his presses and threatened his life in 1837. Fronting on the Mississippi River and located in the southernmost part of the state, Alton (like Cincinnati) teemed with men who supported slavery fervently, who deeply despised abolitionists, and who were eager to do Elijah Lovejoy harm. Seizing his rifle, Lovejoy descended from his second-story office toward his tormentors as they attempted to flush him out with arson. As he descended, they cut him down with a fusillade of gunfire. Thus did white abolitionism enroll its first "martyr." Thus, too, did this unprecedented movement for racial equality begin a momentous transition from a hopeful religious crusade to eradicate slavery to a dogged struggle to resist this formidable institution, protected as it so heavily was by religious denominations, the state, the courts, the two political parties, the bigoted opinions of most white Americans, and now by vigilante violence. In the wake of Lovejoy's murder, Garrison captured perfectly the shocked realization sweeping through the movement that abolitionists must now rethink and revise their fundamental premises: "When we first unfurled the banner of the *Liberator* . . . we did not anticipate that, in order to protect southern slavery, the free states would voluntarily trample under foot all law and order, and government, or brand the advocates of universal liberty as incendiaries and outlaws. . . . It did not occur to us that almost every religious sect, and every political party would side with the oppressor."[20]

19. Ibid. See also George R. Price and James Brewer Stewart, *To Heal the Scourge of Prejudice: The Life and Writings of Hosea Easton* (Amherst: University of Massachusetts Press, 1999), 16–25.

20. For Lovejoy, see Merton L. Dillon, *Elijah Lovejoy: Abolitionist Editor* (Champaign-Urbana: University of Illinois Press, 1965). Also see *Liberator*, December 8, 1837.

Historians have provided clear accounts of the deep divisions that finally shattered the white abolitionist movement once its leaders began acting on this realization. By 1840, three quarreling factions had emerged. One, led by Garrison, argued that the nation's values had now been revealed to be so utterly corrupted that abolitionists must flee from proslavery churches, spurn the proslavery political process, and oppose the proslavery Federal Union with demands for Northern secession. Religious perfectionism and espousals of female equality also seasoned this iconoclastic ideology (referred to as "Garrisonianism" by supporters and detractors alike), and sustained the American Anti-Slavery Society throughout the antebellum decades. A second group, headed by James G. Birney and others, insisted that abolitionists must shift their fight to the political arena, where voters should be exhorted to "vote as they prayed and pray as they voted" for immediate emancipation. This was possible, as they now argued, because the U.S. Constitution derived its organic authority from the Declaration of Independence's assertion that "all men" are "created equal" and thus actually supported a legislative end to slavery. Their Liberty Party first campaigned for the presidency in 1840, garnering no more than seventy-five hundred votes, but continued, undaunted, to field immediatist candidates up to and including the 1860 election of Abraham Lincoln. And finally, a third group, led by Lewis Tappan, founded the American and Foreign Anti-Slavery Society in the hope of sustaining the original version of "moral suasion." To them, Garrisonians were heretical iconoclasts who had deflected the crusade for slave emancipation into a morass of perfectionist, anticlerical heresy while the Liberty Party's initiatives pandered dangerously to proslavery voters.[21]

Yet for all their conflicting approaches, all three factions still felt they relied, just as abolitionists always had, on moral appeals against slavery to "the nation's conscience." All, in other words, saw themselves as remaining wedded to "moral suasion." Certainly none felt suddenly compelled to advocate broadly conceived programs of overt resistance, let

---

21. The fullest, most perceptive analysis of these abolitionist factions and their respective beliefs remains Aileen Kraditor, *Means and Ends in American Abolitionism: Garrison and His Critics on Strategy and Tactics, 1835–1854* (1969; repr., New York: Ivan Dee, 1989).

alone resort to violence. Nevertheless, by the later 1830s, everything had changed, which is precisely what the murder of Elijah Lovejoy symbolized. A seven-year reign of terror now forced these white immediatists to begin exploring, not new approaches for rapidly abolishing slavery, but instead how to grapple successfully with this intransigent institution and its equally intransigent alter ego, white supremacy. In short, they started to fashion the tools of resistance. When Wendell Phillip responded to Lovejoy's death by dramatically embracing the abolitionist cause in 1837, his reasons for so doing illustrate how this process began.[22]

What disturbed Phillips most about Lovejoy's murder was not the sin of slavery (heinous though he thought it was) but instead the institution's seemingly unstoppable capacity to corrupt every aspect of American life, even to the point of destroying those who opposed it in the North, as well as those it kept in chains. The mob that murdered Lovejoy, Phillips insisted, was driven by a soulless, unchecked power in human relations, founded in tyranny, that spread increasing destruction all over America— the institution of slavery. Here, he believed, was "an abnormal element" in American political culture that "no one had counted in. No check and no balance had been provided" in the nation's laws or government to stem its corrupting influences. Phillips, as he explained, suddenly became "conscious that I was in the presence of a power whose motto was victory or death." All that stood between slavery's unchallenged predominance and the last glimmerings of American liberty, according to Phillips, were the abolitionists themselves, few, despised, and powerless though they were.

When Phillips henceforth devoted his life to turning public opinion against slavery with compelling speeches, his participation injected a sharp new tone of resistance to abolitionism. He foreswore pacifism, celebrated the nation's revolutionary traditions of patriotic blood sacrifice, and sought effective political tactics for resisting the "unchecked" onslaught of slavery in the free states. Though Phillips was a staunch Garrisonian when it came to Northern disunion and women's rights, his

---

22. This interpretation of the evolution of white abolitionism is developed most fully in James Brewer Stewart, "Peaceful Hopes and Violent Experiences: The Evolution of Radical and Reforming Abolitionism," *Civil War History* 17 (December 1971): 293–309.

militance spoke to a rapidly growing fear among abolitionists and Northerners more generally that slavery's pernicious influences (race riot, "gag rules," and legislated repression) would surely overwhelm the free states as it had the South unless a new generation of abolitionist patriots rallied to resist it. The contrast between this desperate viewpoint and Garrison's ebullient prediction, six years earlier, that "black skin will soon be not simply endurable, but even popular" measures well how far abolitionists had journeyed from their original hopes of glorious victory.[23]

Yet even as this momentous transition proceeded, African American activists involved in the abolitionist movement also reordered their assumptions and changed direction in a manner that pushed their white associates still further along the pathways of resistance. A review of the evolving roles of Northern black abolitionists in the early white-dominated immediatist movement makes clear how this process unfolded.

From the beginning, black activists such as James Forten, Hosea Easton, and William Watkins had gravely doubted the assumptions of the white "immediatists" that Southern planters would embrace "moral suasion" or that Northern whites would soon cast off their "color phobia." Their long and bitter trials with racial tyranny hardly fostered such optimism. Nevertheless, several reasons compelled them to respond with great enthusiasm to the initial white crusade for "moral suasion." One such incentive involved the white abolitionists' implacable hostility to the American Colonization Society.[24]

No proposition more openly scorned free blacks' claims to citizenship than the idea that they be "returned" to their "homeland" across the ocean, which is exactly what the American Colonization Society proposed. Like so many of the North's black activists, these leaders regarded their ongoing struggles as being rooted in the irrevocable achievement of citizenship that had been attained for all people of color by "colored patriots" who had rallied to the cause during the American Revolution. Wedded to this conviction, they hailed the white immediatists' full-throated condemnations of the American Colonization Society and

---

23. On this aspect of Phillips's career, see Stewart, *Wendell Phillips*, 54–76. For Garrison quotation, see Garrison to Henry Benson, August 29, 1831, Antislavery Collection, Boston Public Library.

24. The best and most recent examination of black abolitionists' resistance to colonization, and of their activism prior to the 1830s, is Newman, *Transformation of American Abolitionism*.

joined them to amplify it as fully as they could. Overburdened by racial bigotry, these Northern black activists also felt understandably heartened by the sudden appearance of whites who took their views seriously when inviting them to abolitionist meetings and publishing their thoughts in the abolitionist press. Black and white abolitionists discovered, furthermore, that they shared many of the same moral values, those stressing piety, thrift, sobriety, self-control, and self-improvement. Black leaders had long been accustomed to advocating these qualities when exhorting their communities to sustain programs of self-help in order to "uplift" themselves to ever higher levels of "respectability." That meant building and strengthening churches and schools as well as sponsoring adult education groups, fraternal organizations, and temperance societies. "Uplift" constituted an ideology well suited not only for fortifying communities of color in Northern cities but also for inviting close collaboration between black community leaders and white immediatists to foster African American "respectability" as a demonstration of racial equality.[25]

Never before in the nation's history had people of color and Euro-Americans worked together so closely for racially egalitarian goals of "uplift" and "respectability." Together they moved decisively during the early 1830s in cities throughout the free states to establish academies, colleges, and libraries and to foster temperance societies and underwrite cultural enrichments such as debating societies, literary clubs, and "juvenile associations." One monument to this brief crescendo of interracial creativity endures to this day, Oberlin College, founded in 1835 as the nation's first institution of higher learning open to students of both genders and of all skin colors. But Oberlin, unfortunately, is all that endures. On every other front, these unprecedented efforts to face down "color phobia" with racial "uplift" backfired by giving the mightiest impetus of all to fears of racial "amalgamation" and the most compelling motives for applying mob rule and legislated repression.[26]

Thus, while white immediatists were responding to racial tyranny by moving beyond "moral suasion," their African American colleagues felt

---

25. For these developments, and for excellent recent studies of black as well as white abolitionism, see ibid.; Rael, *Black Identity and Black Protest*; and Paul Goodman, *Of One Blood: The Abolitionists and the Origins of Racial Equality* (Berkeley: University of California Press, 1998).

26. Goodman, *Of One Blood*, 11–65.

driven to recognize "uplift's" costly limitations and to design militant new approaches of their own. Both groups, in other words, drastically revised their initial strategies and tactics. Most white immediatists turned from efforts to convert the planter class to efforts to resist and unmask slavery's Northern sources of power, as Wendell Phillips did. Northern black activists, for their part, continued to seek the "uplifting" of their communities but only as part of militant new campaigns to face down bigots, demand the rights of citizenship, and assist individual slaves in escaping their masters. On every front, and among those of every complexion, abolitionists displayed an ever more militant spirit of resistance from the 1840s on.

A new generation of talented African American activists that rose to leadership in the 1840s did much to move abolitionism in these new directions. As often as not, these forceful black abolitionists now set agendas for their white associates and had no time for their paternalistic impulses. This was dramatic reversal from the early years of "moral suasion" and African American "uplift" when whites made the most of the basic decisions and expressed, unchallenged, their sense of cultural superiority. Some, like James McCune Smith, Martin Delany, and James W.C. Pennington, had Northern roots and abolitionist educations while others, notably Frederick Douglass, Samuel Ringgold Ward, Sojourner Truth, and Henry Highland Garnet, were survivors of slavery. Whatever their backgrounds, they seldom flinched when confronted by Northern bigotry and they quickly began involving whites like Wendell Phillips in protracted struggles to resist segregation.[27]

It was black David Ruggles, for example, who first refused in 1841 to sit in the "colored-only" sections of steamboats and railway cars operating in Massachusetts. After being physically ejected from several of these conveyances, he filed a series of antidiscrimination lawsuits and invited Phillips and other leading white abolitionists to join him in campaigns of

---

27. The best studies of black abolitionism and its transformation in the 1840s and 1850s are Jane H. Pease and William H. Pease, *They Who Would Be Free: Blacks' Search for Freedom, 1831–1861* (New York: Oxford University Press, 1974); Benjamin Quarles, *The Black Abolitionists* (New York: Oxford University Press, 1965); R. J. M. Blackett, *Building an Antislavery Wall: Black Americans in the Atlantic Abolitionist Movement, 1830–1860* (Baton Rouge: Louisiana State University Press, 1983); Donald Yacovone, "The Transformation of the Black Temperance Movement, 1827–1854," *Journal of the Early Republic* 8 (Fall 1988): 282–97; and Julie Winch, *Philadelphia's Black Elite: Activism, Accommodation, and the Struggle for Autonomy* (Philadelphia: University of Pennsylvania Press, 1988).

civil disobedience. On a warm August day that same year, Phillips thus found himself on the open air "Negro deck" of a steamer bound to New Bedford, Massachusetts, defying segregation by mingling with forty black and white abolitionists, William Lloyd Garrison and Frederick Douglass prominent among them. Soon thereafter individual acts of civil disobedience and concerted efforts by integrated groups against segregated transportation systems spread throughout New England and quickly expanded to address the issue of segregation in the public schools.[28]

In the early 1840s black abolitionists began rallying their communities to boycott segregated schools and, again, found useful allies in white abolitionists. In Massachusetts towns such as Salem, Lynn, New Bedford, and Nantucket such boycotts proved successful, as did another led by Frederick Douglass in Rochester, New York. The most significant struggle, however, took place in Boston, led by previously obscure local blacks and supported by some of the North's most prominent whites. Black abolitionists William C. Nell and John T. Hilton began an antisegregation petition campaign in 1846 to the Boston School Committee, and when their petitions were rejected they launched boycotts and rallied parents in mass demonstrations to prevent students from registering for segregated classes. When the secretary of the Massachusetts School Board, Horace Mann, tried to broker a compromise, Wendell Phillips intervened with bitterly sarcastic speeches and editorials. Meanwhile black and white activists merged assets and expertise to force desegregation by bringing expensive lawsuits. In 1849, black attorney Robert Morris and white attorney Charles Sumner brought a suit against the Boston School Committee on behalf of Benjamin Roberts, whose five-year-old daughter walked each day past five "all-white" elementary schools before arriving at the grossly inferior "colored school" to which she had been assigned. Although these lawsuits failed, continuing agitation led by Phillips and Garrison and energized black communities led by Roberts and Nell finally resulted in victory, when, in 1855, the Massachusetts legislature voted to outlaw segregation in public schools across the state.[29]

28. Carleton Mabee, *The Non-Violent Abolitionists from 1830 through the Civil War* (New York: Macmillan, 1970), and Stewart, *Holy Warriors*, 127–49.

29. Donald M. Jacobs, "The Nineteenth-Century Struggle over School Segregation in Boston," *Journal of Negro Education* 39 (1970): 76–85; Stewart, *Wendell Phillips*, 99–100.

When abolitionists turned their efforts to Northern politics, however, the results were much less satisfying. During the early and mid-1840s, for example, black abolitionist Henry Highland Garnet led a sustained campaign to force the repeal of New York State's two-hundred-dollar property qualification required of all black men who would exercise the franchise. The white abolitionists who came forward to assist him were not Garrisonians but leaders of the emancipationist Liberty Party, such as Henry Brewster Stanton, Joshua Leavitt, and Alvin Stewart—just one of many instances when white Liberty Party members supported black activists' efforts to resist and repeal discriminatory laws. Their efforts resulted in a statewide referendum to repeal the restriction, which whites then rejected in 1846 by a nearly 2-to-1 margin, a fair measure of the power of racial tyranny in one significant free state. In Pennsylvania, white opinion stymied a similar effort before it ever reached the voters.[30]

As abolitionists of all backgrounds knew well, none of these struggles did anything obvious to force emancipation in the South. On a deeper level, however, their challenges to their region's boundaries of inequality magnified as nothing else could a growing conflict of fundamental values between the "free" North and the "slave" South. Below the Mason-Dixon line, granted, slavery continued to flourish and expand in the absence of organized opposition of any sort. But above it, especially in New England, in upstate New York, and in northern Ohio, militant blacks were struggling to liberate themselves from humiliating denials of their citizenship and were joining whites pledged to "immediate abolition" in sustained campaigns to make the law serve racial justice. And most significantly, as in Massachusetts, sometimes they succeeded. To be sure, as the abolitionists' defeat in New York State made clear, the free states remained mired in white supremacy at practically every level. This was particularly so in cities, in deeply conservative Connecticut, in "downstate" New York, and in the central and southern regions of states such as Ohio, Pennsylvania, Indiana, and Illinois. Yet even in these locales, attorneys such as Ohio's Salmon Chase occasionally put their legal expertise at the disposal of African Americans ensnared in a highly prejudicial legal system. Southern congressmen and senators, in turn, marked

---

30. Litwack, *North of Slavery*, 64–112.

these multiplying signs of racial insurgency within the free states and found them increasingly disturbing. In this manner, the abolitionists' turn from reform to resistance increasingly distressed the white South and its supporters during the 1840s and 1850s.[31]

Short of black insurrection, nothing undermined political harmony between North and South more deeply than did abolitionists who aided escaping slaves. In the larger history of slave escapes, to be sure, African Americans involved in the "Underground Railroad" usually relied on one another and distrusted whites' involvement. Starting in the 1840s, however, white abolitionists in ever-increasing numbers grew eager to encourage slaves to escape and to protect them once in residence in the North. By the mid-1840s "slave-stealing" ranked high on slaveholders' lists of complaints and the impact of abolitionist resistance on Southern concerns was becoming increasingly easy to measure.

A few venturesome souls actually moved south, assisted escapees, and were heavily punished for their trouble—Charles T. Torrey, for one. Torrey, from Massachusetts, stood high in the abolitionist Liberty Party before moving to Baltimore in 1844 to engineer slave escapes. Caught, convicted, and sentenced in 1845, he died an abolitionist "martyr" in the Maryland penitentiary the following year. In 1836, "Garrisonian" sea captain Jonathan Walker shipped out of New Bedford, Massachusetts, for Pensacola, Florida, where he assisted fugitives until arrested in 1844, branded with the letters SS (for slave-stealer), and imprisoned for a year. The punishment for the Reverend Calvin Fairbank was far harsher in 1844, fifteen years' hard labor for abetting numerous slave escapes in and around Lexington, Kentucky. William Chaplin, another prominent immediatist, proved the most ambitious "slave-stealer" of all when he visited Washington, DC, in 1848, hired two seafaring adventurers and their transport ship, and laid plans to ferry seventy-seven fugitives to the free states. Since the plot was betrayed just as the ship left port, a pursuing steamer captured it. The angry masters (some influential members of

---

31. A fine study of relationships between legal systems and struggles for equality is Robert Cover, *Justice Accused: Antislavery and the Judicial Process* (New Haven: Yale University Press, 1975). See also Litwack, *North of Slavery*, 247–79.

Congress) sold most of the escapees and made sure that the adventurers received harsh sentences. Drayton and Sayres both languished in prison for several years while Chaplin, who evaded prosecution, was later convicted for abetting fugitive slaves in Maryland.[32]

"Slave-stealers" operating in the free states feared no such punishments (though escapees certainly did). On the contrary, during the 1840s, abolitionists discovered to their surprise that Northerners who were in no sense "immediatists" nonetheless began voicing support for protecting fugitives as a way to express their own growing worries over the political impact of slavery in the nation's affairs. What prompted these feelings were the same general concerns that had so troubled Wendell Phillips about the murder of Elijah Lovejoy—the slaveholders' seemingly unstoppable determination to undermine the freedom of Americans everywhere, not simply rule over those they enslaved. Increasing numbers now joined with the abolitionists not to endorse "immediate emancipation" but instead to express their worry over the "gag rule," the assaults on freedom of speech and assembly, the mobs that disrupted orderly communities, the ransacking of federal post offices, and the terrorizing of innocent African Americans. Compounding these concerns after 1845 was the prospect of adding still more slave states to the union, the result of annexing the Republic of Texas and opening a war of conquest against Mexico. When immediatist James G. Birney warned that "whilst our aristocracy would preserve the domestic peace of the South, they seem totally to disregard the domestic peace of the North" and that "the liberties of those yet free are in imminent peril," he also addressed directly the growing fears of what Northerners now had begun to term the "the slave power." Responding to this growing political concern, Northern state legislatures began enacting "personal liberty laws" that relieved judges and law enforcement officials from the obligation to enforce the 1793 Fugitive Slave Law within their particular state's borders. "States' rights" constitutional arguments now were beginning to furnish a means

---

32. A path-breaking account of abolitionist activities south of the Mason-Dixon line, including "slave stealing," are two books by Stanley Harrold, *The Abolitionists and the South, 1831–1861* (Lexington: University Press of Kentucky, 1995), and *Subversives: Antislavery Community in Washington D.C., 1828–1865* (Baton Rouge: Louisiana State University Press, 2003).

for politicians to oppose the influence of slavery in the free states, as well as a way for slaveholders to protect the institution in the South.[33]

When Boston authorities seized fugitive George Latimer in 1842, Wendell Phillips's angry response captured perfectly why state legislatures felt compelled to enact such laws. His remarks also suggests why the abolitionists' spirit of resistance was now beginning to stimulate such strong sectional feelings in Northern political culture and why his own appeal to Yankee audiences was growing so rapidly. The answer, in both cases, involved revulsion against the "slave power's" invasive attempts to make Northern freemen serve the commands of Southern planters.

Who was really responsible for Latimer's plight, Phillips queried his audience? Not his jailors, the sheriff, or even the slave catcher. "No!" Phillips exclaimed, "they are but your tools. You are the guilty ones. . . . It is you that bolt and bar the door to that poor man's dungeon." Demanding the passage of a personal liberty law, Phillips insisted that the state of Massachusetts "cannot allow her soil to be polluted with the footprints of slavery without trampling on her Bill of Rights and subjecting herself to infamy. . . . She is solemnly bound to give protection who all who may escape the prison of bondage, and flee to her for safety." Clearly, Phillips spoke the feelings of most Massachusetts voters. The following year, the legislature did as he demanded by prohibiting Massachusetts justices from acting under the 1793 Fugitive Slave Law and barring state officials from arresting presumed escapees. By the mid-1840s several other state legislatures had done likewise. Black activists in major cities who had long before established vigilance committees of their own to protect runaways now found their work shielded from interference on the state level. For their part, worried planters now felt quite certain the law of the land in the free states legitimized "slave-stealing." Meeting this threat, they decided, required stringent new measures on the part of the federal government. These they secured as part of the legislative compromise of 1850, designed by Congress to resolve all outstanding

---

33. James G. Birney to Ezekial Webb and others, October 6, 1836, in Dwight L. Dumond, *The Letters of James Gillespie Birney 1831–1857*, 2 vols. (Ann Arbor: University of Michigan Press, 1938), 1:363. The fullest discussion of the relationship between civil liberty concerns and antislavery feelings in the North remains Russel Blaine Nye, *Fettered Freedom: Civil Liberties and the Slavery Controversy* (Ann Arbor: University of Michigan Press, 1949).

sectional disagreements, those raised over slavery's expansion into territories conquered during the Mexican War as well as those raised by fugitive slaves and abolitionists.[34]

Proslavery politicians obtained what they wanted when Congress enacted an extraordinarily harsh new Fugitive Slave Law as part of the compromise measures. It authorized federal commissioners, not state judges, to process escapees and obliged every citizen to assist in their capture. Those who protected fugitives risked severe penalties and the fugitives themselves were stripped of the right to trial by jury and the opportunity to testify. Free blacks found themselves in jeopardy of summarily being claimed as escapees, seized and shipped south without so much as a hearing. Though conflict over slavery's future in western territories, not over fugitive slaves, ultimately propelled the sectional collisions that led to civil war, this repressive new law inspired abolitionists to acts of militant resistance that undermined intersectional goodwill. As conflict over reserving the West for "free soil" or opening it to slavery split Whigs and Democrats irrevocably along North/South lines following the Kansas Nebraska Act (1854), the Kansas border wars (1855–1857) and the Dred Scott Decision (1857), abolitionists hungered for confrontation with "slave-catchers" and open defiance of the federal government. To the heightened dismay of the planters who had demanded this Fugitive Slave Law, "slave-stealing," for abolitionists, now constituted their high moral injunction . To a growing majority of "free soil" minded Northerners who were certainly not abolitionists but who supported the new Republican Party, resistance also seemed imperative if hope remained for arresting the spread of the "slave power." After almost three decades of constant agitation, abolitionists were finally being heard, and in a restricted sense, believed, by powerful blocs of Republican Party voters who certainly opposed the desires of the slave South, but who also promised to leave Southern slavery alone and held no necessary brief for racial equality.[35]

As blacks and whites united in defying the Fugitive Slave Law, resistance sometimes turned violent, as in Christiana, Pennsylvania, where in

---

34. Stewart, *Wendell Phillips*, 120–21.

35. These trends are discussed in greater detail in Stewart, *Holy Warriors*, 151–80.

1851 an abolitionist shot a slaveholder, or in Boston, in 1854 when an attempt to free a fugitive by storming the court house and overpowering his guards led to a fatality. And even when physical violence did not result, oratorical militants such as Wendell Phillips (now the best paid, most highly sought after public speaker in the North) increasingly urged their audiences to physically obstruct federal "slave-catchers" if more peaceable methods failed. On several occasions, well-organized groups of abolitionists overwhelmed the federal marshals and spirited fugitives to safety. On others, they stored weapons, planned harassing maneuvers, and massed as intimidating mobs. In any case, most agreed with Phillips when he declared that any black American "should feel justified in using the law of God and man in shooting [any] officer" attempting to enforce the law.[36]

For African American activists, these appeals to arms and defiance of "slave-catchers" represented nothing new but instead built on militant traditions that traced back at least to David Walker's *Appeal*. Leaders such as Frederick Douglass, Samuel Ringgold Ward, and Henry Highland Garnet were hardly innovators when declaring in the 1850s that the killing of tyrants was obedience to God. Neither were the black insurgents in Detroit who drove away federal marshals with volleys of paving stones. For white abolitionists, by contrast, the journey away from "moral suasion" was full of ambivalence. From one perspective "moral suasion" had yielded so little that more extreme measures seemed perfectly justifiable. More than two decades of peacefully preaching against the sin of slavery had yielded not emancipation but several new slave states and an increase of over half a million held in bondage, trends that seemingly secured a death-grip by the "slave-power" on American life. As for the new Republican Party, its opposition to slavery appeared to many abolitionists, as Garrison put it, "mean, partial, dwarfed and twisted," blighted by white supremacy and an easy acceptance of slavery's continuance in the South. Surely, none of this was progress.[37]

Yet from a second perspective, the white abolitionists' commitment

---

36. Phillips quoted in Stewart, *Wendell Phillips*, 155.

37. Garrison quoted in *Liberator*, October 16, 1857. For a good survey of the increasingly militant methods of abolitionists in the 1850s, see Jane H. Pease and William H. Pease, "Confrontation and Abolition in the 1850s," *Journal of American History* 58 (March 1972): 923–37.

to pacifism upheld their movement's high religious vision at a time when "free soilers" and proslavery settlers slaughtered each other in Kansas and Senator Charles Sumner recuperated from a vicious beating by an enraged South Carolina congressman. Then, too, "nonresistance" had always registered the white immediatists' sincere abhorrence of black insurrection. To jettison that conviction now was, perhaps, to embrace the prospect of servile revolt. That, however, is precisely what many white abolitionists began to do, a few quite consciously but most through a hesitant process of rationalization that left them without defenses when they found themselves in the overpowering presence of formidable John Brown.

"Old Brown" was a truly complex and dangerous man, endowed with a personality of immense authority. His magnetism, his skill at manipulating others, and his prophetic vision of godly retribution helped him to draw frustrated immediatists to support his cause of capturing the federal arsenal in Harpers Ferry, Virginia, arming the slaves, and inciting insurrection. He made a familiar figure of himself at abolitionist meetings during the 1850s, where he came to know many leading immediatists. All were well aware that Brown possessed a killer's instinct. It had been widely documented that he had butchered six unarmed settlers during the Kansas wars in 1857 and that leading abolitionists, Phillips among them, had given him money to purchase rifles and pikes. Now as Brown laid plans for fomenting slave insurrection, immediatists again gave him cash and asked few questions. Some black activists such as Harriet Tubman and Jermain Lougen generally knew that Brown plotted insurrection but not where, when, or how. (Wendell Phillips suspected Brown's intentions but claimed no direct knowledge of them.) And then there were the most violence-prone abolitionists of all, those who knew all that Brown would tell them in exchange for directly financing his attack—Liberty Party leaders Gerrit Smith and Frederick Douglass and four strong Bostonian allies of Phillips's in the struggle against the Fugitive Slave Law—Thomas Wentworth Higginson, George Luther Sterns, Franklin L. Sanborn, and Samuel Gridley Howe. Brown satisfied these men's romantic desires to engage in conspiracy and their yearnings for a dramatic example of direct action that would shatter slavery. After many weeks of preparation he and his band of eighteen descended on Harpers Ferry, seized the arsenal, and were quickly routed by troops commanded by Colonel Robert E. Lee. As abolitionists everywhere rushed to embrace his insurrectionary deeds, Brown was arraigned, tried, sentenced, and hanged by Virginia authorities in December 1859. His raid can perhaps be best understood less as Brown's supreme act of will and more as the predictable result of the abolitionists' frustrating struggles in the unremitting cause of resistance, their ambivalent feelings about the Republican Party, and their mounting desires for a morally definitive confrontation with slavery.[38]

In the aftermath, many abolitionists rushed to embrace Brown's insurrectionary deed, though some, like Garrison, attempted to separate their belief in the slaves' inherent right to rebel from Brown's act of terrorism. As usual, Phillips captured feelings of the insurrectionist's admirers unusually well when proclaiming to an enormous audience in Boston's Faneuil Hall that Brown had "twice as much right to hang Governor Wise [of Virginia] as Governor Wise has to hang him." Brown's deeds, Phillips emphasized, did not aim at creating social chaos. Instead, Brown had sought to destroy a turbulent, anarchic society that had tormented the nation for nearly a century. The South itself was in "chronic insurrection," not John Brown, according to Phillips, peopled by a "barbarous horde who gag each other, imprison women for teaching children to read, abolish marriage, condemn half their women to prostitution and devote themselves to the breeding of people for sale." Brown at Harpers Ferry stood, by contrast "as a representative of law, of government, of right, of justice, of religion." Brown, in short, embodied moral order to Phillips, not insurrection, a rationalization that permitted him and many other abolitionists to celebrate the bloody deeds of the most dangerous resister of all.[39]

With Lincoln's election as President in 1860, the full political significance of the abolitionists long pilgrimage from "moral suasion" to resistance and (finally) to insurrection at last became clear. Long observation

---

38. The literature on John Brown is vast and is effectively introduced by Stephen Oates in his biography of Brown, *To Purge This Land with Blood: A Biography of John Brown* (New York: Harper and Row, 1970), and by Benjamin Quarles, *Allies for Freedom: Blacks and John Brown* (New York: Oxford University Press, 1974). Also see John Stauffer, *Black Hearts of Men: Abolitionism and the Transformation of Race* (Cambridge: Harvard University Press, 2001).

39. Stewart, *Wendell Phillips*, 202–8.

of the abolitionists' behavior over almost three decades had utterly convinced the slaveholders that exactly the opposite of what Phillips believed was the truth. The North, not the South, had collapsed into anarchy. Race mixers, law breakers, and armed insurrectionists had now overrun the (supposedly) free states. What once had been a civil society now wallowed in moral chaos. Despite all their reassurances about never meddling with slavery where it presently existed, Abraham Lincoln and the party he led were actually "black Republicans," no different in the final analysis than Frederick Douglass or Wendell Phillips. Fully alienated, the planters elected secession and commenced with civil war. In this respect the abolitionists influenced the course of the nation's history to an extent greatly disproportionate to their meager numbers. In the process, their work had also done much to prepare a white majority in the free states for its ultimate wartime reckoning with Southern slavery.[40]

Subsequent events would drive white Americans to recreate new forms of racial tyranny that continue into our time. Nevertheless, the history of resistance on the part of the abolitionists makes clear that at least some Americans before the Civil War entertained far more democratic visions of the nation's future. While the abolitionists continued their work throughout the Civil War and well into Reconstruction, their antebellum struggles had already secured their ultimate legacy. From 1831 to 1860, they had engaged the nation and one another honestly, exploring their movement's internal tensions and identifying its most fundamental obligations while making searching critiques of society's deep injustices. It is this compelling example of civic engagement that gives the history of the abolitionists' struggles significance for their own age, and for ours.

---

40. Useful analyses of planters' frightened responses to abolitionism and the Republican Party are found in Stephanie McCurry, *Masters of Small Worlds: Yeoman Households, Gender Relations, and the Political Culture of the Antebellum South Carolina Low Country* (New York: Oxford University Press, 1997); and Cooper, *South and Politics of Slavery.*

Contexts

From its inception to its conclusion, the abolitionist movement constantly struggled with the pervasive and intractable problem of racial prejudice. Those difficulties were all the more complicated by the fact that racial prejudice expressed itself in new and disturbing ways as circumstances changed throughout the pre–Civil War years. In this fundamental respect the most influential contexts within which the abolitionists conducted their movement involved the always volatile prejudices abroad in the nation regarding the meanings of skin-color differences. This essay analyzes what caused those changes in racist attitudes, how these evolving prejudices expressed themselves, and how the abolitionists responded when facing a nation committed to preserving white supremacy.

Modernizing "Difference"
The Political Meanings of Color in the Free States, 1776–1840

As the decade of the 1830s opened, people living in the states "north of slavery" found themselves facing unprecedented dangers and opportunities that resulted from rapidly accumulating racial tensions. As crises multiplied, headlines of that time (even in generic form) conveyed their enormity and potential for violence—Nullification Spirit Sweeps South Carolina—Jackson Demands Cherokee Removal—Slaves Revolt and Murder in Southampton County, Virginia—Walker's *Appeal* Found among Southern Negroes—Garrison Demands Race Amalgamation—Abolitionists Gather Women and Negroes in Promiscuous Assemblies—Mobs Attack Negro Neighborhoods. At no previous time in the history of the "free states" did so many racially charged events overtake one another in such rapid succession. Never before were assumptions about the proper dynamics of "race relations" so suddenly and so heavily questioned, revisioned, and defended. Only during Reconstruction, or later still, during the post–World War II civil rights movement, would people experience trauma more drastic than that which swept the free states in the late 1820s and early 1830s. And only in these much more recent struggles would the trajectory of history so suddenly open similar possibilities for democratic change, for brutal repression, and for new political understandings of what skin color differences ought to mean.

This essay seeks to explain what deeper historical developments led the North to this sudden conjuncture in the late 1820s and early 1830s, what its specific dynamics were, and how its long-term influence reshaped and reinforced the power of "race" to define the modernizing political culture of the free states before the Civil War. Before this watershed moment, from 1790 until around 1830, society in the North, though suffused with prejudice, nevertheless fostered a surprisingly open premodern struggle over claims of "respectability" and citizenship put forward by many social groups, and particularly by free African Americans. This effort to achieve respectability, in turn, stimulated deepening internal and external divisions among people of differing skin colors and finally promoted the unprecedented interracialism of a nascent immediate abolitionist movement. By the opening of the 1830s, the compounding effect of these volatile contests had frayed the social fabric of free states to the point of disintegration. Then came David Walker's *Appeal*, Turner's insurrection, South Carolina's nullification crisis, and, above all, William Lloyd Garrison's *Liberator*. When this publication announced that abolitionists—black and white, male and female—were embarking on a crusade for racial equality, the impact of this extraordinary venture transmuted the North's accumulating racial tensions into a general crisis that exploded into mob violence across the free states.[1]

By the late 1830s, as the mobs dispersed African American neighborhoods and the beleaguered victims began to rebuild their lives, views of racial order had changed dramatically for practically everyone in the

---

1. It is important to acknowledge the influence of the burgeoning scholarship on racial "formation," with its emphasis that meanings of skin-color difference involve shifting ideological formulations and social relations. In this regard, the title of this essay, "Modernizing Difference," registers the idea that the role of race in the political development of the early republic is best understood as a set of rapidly evolving, conflicting ideological expressions by specific social groups over at least three decades that heavily determined the development of the North's two-party system and of the abolitionist movement as well. For discussions of this theme and methodology in current historiography, consult David R. Roediger, *The Wages of Whiteness: Race and the Making of the American Working Class* (London, 1991); Alexander Saxton, *The Rise and Fall of the White Republic: Class, Politics, and Mass Culture in Nineteenth-Century America* (New York, 1990); Joanne Pope Melish, *Disowning Slavery: Gradual Emancipation and the North, 1780–1860* (Ithaca, 1998); Stuart Hall, ed., *Representation: Cultural Representations and Signifying Practices* (London, 1997), 225–97; Barbara J. Fields, "Ideology and Race in American History," in J. Morton Kousser and James M. McPherson, eds., *Region, Race, and Reconstruction: Essays in Honor of C. Vann Woodward* (New York, 1982), 143–78. On the specific pertinence of cultural studies scholarship on race to the history of the early republic, see David R. Roediger, "The Pursuit of Whiteness: Property, Terror, and Expansion, 1790–1860," *Journal of the Early Republic* 19 (Winter 1999): 579–600.

North. The abolitionists' first struggles to secure racial equality had instead spawned an unprecedented upheaval among the vast majority of whites in the free states that solidified into an unmovable political consensus of highly ordered white supremacy. "Color lines" that had hitherto been so sharply contested around conflicting claims of "respect-ability" now had become indelibly drawn. Nearly impossible to revise, they were buttressed by a system of democratic white politics premised on the modern assumption that "nature" had always divided "black" and "white" as inferior and superior, and always must. By the mid-1830s, just as the nation's system of mass participation two-party politics began to take hold, this harsh new spirit of modern racial essentialism was becoming all-pervasive. It obliterated in turn earlier relationships based on deference and "respectability" while profoundly reshaping the funda-mental outlooks of even those who would continue to struggle for racial equality. In all these respects, the white North had emerged into an age of racial modernity, an era much more closely resembling the white supremacist tyranny of the late nineteenth century than the interracial contestation and alliance-building of the decades between 1776 and 1830. Moreover, protest movements contesting this new state of affairs much more resembled the racial activism of the twentieth century than they did those of the postrevolutionary era. How this crisis developed, why it concluded as it did, and what its implications were for the North's sectionalizing political system are the questions this essay seeks to answer.

The premodern racial landscapes of the early republican North gave few suggestions of the monumental upheavals that lay ahead. To be clear, deep-rooted racial prejudice was much in evidence as the dismantling of Northern slavery ran its tortuous course after 1776. Far too many of those emancipated remained ensnared in restrictive apprenticeships, and too many more continued their enslavement until reaching ages re-quired by manumission laws. All found themselves being pushed into a rapidly segregating and unequal social order by strengthening customs and newly enacted statutes. Churches that had once included African Americans now isolated or expelled them. Parades and festivals that had once been purposefully multiracial affairs now proceeded for the benefit of whites only. Court dockets and jail registers listed disproportionately high percentages of people of color.[2]

But from African Americans' perspectives, such trends fired ambitious visions even as they blighted immediate hopes. To the first generation of free African American leaders, racial boundaries in the early republican North were detestably unfair, but it remained unproven that they could not be contested and redrawn. As a result, initiatives multiplied as the new century opened—Paul Cuffee launched an extraordinary quest to create an Africa-based, transatlantic, commercial empire. His kinsman, James Easton, developed an ambitious manual labor school for African American youth at his foundry outside Boston. James Forten also reached outward to Africa while using his remunerative sail loft in Philadelphia to educate young black artisans. Forten's collaborator, Bishop Richard Allen, turned his single congregation into the nursery of an entire denomination, the African Methodist Episcopal Zion Church. New York City's John Teasman successfully promoted tax-supported schools to serve African Americans. Boston's Prince Hall dreamed of returning to Africa but witnessed instead the spread of his idea of uniting free people of color under the banner of Freemasonry.[3]

For all the variety of their plans and visions, these early leaders drew common inspiration from the prospect of free people of color "uplifting" themselves to conditions of "respectability," an approach to securing equality that stressed patient incrementalism, strenuous self-improvement, deference from ordinary community members, and the guidance of patriarchal leaders. Such aspirations permitted free African Americans to

---

2. The literature describing the ending of Northern slavery, the consolidation of free black communities, and the development of white supremacist social practices includes James O. Horton and Lois Horton, *In Hope of Liberty: Culture, Community, and Protest among Northern Free Blacks, 1700–1860* (New York, 1997); Gary B. Nash, *Forging Freedom: The Formation of Philadelphia's Black Community, 1720–1840* (New York, 1991); Graham Hodges, *Slavery and Freedom in the Rural North: African Americans in Monmouth County, New Jersey, 1665–1865* (Madison, WI, 1997); Julie Winch, *Philadelphia's Black Elite: Activism, Accommodation, and the Struggle for Autonomy, 1787–1848* (Philadelphia, 1988); Leonard P. Curry, *The Free Black in Urban America, 1800–1850: The Shadow of a Dream* (Chicago, 1981); and Shane White, *Somewhat More Independent: The End of Slavery in New York City, 1770–1810* (Athens, GA, 1991).

3. See Carol V. R. George, *Segregated Sabbaths: Richard Allen and the Rise of Independent Black Churches, 1760–1840* (1973; repr., Athens, GA, 1991); George R. Price and James Brewer Stewart, *To Heal the Scourge of Prejudice: The Life and Writings of Hosea Easton* (Amherst, 1999); Nash, *Forging Freedom*; Robert J. Swan, "John Teasman: African American Educator and the Emergence of Community in Early Black New York," *Journal of the Early Republic* 12 (Fall 1992): 331–56; and Lamont D. Thomas, *Paul Cuffe: Black Entrepreneur and Pan-Africanist* (Urbana, 1986).

build autonomous institutions that nurtured their sense of themselves as both "African" and "American" and that acted as "uplifting" agencies by which they could interject their egalitarian voices into the nation's political discussions. Persuasive historical analysis has pinpointed the strengths and weaknesses of this approach: it was vital to giving free blacks a sense of cultural solidarity and achievement when facing a hostile white world, but it also deflected primary responsibility for improving "race relations" away from bigoted whites while conveying the fatal impression that African Americans, in their "non-uplifted" state, were, indeed, a "degraded people." But whatever the costs and gains, Cuffe, Easton, Allen, and the others had every incentive to embrace the goals of "uplift" and "respectability" as the 1800s opened.[4]

The strongest of these imperatives, to build solid communities where none had existed, compelled these early leaders to place stern demands on their neighbors, and on themselves. Progress against discrimination, they insisted, required unflagging efforts by each to "uplift" all by living lives of "respectability" and by striving to embrace piety, practice thrift and temperance, comport one's self with well-mannered dignity, and seek all advantage that education offered. Far from registering "white middle-class" values, the distinguished "men of color" who set forth these daunting expectations registered a distinctly premodern African American style of Federalist-era deference politics when giving direction to their own "lesser orders." Their didactic pronouncements responded to the consequences of slave emancipation that made community-building so difficult after 1776, namely, the streams of former slaves from the North, the South, and the Caribbean that flowed into Northern cities, and the hostile critiques of whites who increasingly defined these congregating free people of color as an innately "turbulent, degraded race" that merited segregation and surveillance.

In the face of these obstacles, proponents of "uplift" and "respectability" succeeded magnificently in shaping ethnically diverse groups of

---

4. See works cited in the previous note, and Gary Nash, *Race and Revolution* (Madison, WI, 1990), 57–87. For discussions of the strengths and weaknesses of "uplift" and "respectability" in various formulations of free African American ideology, see Joanne Pope Melish, "The 'Condition' Debate and Racial Discourse in the Antebellum North," *Journal of the Early Republic* 19 (Winter 1999): 651–72; Kevin Gaines, *Uplifting the Race: Black Leadership, Culture and Politics in the Twentieth Century* (Chapel Hill, 1996), 17–91; and Horton and Horton, *In Hope of Liberty*, 125–54.

urban transients into enduring communities. In so doing, they automatically rebutted imputations that blacks constituted a "degraded race" by empowering those very African Americans to demonstrate cultural parity with whites of the highest attainment, to scorn "degraded" slaveholders and racial bigots as inferiors, and to give the lie to those who judged all dark-skinned people by the behavior of a "degenerate" few. To live "respectably" also constituted an assertion of free African American "manhood" and citizenship. It was a demonstration of personal independence embraced by men when protecting and directing their families, which was exactly what enslaved men throughout the South were presumably prevented from doing. Above all, "respectability" connoted the possession of the intellectual and literary skills necessary to allow African Americans to contribute their own authoritative political voices as equals to the nation's ongoing civic discussions. In sum, "respectability" initially expressed the free black elites' deepest abolitionist values.[5]

Judged by the impressive number of churches, schools, and benevolent associations they established by the 1820s, the accomplishments of these "uplifting" leaders were by any measure extraordinary, and the painstaking work of ordinary people all the more so. Yet the price that these successes exacted from many free African Americans was heavy, often requiring drastic alterations of identity and allegiance. Numerous members of "multiracial" families with bloodlines that had mixed African, Indian, and Euro-American ancestors (Eastons and Cuffes prominent among them) now chose in the name of "respectability" to identify themselves as African Americans and, as a result, to allow themselves to be identified as members of the "Negro race," a rapidly compounding aggregate of ostracized dark-skinned peoples of differing origins and genealogies. Left behind in their quests for "respectability" were indigenous traditions that had stressed communal sharing and the suppression of individualism, qualities inimical to the progressive assumptions of "uplift." The embrace of "uplift" also exacted a second, related loss, the disintegration of

---

5. This paragraph and the one preceding it are based on James Oliver Horton and Lois E. Horton, "The Affirmation of Manhood: Black Garrisonians in Antebellum Boston," in Donald M. Jacobs, ed., *Courage and Conscience: Black and White Abolitionists in Boston* (Bloomington, IN, 1993), 128–53; Patrick Rael, "African American Elites and the Language of Respectability" (paper presented at the Annual Meeting of the Organization of American Historians, San Francisco, 1997); and Price and Stewart, *Hosea Easton*, 3–57.

traditional definitions of the "turbulent rabble" that had regulated social relations throughout the eighteenth century. In this earlier setting, the inclusion of dark-skinned people in the ethnically diverse "lower orders" had inhibited naked repression exclusively against black people and fostered multicultural alliances among the poor of a variety of skin colors. But by the opening of the new century, these plebeian connections were beginning to unravel across the North as people of many backgrounds became increasingly caught up in a harsher regime of "race relations" in which the values of "respectability" began exerting greater influence over the minds of Anglo-Americans.[6]

For black New England's elite leaders, the implications of these developments were inescapable. Perforce, they must now undertake their own struggles for "uplift" in order to secure the future "respectability" of their (ever more stringently defined) "race." Though interracial alliances still remained, by the 1800s they involved only the haphazard patronage of individual philanthropists at the apex of the social order—elite Quakers, British reformers, and Federalist scions. Never again would support be found among a mass of poor Euro-Americans. Black Yankees, in short, had no choice but to begin pouring the resources of their "race" into programs that secured their claims to equality by "uplifting" themselves and their neighbors. Little wonder, given these circumstances, that while the Eastons, Fortens, and Allens despised this racial order, they also maintained that they could challenge and reshape it by promoting "respectability." Their impressive personal histories of accomplishment and recognition certainly suggested just how mutable "race relations" actually were and gave them little choice but to believe that a pious, energetic people could, with God's help, incrementally change those relations for the better.[7]

---

6. See James O. Horton's "Comment" in response to James Brewer Stewart, "The Emergence of Racial Modernity and the Rise of the White North, 1790–1840," *Journal of the Early Republic* 8 (Summer 1998): 222–26; Horton and Horton, *In Hope of Liberty*, 30–54; Jeffrey Bolster, *Black Jacks: African American Seamen in the Age of Sail* (Cambridge, MA, 1997), 68–13; and particularly Lois E. Horton, "From Class to Race in Early America: Northern Post-Emancipation Racial Reconstruction," *Journal of the Early Republic* 19 (Winter 1999): 629–50.

7. Linda Kerber, *Federalists in Dissent: Imagery and Ideology in Jeffersonian America* (Ithaca, 1970), chaps. 2–3; Robert Forbes, "Slavery and the Evangelical Enlightenment," in John R. McKivigan and Mitchell Snay, eds., *Religion and the Antebellum Debate over Slavery* (Athens, GA, 1998), 68–106; Joanne Pope Melish, *Disowning Slavery: Gradual Emancipation and "Race" in New England, 1780–1860* (Ithaca, 1998), 84–118; Robert H. Abzug, *Cosmos Crumbling: American Reform and*

By choosing this course of action, free African Americans joined an intense and highly divisive race for "respectability" that set them against a formidable variety of Euro-American competitors. For white Northerners from many walks of life in the early nineteenth century the claim of "respectability" came to serve similar functions as it did for African Americans. It valued and gave value to the achievements of piety, refinement, learning, and political engagement far above one's measurable economic position in a time of deepening inequality. As manufacturing, commerce, personal consumption, and class distinctions reshaped urban life in the North, so did rapid immigration from the British Isles and Western Europe. As a result, divisions grew between hard-pressed wage earners and an increasingly affluent middle class, as did ethnic tensions between long-settled Yankees and immigrants and even between newly arrived ethnic groups themselves. To assert one's "respectability" in the face of such deepening rifts meant insisting that workers and immigrants, rural no less than urban, could overcome foreign and plebian origins and claim parity with all other citizens. It also offered "ordinary" people the hope of upward mobility and republican equality, thanks to the strength of their moral character. From the wealthy, it required philanthropic effort to "uplift" the less fortunate who needed education and the benefits of sound morals in order to contribute to the nation's political life.

The race to attain "respectability," in short, seemed to promise cultural and political remedies for multiplying class divisions, ethnic conflicts, stresses of acculturation, and feelings of personal alienation. Equality was presumably attainable to all the "uplifted," whatever their occupation, income, ethnic group, or, as a Forten or an Easton would add emphatically, skin color. But as this contest unfolded it only intensified the very conflicts that it was presumed to mitigate. As a result, by the opening of the 1820s, people throughout the North found themselves engaged in ever more violent disagreements over how racial boundaries ought to be drawn to accord with conflicting claims of "respectability," citizenship, and heightening color consciousness. This compulsion to

---

the Religious Imagination (New York, 1994), 11–29; Horton and Horton, *In Hope of Liberty*, 55–76, 155–70.

embrace "whiteness" and "respectability" was strongly felt even among new immigrants in the rural North, people well removed from African American population centers, but well aware of "Indian Country" when formulating their initial claims to republican citizenship.[8]

These heightening senses of racial identity among whites and mounting inclinations among free blacks to push across racial boundaries increasingly influenced day-to-day urban life in the North in the early nineteenth century. For example, lower-class men, blacks and whites alike, now formulated understandings of the meaning of "respectability" that were very much in conflict with those of their social "betters." Plebeian blacks and whites quickly developed the habit of mixing in grog houses, cellar bistros, oyster houses, and lottery stalls, all elements of street culture that ran deeply counter to elites' "uplifting" values. Yet this was hardly a return to the interracial fraternization among the "lower orders" of prerevolutionary days. Instead, the situation fostered hostility between working men of differing skin colors over the preservation of "manly self-respect." Working-class whites now exhibited a volatile ambivalence toward African American culture when they burlesqued it in black-faced minstrel shows, even as they also patronized black prostitutes, applauded black musicians, and drank their fill in black speakeasies. Now encountering the traumas of industrial labor, these white male wage earners, many of them immigrants, feared the "blackness" of those with whom they mingled as symbolic of their own personal "degradation." Such feelings in turn spurred their desires for emotional catharsis and became an excuse for aggressive assertions of "manly self-respect." Street-corner tensions deepened as black men responded with assertive

---

8. The discussion of class formation and the ideology of "respectability" derives from Stuart Blumin, *The Emergence of the Middle Class: Social Experience in the American City, 1700–1900* (New York, 1989), 66–230; Richard Bushman, *The Refinement of America: Persons, Houses, and Cities* (New York, 1992), 207–447; Karen Halttunen, *Confidence Men and Painted Women: A Study of Middle Class Culture in America* (New Haven, 1982); John Kasson, *Rudeness and Civility: Manners in Nineteenth-Century Urban America* (New York, 1990); Tamara P. Thornton, *Cultivating Gentlemen: The Meaning of Country Life among the Boston Elite* (New Haven, 1989); Ronald Story, *The Forging of an Aristocracy: Harvard and the Boston Upper Class* (Boston, 1980); Roediger, *Wages of Whiteness*, 133–56; and Jon Gjerde, "'Here in America there is neither king nor tyrant': European Encounters with Race, 'Freedom,' and Their European Past," *Journal of the Early Republic* 19 (Winter 1999): 673–90; and James P. Ronda, "'We Have a Country': Race, Geography, and the Invention of Indian Territory," *Journal of the Early Republic* 19 (Winter 1999), 739–56.

behavior of their own, which fused assertions of gendered identity with those of color.[9]

Meanwhile, on the opposite end of the social spectrum, genteel white philanthropists and public officials who espoused colonizationism also blurred racial boundaries and fostered contention over claims of male "respectability" by inviting African American elites to join them as "gentlemen" in "uplifting" the nation's free blacks. Through their American Colonization Society they proposed to "elevate" free African Americans from oppressive white bigotry by subsidizing their voluntary emigration to the West Africa colony of Liberia. But rather than cementing biracial cooperation among gentlemanly "respectables," this proposition prompted the black elites, including those truly interested in African resettlement, to mobilize their communities against the colonizationists. They denounced colonizationists in an unprecedented outpouring of pamphlets, speeches, sermons, and "indignation meetings" as "degraded" white conspirators who aimed to drive "upstanding" free people of color into exile. Here, in fact, were the first stirrings of both a formally organized elite black abolitionist movement and of a clearly identified "respectable" white opposition to it.[10]

On every social level, then, from barrooms to church meeting halls, the continuing efforts of African Americans to put themselves forward as equals provoked deepening racial resistance from whites preoccupied with their own pursuits of "manliness" and "respectability." When, for example, African American men began staging marches commemorating their two most meaningful political events—Northern emancipation and Haitian independence—whites lampooned them in handbills and showered them with epithets and rocks, scorning their assertion that a citizen's right to the streets belonged as much to African Americans as to anyone. Even the very landmarks that bespoke the elites' successes in

---

9. Eric Lott, *Love and Theft: Blackfaced Minstrelsy and the American Working Class* (New York, 1993); Michael Kaplan, "New York Tavern Violence and the Creation of a Male Working Class Identity," *Journal of the Early Republic* 15 (Winter 1995): 592–617; Roediger, *Wages of Whiteness*, chaps. 3–5.

10. P. J. Staudenraus, *The African Colonization Movement, 1816–1865* (New York, 1967), 94–187; Hugh Davis, "Northern Colonizationism and Free Blacks, 1823–1837: A Case Study of Leonard Bacon," *Journal of the Early Republic* 17 (Winter 1997): 553–75; George Fredrickson, *The Black Image in the White Mind: The Debate on Afro-American Character and Destiny* (New York, 1971), 1–27; Horton and Horton, *In Hope of Liberty*, 196–68; Paul Goodman, *Of One Blood: The Abolitionists and the Origins of Racial Equality* (Berkeley, 1998), 1–35.

promoting "uplift" now served as catalysts for compounding white resentment. Whites rightly regarded the handsome new churches, meeting halls, and school buildings as both symbols of African American communities' high aspirations and as agencies for amplifying the voices of its "uplifted" preachers, pamphleteers, and social activists. Consequently, white harassment increasingly marred Sabbath observances and school-day activities, and the buildings themselves became the targets of the earliest race riots that first erupted in the early and mid-1820s in Boston, New Haven, Providence, Pittsburgh, and Philadelphia.[11]

These violent episodes, unsettling in their own right, were actually skirmishes in a sustained assault against free blacks that gathered strength throughout the North in the 1820s. In the political sphere, state legislatures took the lead, and by late in the decade every one of them had either seriously debated or passed legislation that placed new restrictions on African Americans' voting rights, legal standing, and freedom of migration. To complete this sweeping confirmation of free blacks' ever more uniform "degradation," every legislature also enacted universal male suffrage for whites—the ultimate recognition of masculine social acceptability. The popular mandate supporting this legislation expressed fully in the North's newly emerging mass print culture, where cartoonists and editors found limitless audiences for woodcuts and sketches that demeaned African Americans in nearly every manner conceivable. By ridiculing blacks' physiognomy as simian, their speech as pidgin dialect, and all their attempts at "respectability" as outlandishly grotesque, these cartoons confirmed just how forceful free African American activists had been in pursuing their goals, how much their successes at pushing through racial barriers had unsettled public culture, and how determined whites now were to suppress all such "uplifting" endeavors. What had begun in the 1790s as a quest for equality by "uplifted" African Americans was evolving by the late-1820s into a white crusade against free blacks

---

11. Emma Jones Lapsansky, "'Since They Got Those Separate Churches': Afro-Americans and Racism in Jacksonian Philadelphia," *American Quarterly* 32 (Spring 1980): 54–79; Shane White "'It Was a Proud Day': African Americans, Festivals, and Parades in the North, 1741–1834," *Journal of American History* 81 (June 1994): 13–50; Paul J. Gilje, *The Road to Mobocracy: Popular Disorder in New York City, 1763–1834* (Chapel Hill, 1987), 145–62; Patrick Rael, "'Besieged by Freedom's Army': Antislavery Celebrations, Black Leaders, and Black Society in the Antebellum North," unpublished paper in the author's possession.

in general. That such a crusade licensed terrorism became obvious when whites in Cincinnati launched vicious attacks on their black neighbors in 1829, leaving several hundred homeless and driving an undetermined number into exile in Canada.[12]

Among free blacks, such horrifying events evoked an understandable mixture of fear, anger, and alienation. Some elite leaders explored emigrating to Haiti or Upper Canada. Others speculated that violence-prone white Americans must have sprung from corrupted European origins and compared them to patiently struggling blacks who surely carried the legacy of culturally superior African beginnings. Nearly all responded warmly to the passionate writings of David Walker, whose extraordinary *Appeal* was published in 1829. In it he scorned the efficacy of African American "uplift" without militant self-transformation, condemned colonization in unusually sweeping terms, and called for black people to defend their rights by force when necessary. The angry African Americans in several cities who protested the recapture of fugitives by hurling paving stones at whites obviously saw matters much as Walker did. Torn between the questionable alternatives of armed resistance, quiet submission, or self-exile, free blacks in the North faced a terrible impasse as the 1830s opened.[13]

Given these circumstances, the sudden appearance in 1831 of a militant white abolitionist movement must have seemed a godsend to free black leaders for, as crises deepened for free African Americans, racial tension erupted nationally as well. In South Carolina, militant planters courted civil war when they demanded the right to "nullify" on behalf of slavery. A massive slave insurrection in Jamaica, Nat Turner's rebellion in Virginia, and the discovery of Walker's *Appeal* in the possession of Southern blacks stimulated premonitions among whites of an impending race war. President Andrew Jackson's crusade to remove the Cherokee Nation

---

12. The fullest overview of these developments remains Leon Litwack, *North of Slavery: The Negro in the Free States, 1790–1860* (New York, 1961). See also Richard C. Wade, "The Negro in Cincinnati, 1800–1830," *Journal of Negro History* 35 (Jan. 1954): 39–51; John M. Werner, "Race Riots in Jacksonian America, 1824–1849" (Ph.D. diss., University of Indiana, 1973). For a closely related analysis of these trends and their deeper meanings within the slave states, see Lacy K. Ford Jr., "Making the 'White Man's' Country White: Race, Slavery, and State-Building in the Jacksonian South," *Journal of the Early Republic* (19 Winter 1999): 713–37; and respecting Cherokee removal, Ronda, "We Have a Country."

13. Peter Hinks, *To Awaken My Afflicted Brethren: David Walker and the Problem of Antebellum Slave Resistance* (University Park, PA, 1997); Bruce Dain, "Haiti, Egypt, and Early Black Racial Discourse in the United States," *Slavery and Abolition* 14 (Dec. 1983): 139–61.

linked racialized state coercion with mass expulsion in an unprecedented fashion. To African American activists and white abolitionists, this only cast the American Colonization Movement in a still more ominous light. Little wonder, therefore, that when Garrison and his associates, encouraged by activist African Americans, pledged to unmask that society, to promote equality for the North's free blacks, and to demand slavery's immediate abolition, the black elite responded enthusiastically. Yet in the light of the increasingly volatile, gender-focused racial contentiousness of the late 1820s, compounded now by nullifiers and insurrectionists, it is impossible to imagine any event more disruptive than the sudden appearance of a biracial abolitionist movement that included women as well as men. Never before had struggles over racial boundaries and the masculine attributes of "respectability" carried such potential for violence as they did in 1831, when white Garrisonians invited people of all skin colors and both genders to crusade to "uplift" the free black community in the North and hasten the end of Southern slavery.

Viewed from this perspective, the white men who mobbed abolitionists and terrorized black neighborhoods until the later 1830s should be understood as having been absolutely correct when decrying their victims as racial "amalgamationists." For these new white abolitionists, "respectability" constituted a highly charged interracial imperative that black and white reformers, female as well as male, must collaborate to "uplift" Northern African Americans into a racially inclusive middle class. This, they maintained, was essential to their overarching goal of obliterating caste oppression in all of its forms. To the men of the African American elite, however, the prospect of an alliance with fellow "Christian gentlemen" such as Garrison, Lewis Tappan, and William Jay relieved their terrible impasse. Here, with unprecedented white assistance, was a unique opportunity once again to take action against white supremacism while recommitting their communities to the quest for "respectability."[14]

---

14. Stewart, "Racial Modernity"; Bertram Wyatt-Brown, *Lewis Tappan and the Evangelical War against Slavery* (Cleveland, 1969), 78–125; James Brewer Stewart, *William Lloyd Garrison and the Challenge of Emancipation* (Arlington Heights, IL, 1992), 40–74; Richard Newman, "The Transformation of American Abolitionism: People, Tactics, and the Changing Meaning of Activism from the 1780s to the 1830s" (Ph.D. diss., State University of New York, Buffalo, 1997); James Huston, "The Experiential Basis of the Northern Antislavery Impulse," *Journal of Southern History* 56 (Nov. 1990): 609–41; Mary Hershberger, "Mobilizing Women, Anticipating Abolition: The Struggle against Indian Removal in the 1830s," *Journal of American History* 86 (June 1999): 16–40.

Whatever their motives, white and black abolitionists shared the revolutionary belief that African Americans had every right to speak the harshest truth to their "unregenerate" oppressors and to "rise" to social equality as rapidly as possible. For this reason African American authors were heavily featured in white abolitionists' publications, an abrupt and unprecedentedly forceful intervention by African Americans into the nation's "marketplace of ideas." Meanwhile, white reformers also made unprecedented interventions by becoming deeply involved in renewed African American campaigns of community "uplift" that blossomed in the early 1830s. They eagerly welcomed African Americans into their rapidly multiplying antislavery societies and roundly denounced "color-phobia" among whites as supremely sinful and ignorant. But to the vast majority of Northern white men in this already polarized racial order, the very idea that blacks and whites of both genders would presume to "elevate" free African Americans to equal middle-class status and dictate morality to Euro-Americans "beneath" them meant unspeakable "degradation." As prominent colonizationists, leading politicians, and ordinary day laborers prepared for mob action, it was clear to all but the abolitionists themselves that their entrance into the highly contested race for "respectability" guaranteed the rapid suppression of the movement.

A survey of the antiabolitionist violence that tore through practically every major Northern city and so many smaller towns amply confirms this truth. In nearly all of these thoroughly studied events, mob activity from 1831 to 1838 was triggered initially by a highly visible action that abolitionists regarded as part of their "respectable" promotion of African American "uplift" but that whites of all classes abominated as degrading racial and sexual "amalgamationism": proposals for manual labor schools for black youths in New Haven, Connecticut, and in Canaan and Dover, New Hampshire; attempts to establish academies for young African American women in Canterbury, Connecticut, and in Cincinnati and Zanesville, Ohio; the "promiscuous" gatherings of abolitionists of both races and genders in public meeting halls in Boston, Utica, Pittsburgh, and New York City; and the "amalgamated" funding and leadership involved in building Philadelphia's Free Speech Hall. Equally predictable were the specific targets of mob action—abolitionists of both races and genders whose pretenses to "respectability" had to be violently obliterated, and African American neighborhoods, those magnets of "vice" and "debasement," where racial boundaries and white identities had been contested and compromised far too long.[15]

The complementary roles played throughout the rioting by white men on opposite ends of the social order were also consistent. As urban workers tore into black neighborhoods and shut down abolitionists' meetings, prominent businessmen, politicians, and editors, many of them colonizationists, condemned the abolitionists as instigators of the riots, deploring only the mobs' "excesses." As abolitionists remarked at the time and as modern scholarship has since confirmed, the lower-class "tail" of urban white society worked easily with those at its "head" as both rich and poor whites drew from the cathartic violence an unprecedented sense of their brotherhood as the dominating "race." Theirs was a profoundly heightened activist identity that quickly expressed itself at the ballot box as well as in the streets.[16]

In retrospect, it seems all but inevitable that the abolitionists' drive for racially "respectable" inclusiveness would be overwhelmed by the growth of modern, white supremacist two-party politics. The spread of mob violence and the development of the second-party system quickly linked rioters, their apologists, party spokesmen, and voters in common electoral purposes. Historians have long recognized the close relationship between the rise of universal white manhood suffrage and the

---

15. The generalizations developed here regarding the importance of gender as well as racial antagonisms follow works that have carefully studied specific instances of antiabolitionist and anti-free-black rioting in New England, New York, and Pennsylvania. In addition to Leonard L. Richards, *"Gentlemen of Property and Standing": Antiabolitionist Mobs in Jacksonian America* (New York, 1971), 20–155; Roediger, *Wages of Whiteness*, 107–110; and Lott, *Love and Theft*, 28–29, 131–35, consult Susan Strane, *A Whole-Souled Women: Prudence Crandall and the Education of Black Women* (New York, 1990); Donald Yacovone, *Samuel Joseph May and the Dilemmas of the Liberal Persuasion, 1797–1871* (Philadelphia, 1991), 43–55; Margaret Hope Bacon, "By Moral Force Alone: Antislavery Women and Non-Resistance," in Jean Fagin Yellin and John Van Horn, eds., *The Abolitionist Sisterhood: Women's Political Culture in Antebellum America* (Ithaca, 1994), 285–90; John Runcie "'Hunting the Nigs' in Philadelphia: The Race Riot of August, 1834," *Pennsylvania History* 39 (Apr. 1972): 187–218; Werner, "Race Riots," chaps. 3–4; Linda K. Kerber, "Abolitionists and Amalgamators," *New York History* 48 (Jan. 1967): 28–39; and Kaplan, "New York Tavern Violence."

16. For sources pertinent to this paragraph and the one preceding it, see Leonard L. Richards, *"Gentlemen of Property and Standing"*; Kerber, "Abolitionists and Amalgamators," 28–39; Lott, *Love and Theft*, 63–88; Kaplan, "New York City Tavern Violence"; David Grimsted, "Rioting in Its Jacksonian Setting," *American Historical Review* 77 (Apr. 1972): 361–97; Dale Knobel, *Paddy and the Republic: Ethnicity and Nationality in Antebellum America* (Middletown, CT, 1986), 39–68; and Julie Roy Jeffrey, *The Great Silent Army of Abolitionism: Ordinary Women in the Antislavery Movement* (Chapel Hill, 1998), 14–95.

systematic suppression of free African Americans' rights. As part of this process, they have also stressed the Northern Democratic Party's success in the 1830s in uniting its Northern constituents through endorsements of bigotry and mob activity. Less understood, but equally important, was the Northern Whigs' transformation of colonizationism from a poorly funded voluntary association into a major component in their party's ideology of "race." Throughout the early and mid-1830s, while many free-state Democrats endorsed racial violence, Northern Whig editors and party leaders generally mixed condemnations of abolitionist "amalgamationism" and working-class "mob rule" with praise for the temperate statesmanship of Henry Clay, Edward Everett, and Daniel Webster, colonizationism's most prominent political spokesmen. In 1840 and 1844, when the national Whig Party nominated presidential candidates, it was no accident that its choices were the planter–colonizationists William Henry Harrison and Henry Clay.

By adopting this strategy, Northern Whigs found an effective means of distinguishing their positions on issues of slavery and "race" from those of Northern Democrats while satisfying fundamental rules that both parties obeyed—intersectional harmony and white supremacist solidarity. Though some Whigs, like Clay, believed deeply in voluntary emigration, most in the North who endorsed colonization were simply contrasting their party's new distinctive formulation of white supremacist politics to that of their Democratic opposition by stressing that free African Americans, ideally, should be "sent back to Africa." Their own allegiance to "whiteness" thus established, Northern Whigs were free to attack their free-state Democratic opponents in sectional terms by condemning them as "tools" of Southern planters because of their promotion of riots and their support for suppressing antislavery petitions in Congress. These tactics, however, did not undermine their party's unity, since Southern Whigs appreciated the deeper support for slavery and white supremacy that underlay them, as well as the fact that they strengthened the party's overall performance against the Democrats in national elections.[17]

---

17. For analyses of the Whig and Democratic parties, slavery, colonization, white supremacy, and partisan loyalties that inform this paragraph and the one preceding it, see Leonard L. Richards, "The Jacksonians and Slavery," in Lewis Perry and Michael Fellman, eds., *Antislavery Reconsidered: New Perspectives on the Abolitionists* (Baton Rouge, 1979), 99–118; Richards, *"Gentlemen of Property and*

Despite this approach, the Whig Party had to accommodate the supporters of maverick politicians such as John Quincy Adams and Joshua R. Giddings, who genuinely did hate slavery and its incursions on "Northern rights" and who were truly disturbed by the plight of dark-skinned Americans. Soon too, strong criticisms also surfaced from a handful of antiabolitionist Northern Democrats like Benjamin Tappan, who nevertheless despised "aristocratic" slaveholders and advocated the rights of their "chattel laborers" to freedom. In this respect, two-party racial politics ultimately stimulated authentic disagreements over the status of African Americans that wove themselves into conflicts over slavery's westward expansion. But in the meantime, the Democrats' blunt appeals to "white manhood" and the Whigs' more polished espousals of colonization conveyed identical conclusions regarding the newly modernized political meanings of color in the North. No matter how estimable their qualities or accomplishments, free African Americans had to be denied their claims of equal "respectability" and to be treated categorically as an "inferior race." Voters, in turn, had to express their party allegiances in terms of "white identity politics," rejecting all that was symbolized by both "abolitionism" and the possession of dark skin. Considering these precedents, it is little wonder that in later years Northern free-soil ideology and white racial bigotry were so often to become intertwined in the political crises leading to civil war.[18]

Standing," 8–10, 18, 29, 87, 114–22; Daniel Walker Howe, *The Political Culture of the American Whigs* (New York, 1980), 18–37, 165–80; John M. McFaul, "Expedience vs. Morality: Jacksonian Politics and Slavery," *Journal of American History* 62 (June 1975): 24–39; John Ashworth, *Slavery, Capitalism, and Politics in the Antebellum Republic,* vol. 1, *Commerce and Compromise, 1820–1850* (New York, 1995), 323–50; Michael F. Holt, *The Political Crisis of the 1850s* (New York, 1978), 17–33; James Brewer Stewart, "Abolitionists, Insurgents, and Third Parties: Sectionalism and Partisan Politics in Northern Whiggery, 1836–1844," in Alan Kraut, ed., *Crusaders and Compromisers: Essays on the Relationship of the Antislavery Struggle to the Antebellum Party System* (Westport, CT, 1983), 26–43.

18. A convenient, highly readable overview of Whig antislavery impulses is found in Leonard L. Richards, *The Life and Times of Congressman John Quincy Adams* (New York, 1986). See also Ashworth, *Slavery, Capitalism, and Politics,* 350–61; and James Brewer Stewart, *Joshua R. Giddings and the Tactics of Radical Politics* (Cleveland, 1970). For discussions of Democratic Party expressions of extreme antislavery sentiment (rare though they were in the 1830s and early 1840s), see esp. Daniel Feller, "A Brother in Arms: Benjamin Tappan and the Antislavery Democracy," paper delivered at the Annual Meeting of the Society for Historians of the Early American Republic, Lexington, KY, July 16, 1999; Sean Wilentz, "Slavery, Antislavery, and Jacksonian Democracy," in Melvyn Stokes and Stephen Conway, eds., *The Market Revolution in America: Social, Political, and Religious Expressions* (Charlottesville, VA, 1996), 202–23; and Goodman, *Of One Blood,* 161–75. The most discerning analysis of the relationships between white supremacy, racial egalitarianism, and Northern opposition to slavery's westward expansion remains Eric Foner, *Free Soil, Free Labor, Free Men: The Ideology of*

As their travails continued into the later 1830s, Garrison and his white associates also developed a quite new and unmistakably more modern understanding of racial identity and the political meaning of skin color. During the height of racial violence, all agreed that their crusade could no longer sustain its struggle for black "respectability." Especially in urban areas, abolitionists' efforts of racial "uplift" abruptly halted. The "moral bankruptcy" of their own white "race" caused these reversals, they now concluded; the sins of black enslavement in the South had now been shown to be powerfully reinforced by equally heinous crimes of politically mobilized whites throughout the free states. And as Garrison and his white coworkers reflected further, they also understood how deeply alienated they had become not only from the unrepentant slave holders in the South but also from the vast majority of their fellow Northern whites.[19]

The schisms that shattered white abolitionism in 1840 had many causes, but basic among them were deep disagreements over what these reformers believed was required of them now that they had become so self-consciously estranged from the white North. All concurred that their efforts must now be redirected to transforming the white majority's "corrupted" values, and as a result, for the first time in the nation's history, a white social movement put highest priority on wholesale ideological opposition to the Northern racial prejudice of its own "race" rather than on attempting to lessen it by assisting free blacks to "rise." But almost immediately, white abolitionists also began articulating irreconcilable

---

the Republican Party before the Civil War (New York, 1970), 261–317. Michael A. Morrison, *Slavery and the American West: The Eclipse of Manifest Destiny and the Coming of the Civil War* (Chapel Hill, 1997), contextualizes these racial themes in struggles between Northern and Southern politicians over conflicting understandings of the shared political traditions of republicanism. For Foner's most recent statement on issues of race, class, gender, and contested definitions of freedom in antislavery ideology, see his trenchant and widely focused "Free Labor, Wage Labor and the Slave Power," in Stokes and Conway, *Market Revolution in America*, 128–46.

19. The most detailed and substantial analysis of the deeper issues involved in the schisms among white abolitionists and their relationship to issues of race and white supremacy remains Aileen Kraditor, *Means and Ends in American Abolitionism: Garrison and His Critics on Strategy and Tactics, 1834–1850* (New York, 1969). See also James Brewer Stewart, "Peaceful Hopes and Violent Experiences: The Evolution of Conservative and Radical Abolitionism, 1831–1837," *Civil War History* 17 (Dec. 1971): 293–309; Stewart, "Racial Modernity"; Alan Kraut, "'Vote as You Pray, Pray as You Vote': Church Oriented Abolitionism and Antislavery Politics," in Kraut, *Crusaders and Compromisers*, 179–205; and Lawrence J. Friedman, *Gregarious Saints: Self and Community in American Abolitionism, 1830–1870* (New York, 1982), 43–67.

versions of their own "identity politics" as they disagreed over how best to challenge white supremacy in some fundamental way. As discord deepened, it became clear that their trials by violence had deeply altered their understandings of the political meanings of color in the North.[20]

To Garrison and his supporters, only a comprehensive espousal of women's rights, religious perfectionism, and nonresistance—the moral antipodes of mobs and mass parties—could inspire the transformation of "corrupted" majority values. To many of Garrison's opponents, however, it was the North's white voters, "enslaved" to the Whigs and Democrats, who must be morally liberated, and this could only be done by founding an emancipationist Liberty Party. But beneath these controversies, serious as they were, lay the deeper acceptance by all parties that their overriding political challenges arose from bigoted constructions of "whiteness" that inspired mob rule and political repression within the free states. Both factions, in other words, now sought the liberation of the entire black population by overthrowing the North's newly organized white supremacist polity. No longer fixated on interracial "respectability," they were now eager to seek categorical equality for all Northern blacks, "uplifted" or not, by challenging their own white "race."[21]

For Liberty Party members this objective required a concentrated effort in culturally homogenous rural areas such as Ohio's Western Reserve, western Massachusetts, and New York State's "Burned-Over District" where blacks and immigrants were few, where evangelical Yankees dominated, and where abolitionist sympathizers could be rallied to challenge the two major parties on egalitarian grounds. For Garrisonians it meant the wholesale condemnation of fellow whites of all institutions that nurtured "unregenerate" bigotry: religious denominations, electoral processes, courts of law, the constabulary, and the Federal Union itself.

---

20. Stewart, "Racial Modernity," 210–13.

21. Vernon Volpe, *The Forlorn Hope of Freedom: The Liberty Party in the Old Northwest, 1838–1848* (Kent, OH, 1990); John W. Quist, "'The Great Majority of Our Subscribers are Farmers': The Michigan Abolitionist Conspiracy of the 1840s," *Journal of the Early Republic* 14 (Fall 1994): 326–38; Alan Kraut, "Forgotten Reformers: A Profile of Third Party Abolitionists in Antebellum New York," in Perry and Fellman, *Antislavery Reconsidered*, 119–45; James Brewer Stewart, *Wendell Phillips: Liberty's Hero* (Baton Rouge, 1986; 1986; repr., 1998), 97–145; Stewart, "Boston, Abolitionism, and the Atlantic World, 1820–1861," in Jacobs, *Courage and Conscience*, 102–25; Friedman, *Gregarious Saints*, 43–126, 160–95; Jeffrey, *Great Silent Army of Abolitionism*, 134–70.

But whatever the particular strategy, behind it lay the white abolitionists' shared imperatives to pursue categorical equality for all black people by attacking white society for its uniform racial bigotry rather than by promoting the "uplifting" of individual African Americans.

Black activists, very predictably, adamantly embraced this agenda, and by 1840 were developing new political approaches that anticipated struggles for racial equality more familiar to our time. Utterly convinced by this time that equality could never be "respectability's" reward, African American activists now embraced racial independence. As they did, these reformers helped to inaugurate a recognizable antecedent of the modern civil rights movement, for their stress was now on independent black leadership, mass participation, the development of distinctive black ideologies, and the importance of political coalition-building. Speaking no longer as individual exemplars of "uplift," they instead saw themselves as architects of a militant black movement that could ally with white reformers without compromising their own distinctive ends.

As a result, by the opening of the 1840s, broad-based interracial collaborations multiplied. In states where black men could vote, for example, African American abolitionists worked with the white-led Liberty Party by campaigning and casting ballots for emancipationist candidates while simultaneously helping to build abolitionist constituencies. In certain states they also joined with sympathetic whites to agitate for color-blind male suffrage and the repeal of discriminatory "black codes," activities unthinkable in the 1820s and 1830s. Coalitions also developed between African American activists and white Garrisonians that reflected an equally modern spirit. These alliances engaged in epochal battles against segregated schools and public facilities, which mobilized black communities for sustained periods while white reformers also played prominent roles. Henceforth, until at least 1861, when black and white abolitionists worked together, it was invariably as a collaboration between members of distinct "races" united in the cause of unconditionally equal treatment for all African Americans, not as an alliance of "respectables," intent on incremental programs of melioration. Thus did abolitionists both black and white become egalitarian practitioners of modern racial politics, a fitting reversal of the essentialist white supremacist principles embraced in the 1830s by Whigs and Democrats when first inaugurating mass participation politics.[22]

Having moved in this fashion beyond the traumas of white supremacist politics, abolitionists also opened path-breaking ideological debates during the 1840s and 1850s that sustained the movement's vitality, deepened its radicalism, and documented its transformation into a recognizably modern enterprise. A simple listing of the topics that prompted their ideological disagreements suggests just how far these crusaders had evolved from their original commitments to "uplift," and just how closely their outlooks prefigured more recent struggles for racial equality: the conflicting values of racial integration and black separatism; the problems of racial bias and cultural antagonism between black and white egalitarians; the necessities and perils of pacifism and political violence; the contested positions of women, black and white, in a movement dominated by men; the multiple meanings of "Africa," emigrationism, and "pan-African" identity for African Americans; the debatable equation of the rights of citizenship with the imperatives of social justice. In the process, abolitionists clearly began recognizing some of the deeper complexities of color, gender, and cultural and class difference.[23]

When Donald Yacovone, a talented historian of abolitionism, observed to this writer that "there is no controversy in today's struggle for racial

---

22. Studies that document this crucial shift particularly well include Donald Yacovone, "The Transformation of the Black Temperance Movement, 1827–1854: An Interpretation," *Journal of the Early Republic* 8 (Fall 1988) 282–97; Richard Newman, "Black Radical Politics in Jacksonian America," paper delivered at the Annual Meeting for the Society of Historians of the Early American Republic, Lexington, KY, July 16, 1999; and, more generally, C. Peter Ripley, Roy E. Finkenbine, Michael F. Hembree, and Donald Yacovone, eds., *Witness for Freedom: African American Voices on Race, Slavery, and Emancipation* (Chapel Hill, 1993), 1–17. The most extensive study of black and white coalition-building in the name of racial integration and political equality remains Carleton Mabee, *Black Freedom: The Non-Violent Abolitionists* (New York, 1970). Other works that elucidate important aspects of this collaborative dynamic include Milton Sernett, *Abolition's Axe: Beriah Green, the Oneida Institute, and the Black Freedom Struggle* (Syracuse, 1986); Horton and Horton, *In Hope of Liberty*, 64–65, 109, 126, 129, 152, 203–36; and James Brewer Stewart, *Holy Warriors: The Abolitionists and American Slavery* (New York, 1996), 127–49.

23. For a most accessible primary-source sampling of this range of discussion among African Americans, consult Howard Holman Bell, ed., *Minutes of the Proceedings of the National Negro Conventions, 1840–1864* (New York, 1969). See also Jane H. Pease and William H. Pease, "Black Power: The Debate of 1840," *Phylon* 29 (Spring 1968): 19–26; Floyd J. Miller, *The Search for Black Nationality: Black Emigration and Colonization, 1787–1863* (Urbana, 1975), 90–249; and Howard Zinn, "Abolitionists, Freedom Riders, and the Tactics of Agitation," in Martin Duberman, ed., *The Antislavery Vanguard: New Essays on the Abolitionists* (Princeton, 1965).

justice that the abolitionists failed to address before the Civil War," he wisely identified why these now long-dead reformers continue to have so much to tell the generations of scholars who study them. Indeed, the abolitionists' presence has become inescapable in our historical vocabulary as we continue to struggle over the political meanings of color. On the most general level, representations of Frederick Douglass, Harriet Tubman, and Sojourner Truth join those of Martin Luther King and Malcolm X to dominate elementary and secondary curriculum. At the opposite end of the academic continuum, contemporary historiography, that extraordinary explosion of scholarship on abolitionism in all its varieties, now reverberates far beyond departments of history. It is a "supernova" of research and analysis radiating across the humanities that as often inspires professors of literary and cultural studies to excel in the historian's craft as it compels historians to pioneer in interdisciplinary endeavor. In every academic setting abolitionism speaks at least as urgently to as many today as it did to the "neo-abolitionist" feelings of scholars and civil rights activists in the 1960s.[24]

In the last analysis, this contemporary sense of the abolitionists' immediacy best demonstrates just how modern their racial politics actually became after 1840. By the opening of that decade they had lived through the terrible process that had forged democratic white supremacy's "iron cages." While *herrenvolk* democracy was being built in the North on the wreckage of the abolitionists' hopes for immediate abolition and the "elevation" of "respectable" African Americans, their responses inaugurated an ever-compounding challenge to white supremacy even as civil war drew closer. Moreover, they mounted these challenges when facing a white South increasingly united by its own successful modernization of white supremacist political culture. From 1840 on, therefore, abolition-

---

24. Yacovone's comment is quoted with his permission from a longer discussion with the author on the subject of the "modernity" of abolitionism in the 1840s and 1850s at Legal Seafood Restaurant, Copley Plaza, Boston, Mar. 18, 1997. For instances of recent scholarship by members of departments of literature that eschew "poststructural" and cultural studies approaches in favor of almost "Rankean" efforts to reconstruct factual narrative, see Gary Collison, *Shadrach Minkins: From Fugitive Slave to Citizen* (Cambridge, MA, 1998); and Albert Von Frank, *The Trials of Anthony Burns: Freedom and Slavery in Emerson's Boston* (Cambridge, MA, 1997). For examples of historians of abolitionism whose work crosses over into interdisciplinary approaches, see David Blight, *Frederick Douglass's Civil War: Keeping Faith in Jubilee* (Baton Rouge, 1989); Nell Painter, *Sojourner Truth: A Life, a Symbol* (New York, 1997); and Horton and Horton, *In Hope of Liberty*. For a useful discussion of these interdisciplinary trends, consult Roediger, "Pursuit of Whiteness."

ists' immediate victories were rare and equivocal. Yet it is also difficult to deny that during this same period they did, indeed, strip white supremacism of its intellectual pretension, claims of moral sanction, and unchallenged power to shape social relations, thereby setting precedents and standards that continue to furnish some of our most compelling historical references. Had they chosen otherwise, the impoverishment of our efforts to convey the moral challenges of our history is easy to estimate. All we need do is imagine the duration of our silence.

Acknowledgments

I wish to thank the following colleagues and friends for their critical contributions to the development of this essay: Dickson D. Bruce, Peter Hinks, James O. Horton, Lois Horton, Carol Lasser, Joanne Pope Melish, Michael A. Morrison, Gary Nash, Rich Newman, George Price, Patrick Rael, Jean Soderlund, Clay Steinman, Dorothy C. Stewart, Ronald Walters, and Donald Yacovone.

Commitments

There is no more difficult challenge for historians, particularly for historians of abolitionism, than that of explaining motivations. What circumstances made the abolitionists decide to take on such an unpopular, even dangerous and seemingly impossible task? Once they had committed themselves to ending slavery, what allowed them to persist so tenaciously for so long against such entrenched and successful opponents? Rather than attempting to generalize about the movement as a whole, these two essays seek to understand motivations by closely examining the lives of several of the movement's most prominent leaders and the impacts these leaders had on their co-workers.

The Roberts Case, the Easton Family, and the Dynamics of the Abolitionist Movement in Massachusetts, 1776–1870

With George R. Price

As one of Boston's most militant black abolitionists, Benjamin Roberts surprised no one when he filed a desegregation lawsuit against the city school committee in 1848. This familiar and important story ultimately set formidable precedents in the struggle for racial equality and in the history of American law. The plaintiff in *Roberts v. the Boston School Committee* sought admission of his five-year-old daughter, Sarah Roberts, into the city's all-white public school system and an end to the grossly inferior facility reserved exclusively for "colored" Americans (as these Bostonians preferred to call themselves). By demanding the integration of all Boston public schools—and six hundred dollars in damages—Roberts's suit began a seven-year battle that led first to stinging defeat and then to unexpected victory. After Massachusetts Chief Justice Lemuel Shaw issued his infamous decision against Roberts that enunciated the doctrine of "separate but equal," the controversy moved into the streets. Demonstrations, boycotts, and petitions mobilized the state's abolitionist community and antislavery-minded politicians. In 1855, the state legislature finally passed a law forbidding segregated education within the Commonwealth. Benjamin Roberts and his allies deserved the credit for this unprecedented victory for equal school rights. Segregationists

Originally published in co-authorship with George Price as "The Roberts Case, the Easton Family and the Dynamics of the Abolitionist Movement in New England, 1776–1870," *Massachusetts Historical Review* 4 (2004): 89–115. Reprinted with permission. George R. Price teaches in the Native American Studies and African American Studies departments at the University of Montana and is currently working on a multigenerational biography of activists in the Easton family. We are deeply indebted to two unusually talented editors, Donald Yacovone and Ondine Le Blanc of the Massachusetts Historical Society, who have improved this essay immeasurably at practically every turn.

ultimately triumphed on the national level, however, when, in 1896, the United States Supreme Court cited Shaw's "separate but equal" doctrine as its leading precedent in its *Plessey v. Ferguson* decision that legalized segregation throughout the country. Not until 1954, of course, did the Supreme Court overturn that doctrine in *Brown v. Board of Education of Topeka*, a historic decision that helped mark the emergence of the modern civil rights movement.[1]

Embedded in the early portion of this important narrative lie revealing but heretofore unexplored issues concerning the social construction of race and identity in nineteenth-century New England. Roberts's story compels us to investigate his life and character in greater detail, including how his words and deeds reflected his self-perceptions; the values, traditions, and imperatives he saw himself upholding; and why he chose to express his equalitarian commitments through the education of his five-year-old daughter. By considering Roberts's career, we may also achieve a deeper understanding of the personal motives and frameworks of identity that supported a "colored" (or if one prefers, African) American's commitment to abolitionism. To be sure, a significant body of writings already exists about the personal meaning of activism for uniquely situated and richly self-documented fugitives-turned-activists, such as Frederick Douglass and Harriet Jacobs, and about activism as a source of civic values within free African American communities.[2] Nevertheless, historians have largely settled for the obvious regarding New England abolitionists of color, concluding that a personal hatred of discrimination and slavery alone drove their commitment to abolitionism.

As their many sophisticated studies amply testify, biographers and historians working in this field recognized long ago that the brute facts of racial exploitation, in and of themselves, do not sufficiently explain the

---

1. Carleton Mabee, *Black Freedom: The Nonviolent Abolitionists from 1830 through the Civil War* (New York, 1970), 91–127; *Sarah C. Roberts vs. the City of Boston*, Supreme Court of Massachusetts, Suffolk, 59 Mass. 198, 59 Cush.19; Donald M. Jacobs, "The Nineteenth-Century Struggle over School Segregation in Boston," *Journal of Negro Education* 39 (1970): 76–85; Leonard W. Levy and Harlan B. Philips, "The Roberts Case: Source of the 'Separate But Equal Doctrine,'" *American Historical Review* 56 (1950): 510–18; *Liberator*, Aug. 6, 1849, Apr. 4, 1851.

2. See, for example, David Blight, *Frederick Douglass' Civil War: Keeping Faith in Jubilee* (Baton Rouge, 1989); and Jean Fagin Yellin, *Women and Sisters: The Antislavery Feminists and American Culture* (New Haven, 1989), 77–99.

commitments of white activists. As many recent studies have emphasized, the vast majority of Northern whites had little but contempt for African Americans and abolitionists, and they harbored few reservations about slavery's continued existence. Likewise (as African American activists repeatedly lamented), most free people of color grew demoralized and distracted, not energized and politicized, by the terrible toll exacted by racial bigotry.[3] If abolitionism drew public attention to one's dark complexion, then incessant personal risk and concerns for the safety of one's family and community complicated individual challenges enormously. Being an abolitionist, black or white, could be a dangerous way to live. With so many forces against them, one might well marvel that so many Northern blacks accepted a public abolitionist role.

Clearly, we must learn more about what motivated these exceptional free people of color to venture so far from the safety of conventional norms and how their commitments differed from those of their white associates. This inquiry into the life of Benjamin Roberts offers such an opportunity. It also invites a fuller understanding of the dynamics of color consciousness within New England abolitionism. Approached in this manner, the material allows several broad but tentative hypotheses to take shape. Specifically, Roberts's biography has convinced us that the abolitionist commitment for African Americans and whites involved differing psychological and historical dynamics and produced contrasting constructions of color consciousness. Abolitionism, in this case, allowed Benjamin Roberts to embrace the family legacy of activism established by his formidable grandfather, James Easton, during and immediately after the American Revolution. Through and for abolitionism, Roberts internalized powerful historical continuities. Moreover, the Roberts family history would not permit the white practice of classifying humanity by pigmentation. Long before 1776, as Roberts acutely understood, his forebears had created a family tree without rigid categories of race, one that mingled the bloodlines of Indians, English, and Africans. Roberts

---

3. Joanne Pope Melish, *Disowning Slavery: Gradual Emancipation and Race in New England, 1780–1860* (Ithaca, 1998); Leon Litwack, *North of Slavery: The Negro in the Free States* (New York, 1961); James Oliver Horton and Lois Horton, *In Hope of Liberty: Culture, Community, and Protest among Northern Free Blacks, 1700–1860* (New York, 1996).

acted decisively on the realization that his family and his ancestors shared a long history of revolutionary struggle and a multicultural lineage that confounded the accepted "reality" of black and white races.

White abolitionists could forge a commitment to "the cause" without questioning the reality of their own race. But New Englanders such as Wendell Phillips and William Lloyd Garrison saw in abolitionism a disjunctive opportunity to be "reborn." Rather than questioning the "fact" of race or defending their raced selves in a hostile community, white abolitionists remade their identities around the radical insight that two sharply distinguished races—a reputedly degraded black one and a supposedly superior white one—were, in truth, equal. Furthermore, white abolitionists rebelled against the legacy of the founding fathers, whom they deemed hypocritical for upholding slavery while espousing equality.[4] By contrast, most black abolitionists staked their claim for equal rights firmly in the heritage of the Revolution. These differing frameworks, however, changed significantly as the abolitionist movement in New England itself evolved. By the 1840s and 1850s, black *and* white abolitionists drew powerful inspiration from New England's revolutionary past in order to challenge white supremacy in Massachusetts and to create the nation's first civil rights movement.

Let us begin with Roberts's own 1870 reflections on Massachusetts's long struggle for equality, "Our Progress in the Old Bay State," published in the nationally circulated *New Era*, a newspaper edited by lifelong abolitionists. Quite likely, Roberts wrote the article to mark ratification of the Fifteenth Amendment, which secured national voting rights for African American men. Many abolitionists considered this final constitutional amendment of Reconstruction the culminating triumph of their long crusade. From this heady perspective, Roberts felt moved to present his own triumphant history to a national audience as he recounted the trials and victories of three generations of African Americans in Massachusetts. The piece opens with a celebration of the egalitarian achievements of the illustrious "colored" patriots who rallied as equal citizens of Massachusetts in the American Revolution, fighting "side by side with

---

4. The fullest recent explanation of this process is Robert B. Abzug, *Cosmos Crumbling: American Reform and the Religious Imagination* (New York, 1994), esp. 129–229.

white soldiers." In the spirit of Crispus Attucks, "their ashes . . . mingled with the slain who fell defending the right." The narrative then chronicles Massachusetts's post-Revolution declension into six decades of racial tyranny, during which a brutal white majority subverted the struggle for equality at every turn. "Colorphobia deprived us of common schools and many other privileges: we were assailed and hooted at in the streets . . . and it was a dark day for all of us," Roberts emphasized. To document this dispiriting trend, he referred briefly to the futile efforts of "a black man named James Easton born in Middleboro," a "Revolutionary soldier" whose ambitious manual labor school for African American youth was undermined in the 1820s by white prejudice and black apathy. This passing reference to Easton, Roberts's grandfather, as it turns out, is the key to appreciating fully the significance of this published account.[5]

The tide turned in Massachusetts, in Roberts's account, in the 1840s. The state's regeneration, according to Roberts, began in Boston as a result of the protracted struggle, waged against the "old fogies of that day, both black and white," to end segregation in the schools—a struggle initiated by an unidentified "young man" (as Roberts obliquely referred to himself) who had filed a lawsuit on behalf of his young daughter. Years of collective abolitionist effort secured the victory over segregation in 1855, at long last redeeming the promise of the Revolution. From the perspective of 1870, racial tyranny in Massachusetts had been shouldered aside. The 1855 success appeared as a glorious prelude to the destruction of white oppression following the Civil War, when the federal government enacted emancipation and constitutional guarantees of African American citizenship. In Roberts's final estimation, the democratic regeneration of Massachusetts foretold that of the United States itself.

> Our children do not feel as their predecessors felt a thousand times when passing the schoolhouse as *inferiors and outcasts.* To them, new ideas are opened . . . and it will not be many years ere the full results will find our successors in the full possession of positions of honor and emolument and amply competent to cope with the most distinguished citizens of our community. . . . The man of yesterday, borne down by servile oppression,

---

5. Benjamin F. Roberts, "Our Progress in the Old Bay State," *New Era,* Mar. 31, 1870.

a stranger in the land of his nativity, his limbs galled by chains and fetters and naught but black despair settled upon his troubled mind . . . now wrested by the powerful arm of justice from his tormentors and placed on the moral platform untrammeled, free and supplied with all that is necessary to a fully developed member of the brotherhood of man. . . . Who among us can refrain from giving vent to highest exultation over these remarkable events?[6]

Thus, Roberts closed his history on a high note, exhorting his readers to continued success with a renewed awareness of the obstacles already overcome and the inspirational legacy of black activism.

On a first reading of Roberts's narrative, one might not sense in it any motive other than a desire to secure for the abolitionists an exalted place in history and to memorialize the school desegregation crusade. A second reading, however, especially one informed by certain historical facts, can shed light on the complex, personal motives that inspired Roberts to write. The clue that opens up Roberts's essay is his sketchy characterization of James Easton, the "Revolutionary soldier . . . born in Middleboro," and the brief description of Easton's ambitious project to educate African American youth and its defeat. To Roberts's contemporaries, who knew that Easton was his grandfather, his essay voiced (for all its apparent modesty) an eloquent justification of his own activism and that of three generations of his forebears. They could see the ideological and genealogical continuity over time. Between 1776 and 1870, revolutionary promise had given way to a desperate conflict with racial tyranny, which in turn developed into a broad struggle for legislated equality. To historians today, to whom the personal connection has become invisible, only the general meaning remains: the essay documents how African American abolitionists in New England lived out their crusade in the midst of evolving racial politics.

The more we know about Easton, the more we will understand how the counterpoint between individual history and activism shaped Roberts's commitments to abolitionism. His sense of the movement's

---

6. Ibid.

historical development, fundamentally different from that of any white abolitionalist, grew out of his personal inheritance from James Easton; Easton's predecessors from England, Africa, and North America; and Easton's children, who continued in various ways to demand an end to discrimination in New England.[7] Furthermore, the inheritance was not a distant one: James Easton lived long enough for Benjamin Roberts to know him and his career intimately. By making James Easton's educational venture the historical prelude to his own victory over segregation, Roberts explained how he had upheld Easton family honor, vindicated his grandfather's work, and set an example for future generations.

When we examine James Easton's origins, we enter a New England without races—at least as we have come to understand that term. Although from the first, Anglo-Americans perceived Africans as black and therefore markedly "different," social conditions in colonial New England greatly complicated the consequences of this understanding. Before the Revolution, as Lois Horton and Joanne Melish have explained, American Indians and people of African descent often shared common conditions of enslavement and intermarriage. The results defy our modern understandings of terms such as "Negro," "colored," "black," "mulatto," and "Indian." Whites, in fact, invented these terms when seeking to categorize and control dark-complected people in New England, regardless of ancestry. English settlers, for example, generally considered all slaves black and of African descent, and from their perspective "black," "African," and "enslaved" were closely overlapping terms that described a system of coerced labor. Indigenous and African peoples, by contrast, customarily regarded each other not by skin color but by group or tribal names—"Wampanoag," "Narragansett," "Gambian," "Ibo," and so forth. The resulting struggle over conflicting identifications created ambiguous situations in which whites regarded some "Indians" as black, others as "red," and indigenous groups with African members as "Negro Indians." Religious practices also reflected these ambiguities. Before the Revolution and for several decades after, some New England churches

---

7. For James Easton's biography and a history of the Easton family, see George R. Price and James Brewer Stewart, eds., *To Heal the Scourge of Prejudice: The Life and Writings of Hosea Easton* (Amherst, 1999), 1–47.

served "colored"—whether African or Native American—parishioners as well as white, sometimes by allowing integrated worship and sometimes by demanding segregated seating.[8]

Still more perplexing terminology arose once European-descended settlers began referring to "mixed" individuals as "mustees," "mullatos," and "colored," terms that could indicate the presence of a white lineage, as well as "black" or "red." Further confounding the racial terrain, some emancipated slaves of African descent made their way into white New England, usually by becoming farmers, artisans, sailors, or semiskilled laborers. Others retreated into isolated indigenous communities, gaining kin support and personal security by creating or joining mixed families. Other native or indigenous people, meanwhile, represented themselves as "Negroes" in order to claim legal advantages and political rights—a situation that remained true through the Civil War. For our understanding of Benjamin Roberts, all this confusion documents one crucial point: the rigid categories of "red," "black," and "white" that Euro-Americans enforced so ruthlessly during Roberts's antebellum days would have seemed wholly irrational, oppressive, and unprecedented to dark-skinned New Englanders of James Easton's generation. Although we cannot know fully what Easton meant when he described himself as "colored," he most certainly meant it as a repudiation of the hardening white definitions of his era.[9]

The Easton family can trace its roots to Newport, Rhode Island, during the 1670s, when Quakers Peter and Nicholas Easton began manumitting their slaves. By 1690, the white Eastons had freed eight slaves, or "servants"; two they designated as "negroes," two as "Indian," and four received no racial designation. By the mid-eighteenth century, local records were littered with mentions of "black," "colored," "indian," or "mulatto" Eastons or Easons—none enslaved. Two of these early emancipated slaves, Richard and Mary Eas(t)on, lived in a small village near

8. See Melish, *Disowning Slavery*; Joanne Pope Melish, "The Narragansett Indians: A Nineteenth-Century History of Racial Extinction" (paper presented at the Annual Meeting of the Society for Historians of the Early American Republic, Buffalo, NY, July 2000); and Horton and Horton, *In Hope of Liberty*, chaps. 3–5.

9. Melish, "Narragansett Indians"; Dickson D. Bruce, *The Origins of African American Literature, 1680–1865* (Charlottesville, VA, 2001), 1–92.

the town of Middleborough, where in 1754 Mary gave birth to James Easton. After 1754, the family disappears temporarily from the historical record, suggesting that the Eastons moved to one of the several small Indian communities just outside Middleborough; since 1694, the town had banned Indians from living within its boarders. When James Easton married Sarah Dunbar, a woman of possibly similar mixed-race heritage, the Easton name returned to visibility.

The tradition of Indian–African intermarriage continued as well. John Wainer, a Wampanoag and the nephew of the famous international commercial trader Paul Cuffe of New Bedford, married Mary Easton, one of James's daughters, thereby beginning a long and complex connection between the two families. Caleb, one of Easton's sons, married Chloe Packard, a white woman from a leading North Bridgewater, Massachusetts, family; three of their six children would be classified as white in the 1880 census. Thus, to insist that James Easton and his family belonged to a "separate [let alone inferior] race," whether black or red, would simply scorn reality. Such a characterization meant that the Eastons would be forced into an "uninhabitable category" (Melish's telling description), constructed for them by prejudiced whites. Yet this precise tragic predicament awaited James Easton and all dark-skinned people living in New England at the close of the Revolution.[10]

When James Easton joined the patriot cause, however, his quest for better prospects outran his equalitarian principles. Like many other dark-skinned New Englanders who enlisted into the military, he declined to identify himself as African American, Indian, or as anything else in the white vocabulary for designating color distinctions. It was a choice that he and thousands of others, Indian- and African-descended alike, made for practical reasons. Heavy legal sanctions against Indians' rights to assemble, bear arms, and trade freely would have nullified their prospects for revolutionary citizenship and relegated them to isolated enclaves. Seeking to destroy these barriers, numerous Wampanoags and Narragansetts, groups from whom James Easton descended, rallied unannounced to the patriot cause. At the same time, African-descended individuals not

---

10. For a detailed presentation of the Easton family genealogy, see Price and Stewart, *To Heal the Scourge of Prejudice*, 3–6.

classified as Indians suffered no such disabilities in Massachusetts. For them, the Revolution likewise offered promises of civic participation and expanding opportunity—certainly James Easton's hopes.

After digging breastworks for George Washington on Boston's Dorchester Heights in 1776, Easton campaigned as a foot soldier in the regiment of Gamaliel Bradford, a veteran of the French and Indian War also from Middleborough. Bradford's regiment occupied various towns in the Hudson River Valley before participating in the fall of Fort Ticonderoga the following year. Easton's next three years remain undocumented, but we know that he mustered out of service and in 1780 moved to North Bridgewater (now Brockton), his family home for the rest of his busy life.[11]

What did Easton believe he had fought for? What new kind of world did he think the Revolution should bring to him and his growing family? Nothing in his own words survives to instruct us, but two closely related sources provide reliable answers. Easton's son Hosea published the first of these, his *Treatise*, in 1837, and his views on exactly these questions most likely expressed the opinions of his deeply revered father, who had died only seven years earlier. The scattered records that document James Easton's remarkable career constitute the second.

According to Hosea Easton, the Revolution made all Americans equal—without exceptions. "When the country belonged to Great Britain, the colored people were slaves," he granted. But once the Declaration of Independence had been promulgated, slaves "were no longer held by any legal power." As a result, Easton argued, the Revolution had proceeded as a massive exercise in mandating racial equality. Nothing, he insisted, had restricted the "color of the attendants" in revolutionary town meetings, "not a word was said about color" when "convoking the Continental Congress," and there was "not a public document of the [federal] government," he claimed, "which recognized the colored man as a slave." In the light of all this compelling evidence, Hosea Easton wondered, How "can it be said that the colored people are not recognized as

---

11. Price and Stewart, *To Heal the Scourge of Prejudice*; William C. Nell, *Colored Patriots of the American Revolution* (Boston, 1855), 32–33; "Memoir of Gamaliel Bradford," *Collections of the Massachusetts Historical Society*, 3d ser., vol. 1 (1825): 203–4. Bradford later served in the state legislature as the representative from Plymouth County.

citizens?" Thus, any "civil and political disabilities of the colored people are the effect of usurpation," gross transgressions against the nation's founding values that summoned his palpable rage: "A highwayman or an assassin acts on principles far superior in comparison with those under which the administrators of the laws of church and state act . . . [when] withholding the *inalienable rights* of one part of the subjects of this government. . . . Were I capable of dipping my pen in the deepest dye of crime, and of understanding the science of the bottomless pit, I should then fail in presenting . . . the true nature of American deception."[12]

Much of Hosea Easton's bitter tone registers the terrible personal costs exacted by his own unavailing struggles against racial bigotry. His words also project the convictions of his equally angry father, a war veteran who had staked his family's future on the promise of multicultural democracy, whose personal lineage mixed people of differing complexions, and who, as a result, wholly loathed racial bigotry.

Although James Easton left no written tract of his opinions, his public actions, captured in other records, express his determination no less eloquently. In 1800, James Easton led his family in its first public stand against segregation. The event took place at Bridgewater's Fourth Church of Christ. The controversy began with the construction of a "Negro gallery," in which the white congregation forced the Eastons and all other dark-skinned members to sit. This galling change represented a sudden departure from the earlier policy of integrated pew benches and thus marked the increasing racial bigotry of white New Englanders. James Easton refused to submit; church records mention "a disturbance in time of public worship," deceptive language for the Easton family's act of defiance. Rather than sit in the "Negro gallery," Easton bought a family pew from a sympathetic white member and occupied it until exasperated white congregants ejected them by force.

More of this incident emerges from an 1855 account by the African American historian William C. Nell, who lived near the Roberts family residence in Boston and who became a leading force in the struggles

12. Hosea Easton, *A Treatise on the Intellectual Character, and the Civil and Political Condition of the Colored People of the U. States and the Prejudice Exercised toward Them: With a Sermon on the Duty of the Church toward Them* (Boston, 1837), reprinted in Price and Stewart, *To Heal the Scourge of Prejudice*, 90–98.

against school segregation. There can be no question that Nell repeated what Benjamin Roberts had told him when he recounted the incident: "The family were victims . . . to the spirit of colorphobia . . . and were persecuted even to the dragging out of some of the family from the Orthodox Church . . . in which, on its enlargement, a porch had been erected, exclusively for colored people. After this disgraceful occurrence, the Eastons left the church."[13]

Thus concluded the first of six clearly documented Easton family protests between 1800 and 1827—and it is likely even more took place. Most appear only briefly in the church records.

One truly extraordinary series of events offers a stunning glimpse of Easton family tenacity. Again, we have William C. Nell to thank for preserving Benjamin Roberts's account of his grandfather's actions: They afterward purchased a pew in a Baptist Church in Stoughton Corner, which excited a great deal of indignation. Not succeeding in having the bargain canceled, the people tarred the pew. The next week the family carried [their own] seats in the waggon. The pew was then pulled down: but the family sat in the aisle. These indignities were continued until the separation of the family [from the church].[14]

Every Sunday morning until the membership expelled them, the Easton family (doggedly? angrily? fearfully? sadly?) returned to their church, set up their own chairs, and defied the Christian bigots of Stoughton. These epic moments forged searing memories, potent family stories, and lifelong recollections for James Easton. Surely, we can now understand why Benjamin Roberts took up the challenge of defending his young daughter against the segregationists and why he paid such heartfelt homage to his grandfather.

As monumental as his public stand against segregation was, it constituted neither the whole of his life nor the whole of his work for social change. Self-educated, Easton mastered the arts of commercial iron-working—which explains his choice of North Bridgewater as his home. Practically no people of color other than the Eastons lived in the area, which meant the family lacked social as well as financial capital.

---

13. Nell, *Colored Patriots*, 33.
14. Ibid.

Nevertheless, the location possessed clear professional advantages: it had plentiful raw materials for smelting and casting, and its proximity to Boston—twenty-six miles away—insured Easton access to clients, markets, and the city's activist community. Soon after setting up house in the town, he established his own shop, which specialized in the manufacture of edge tools (plows, axes, and so forth), anchors, sea chains, and other seafaring gear, and schooled his sons in the business. The Eastons also made special-order items, such as grillwork for Boston's new Tremont Theater and track for the new Marine Railway (upon which workers wheeled newly constructed vessels from shipyards to launching berths). As a contractor and skilled artisan, he possessed the dignified bearing of a gentleman at ease in Boston's blossoming commercial culture. "He was welcomed in the business circles of Boston as a man of strict integrity," wrote William Nell, "and the many who sought his advice on complicated matters styled him 'the black lawyer.'"[15]

James Easton's success did not, however, single him out as a unique figure. His imposing leadership and unimpeachable reputation, rather, identified him as a member of a "colored" elite that rose to prominence soon after the Revolution in cities across the eastern seaboard. A civic-minded group of businessmen, clergymen, and educators, these accomplished individuals preached the values they emphatically practiced of "self-improvement, piety and personal rectitude." They founded the churches, schools, fraternal groups, and voluntary associations that solidified communities of color throughout New England. From the close of the Revolution through the 1820s, men such as Easton exhorted all people of color to "uplift" themselves by embracing the "respectable" values of temperance, thrift, religiosity, and, above all, education. Well suited to the challenges of James Easton's era, this ideology of moral rectitude and self-improvement underpinned the rising "colored" communities of the North. Through it, Easton and his peers sought to guarantee realization of the Revolution's egalitarian promises, even as white racial prejudice deepened throughout New England. Capitalist in economic spirit and republican in social vision, this ideology personally empowered Easton

---

15. Ibid.. For parallel developments in Philadelphia, see Julie Winch, *A Gentleman of Color: The Life of James Forten* (New York, 2002).

as it expressed so well his fervent American nationalism, forged in the Revolution by whites and dark-skinned patriots like himself.[16]

Subscribing to these beliefs came at a price. Easton's claims for republican equality and his rise to leadership in the affairs of "colored Americans" necessitated that he suppress his "Indian" (noncitizen) heritage. One might speculate that his searing hatred of racial bigotry arose in part from having been driven to so painful a choice. Whatever his deeper uncertainties, Easton's commitment to "uplift" inspired the extraordinary project he undertook in the mid-1810s. His decision to incorporate a manual labor school for promising "colored youth" into his family-run foundry represented a visionary experiment unprecedented for its time. It also projected influence five decades into the future, becoming a touchstone in his grandson's own pathbreaking struggles against segregation.

Easton designed the school to combat illiteracy and unemployment among young "men of color." As Easton's eldest son, James Jr., explained to his wealthy merchant relative, Paul Cuffe, when seeking to borrow a thousand dollars for the school in 1816, "for Wount [want] of Sufficient Education we fail of accomplishing Eny Cind [any kind] of bisnis of a Publick nature. Besides, ignorance Produces a great Deel of jealousy." (James Jr. would improve his spelling before he achieved distinction as one of the nation's first African American practitioners of homeopathic medicine.) The enterprise underwrote the education of twenty young scholars who divided their days between academics and apprenticing as smiths, farmers, and shoemakers. The Eastons and their fellow teachers fostered "uplift" by insisting on hard study and respectable comportment. Hosea Easton, whose writings confirm his own participation (Benjamin Roberts was old enough at the time to have visited), described the enterprise's directors as insisting on principles of "rigid economy" and "rules of morality" that they "supported with surprising assiduity." Dedicated "colored men of master spirits and great minds" instructed the students. Along with Easton and other benefactors, they all invested

---

16. Gary B. Nash, *Forging Freedom: Emancipation in Pennsylvania and Its Aftermath* (Cambridge, MA, 1988), 101–279; Patrick Rael, "African American Elites and the Language of Respectability in the Antebellum North" (paper presented at the Annual Meeting of the Organization of American Historians, 1997, San Francisco); Patrick Rael, *Black Identity and Black Protest in the Antebellum North* (Chapel Hill, NC, 2002).

"many thousands of dollars" into the school. Nothing in the development of education in the United States to that point approached the originality and ambition of Easton's school.[17]

For approximately fourteen years, until 1829 or 1830, Easton conducted the school with success. Then, the school's finances collapsed. Shortly after, James Easton died. Roberts's uncle Hosea likely spoke for the entire family when he concluded that the shock of the school's closing had hastened his father's death: "The enterprise ended in total failure. . . . By reason of the repeated surges of the tide of prejudice the establishment, like a ship in a boisterous hurricane at sea went beneath its waves, richly laden, well manned and well managed, and all sunk to rise no more. . . . It fell, and with it fell the hearts of several of its undertakers in despair, and their bodies into their graves." The Easton school's collapse, no isolated event, symbolized the many disasters that people of color endured in the 1820s and 1830s.[18]

In the final years of Easton's life and beyond, African Americans across the North found hopes for full citizenship overborne by "the tide of prejudice" that Hosea Easton described. The racial tyranny that arose in the 1820s originated immediately after the Revolution, when African Americans freed by gradual emancipation had started to create their own communities. Fearful and suspicious of the growth of what they perceived to be an unruly and degraded class, white New Englanders intensified segregation—the very kind directed by white congregants at James Easton and his family. In the 1820s, spreading industrialization and unprecedented British immigration reshaped Northern cities. As a consequence, troubling new class divisions, competition for employment, and public debates over the meaning of skin color intensified white racial bigotry.[19]

When first encountering the stresses of industrial wage labor, ordinary

---

17. Roberts, "Our Progress in the Old Bay State"; Nell, *Colored Patriots*, 34; Hosea Easton, *Treatise*, 110–11; James Easton Jr. to Paul Cuffe, Oct. 8, 1816, in *Captain Paul Cuffee's Logs and Letters, 1808–1817*, ed. Rosalind Cobb Wiggins (Washington, DC, 1996), 468–69.

18. For a discussion of the dates during which the school operated, see Price and Stewart, *To Heal the Scourge of Prejudice*, 42 n. 9; Easton, *Treatise*, 110–11.

19. For a detailed analysis of these trends, see James Brewer Stewart, "The Emergence of Racial Modernity and the Rise of the White North, 1776–1840," *Journal of the Early Republic* 18 (Summer 1998): 181–236.

white workers began to see their dark-skinned neighbors as unwelcome competitors in the labor market and as visual symbols of their own diminishing status and prospects. Resenting the African American elites for their forthright assertions of citizenship and threatened by urban communities of color that engaged aggressively in "uplift," lower-class whites began harassing African Americans' Sabbath observances and school-day activities. Harassment soon turned to street-corner bullying and then to invasions of black neighborhoods by outraged white rioters in several Northern cities, Boston included. The worst example took place in Cincinnati in 1829, when a white mob all but destroyed the city's community of color and drove out several hundred residents. Handbills filled with vicious cartoon stereotypes grew ever more popular. Politicians revised Northern state constitutions to deny African Americans' civil rights (Massachusetts almost did so in 1821). They also created two mass parties—Whigs and Democrats—that catered heavily to white voters' racial prejudices. Beginning in 1816, the popular American Colonization Society advocated "returning" free people of color to their "homeland" in West Africa since, its leaders claimed, prejudice against them within the United States was too deep to overcome.[20]

Responding to these multiplying threats, members of the black elite from cities across the North convened the first annual National Convention of Free People of Color in Philadelphia in 1831. Hosea Easton attended, representing Boston, along with his brother-in-law Robert Roberts (Benjamin Roberts's father), Samuel Snowden, and James Barbados. The delegates agreed on an unprecedented new measure to advance the cause of "uplift" by collecting funds to establish a truly distinguished manual labor school for young men of color in New Haven, Connecticut, in partnership, they hoped, with Yale University. Two wealthy white businessmen from New York City, abolitionists Arthur and Lewis Tappan, pledged to help underwrite the project by matching all funds raised by the convention, to a maximum of ten thousand dol-

---

20. See David Roediger, *The Wages of Whiteness: Race and the Making of the American Working Class* (New York, 1991); Paul J. Gilje, *The Road to Mobocracy: Popular Disorder in New York City, 1763–1834* (Chapel Hill, NC, 1987); Melish, *Disowning Slavery*; Noel Ignatiev, *How the Irish Became White* (Cambridge, MA, 1994); and Leonard L. Richards, *"Gentlemen of Property and Standing": Antiabolitionist Mobs in Jacksonian America* (New York, 1971).

lars. The Tappans' close associate, Boston editor William Lloyd Garrison, issued glowing endorsements of the plan in his militant new abolitionist newspaper, the *Liberator*, and announced that he would visit England in search of further funding.[21]

To Hosea Easton, this proposal revived the vision of his just-deceased father, but more grandly and boldly than even he could have imagined. On a still larger scale, the proposed school offered a promising way for the National Convention to join with sympathetic whites in resisting the rising tide of bigotry. As the plan took shape, the imperatives of "uplift" and "respectable" equality that the Eastons had always lived by sprang back to life. Hosea returned to Boston soon after the convention adjourned and began soliciting donations. His brother Joshua, brother-in-law Robert Roberts, sister Sarah, and her sixteen-year-old son, Benjamin Roberts, all quite likely shared his excitement and perhaps in his fund-raising efforts as well.

The involvement of William Lloyd Garrison and the Tappan brothers in the work of the Colored Convention marked the appearance of an unprecedented moral crusade for "immediate abolition." After 1831, Garrison and other white crusaders demanded that slavery be obliterated in an instant—a position that reflected a new consciousness of slavery as a vicious institution and an abomination in the eyes of a just and angry God. Since "immediatists" held that God had created all humanity "in one blood," they argued further that people of color living in the North should be "elevated" to civic and social equality. This radical ideology goes far to explain the sudden interest among these white reformers in the welfare of Northern blacks and their eager support for the New Haven school. Never before had so many black and white activists collaborated so extensively in pursuit of such egalitarian projects aimed at racial "uplift." Sabbath schools, debating and literary societies, private academies, and temperance organizations sprang up in towns and cities across the free states. So did militant antislavery societies that daringly "mixed" women with men and African Americans with whites all

---

21. Howard Holman Bell, ed., *Minutes of the Proceedings of the National Negro Conventions, 1830–1864* (New York, 1969), 6; Howard Holman Bell, *A Survey of the Negro Convention Movement, 1830–1861* (New York, 1969), 20–26; James Brewer Stewart, *William Lloyd Garrison and the Challenge of Emancipation* (Arlington Heights, IL, 1992), 60–61.

condemning slavery and demanding racial equality. For the Tappan brothers, the Easton family, and abolitionists everywhere, the early 1830s promised truly revolutionary developments, exactly what most Northern whites feared beyond all else.[22]

Throughout the free states during the 1820s, whites had responded to the mounting economic stress of industrialization and personal insecurities with ever more frequent acts of racial hostility. As the 1830s opened, they united across class lines to crush the threat of racial and gender "amalgamation" they saw in the new abolitionist movement. Building on the mob violence that already marked the previous decade, angry crowds in towns and cities across the North disrupted abolitionists' meetings and, far more ominously, terrorized free African American communities. All hopes that James Easton's descendents might have entertained for furthering his educational vision disintegrated in 1831 when Yale's administrators scorned cooperation with the Colored Convention and leading ministers denounced the idea of the school. When New Haven's white working class learned of the project, they attacked Lewis Tappan's home, threatened African American churches, and invaded any business that catered to people of color. Mob violence again erupted in a succession of major cities—Boston, Philadelphia, Hartford, Pittsburgh, and New York—as well as in the countryside at Dover, New Hampshire; Canterbury, Connecticut; Granville, Ohio; and Alton, Illinois. Although the abolitionist movement slowly grew over the next two decades, whites succeeded in crushing its initial crusade for racial "uplift" and "immediate emancipation." As Benjamin Roberts recalled decades later, "Colorphobia deprived us of our common schools and many other privileges. We were assailed and hooted at in the streets . . . and it was a dark day for all of us."[23]

Besieged and with their hopes blasted, abolitionists responded in varying, sometimes desperate, and often conflicting ways. To a large measure, their reactions depended upon their original commitment. white

---

22. James Brewer Stewart, *Holy Warriors: The Abolitionists and American Slavery* (New York, 1996), 51–74; Paul Goodman, *"Of One Blood": Abolitionism and the Origins of Racial Equality* (Berkeley, 1998), 1–54.

23. Richards, *"Gentlemen of Property and Standing"*; Robert Austin Warner, *New Haven Negroes: A Social History* (New Haven, 1940), 1–68; Roberts, "Our Progress in the Old Bay State."

abolitionists, largely rebellious and religiously orthodox young men and women, sought to break free of established identities through the wrenching "born again" evangelical experience. Even those of Quaker or Unitarian backgrounds approached abolitionism as a test of religious faith. In all cases, their antislavery inspiration, extremely individualistic and nascent, had just begun to solidify when riot and repression suddenly engulfed them. For these reasons, the cumulative impact of violent and relentless racial tyranny proved profoundly unsettling. With few well-established precedents to guide them, reformers disagreed bitterly over the direction of their movement. Some who followed William Lloyd Garrison embraced nonresistance, anticlericalism, women's rights, and religious perfectionism. Only by rejecting all "godless" authority, they argued, could the nation wipe away the sin of slavery. Some abolitionists who opposed Garrison, such as the Massachusetts Quaker John Greenleaf Whittier, proposed the founding of a third political party. Still others, agreeing with Lewis Tappan, attempted to keep the movement faithful to its original antislavery principles. Whatever their positions, the new crisis drove white abolitionists to revisit their initial motives and assumptions, a process that often resulted in radically new approaches and discord.[24]

The first generation of African American activists, which included the Eastons, endured no such agonizing reassessments or unbridgeable divisions in the later 1830s. Seasoned by decades of struggle against racial tyranny and personally anchored in a keen sense of the past, they were deeply discouraged but not surprised by the violence of the 1830s. When, for example, Hosea Easton endured disillusioning attacks in the mid-1830s, he suffered no fundamental questioning of himself as an abolitionist. Widely recognized as a compelling thinker and sermonizer, Hosea Easton filled the pulpit of an African American church in Hartford, Connecticut, in 1836. He struggled to protect his congregation against violent whites as local harassment turned into rioting, exchanges of gunfire, the sacking of parishioners' homes, and, ultimately, the burning

---

24. Abzug, *Cosmos Crumbling*, 124–229; Aileen Kraditor, *Means and Ends in American Abolitionism: Garrison and His Critics on Strategy and Tactics, 1834–1854* (New York, 1969); James Brewer Stewart, "Peaceful Hopes and Violent Experiences: The Evolution of Conservative and Radical Abolitionism, 1831–1837," *Civil War History* 17 (1971): 293–309.

of his church. After this experience, Easton discarded his lifelong belief that African Americans could "raise" themselves to equality by their own efforts. In 1837, he published an angry and pessimistic inquiry into the origins, development, and nature of white racial prejudice and its devastating impact on people of color. Although "uplift" remained his central creed, Easton now believed that repentant white oppressors must be the guarantors of "elevation." It was a shift in emphasis, but still Hosea Easton held tenaciously to his father's legacy, drawing on the intergenerational continuities of New England's black abolitionists.[25]

Sarah Easton, Benjamin Roberts's mother, also embodied these enduring intergenerational ties. After moving to Boston, Sarah married a man in 1813 who bore uncanny similarities to her father, James Easton. Like Easton, the self-educated Robert Roberts moved with confidence among Boston's moneyed elite: during the 1820s, he managed the households of Nathaniel Appleton and Christopher Gore, scions of the Commonwealth's most opulent families. Roberts's first wife, like Sarah Easton, had been the daughter of a famous "colored" Revolutionary War veteran equal in prominence to Easton. Soon after Roberts arrived in Boston from Charleston, South Carolina, in 1805, he formed numerous attachments with the Easton family. After his marriage to Sarah, he grew close to the influential Cuffe family, longtime Easton kin and business associates. In the late 1820s and early 1830s, he joined his brothers-in-law, Hosea and Joshua Easton, in opposing the American Colonization Society and supporting the ill-fated New Haven manual labor school. Moreover, much like James Easton, Roberts promoted activism within his church, Boston's First Independent (African) Baptist Church, which welcomed white abolitionists such as Garrison. James Easton and Robert Roberts undoubtedly profoundly influenced the entire extended family during their seventeen years together as father- and son-in-law. That much became clear when Sarah and Robert Roberts named their first-born son James Easton Roberts, to honor the family patriarch, and their second child Benjamin Franklin Roberts, to symbolize James Easton's antiracist revolutionary ideology and ideals of personal independence.

---

25. Price and Stewart, *To Heal the Scourge of Prejudice*, 1–47.

These imposing paternal figures placed powerful examples of activism before young Benjamin Roberts.[26]

Robert and Sarah Roberts also encouraged their children to master practical skills, and Benjamin became an accomplished printer and editor. Other siblings, for whatever reasons, either chose not to follow the family path into activism or did so in ways that have escaped documentation. Thus, Benjamin Roberts emerged as the sole heir to his grandfather's role as a reformer. At the age of twenty-three, Roberts formally took up the role of the family's next "James Easton" and in 1837 announced his intention to publish a new abolitionist newspaper, the *Anti-Slavery Herald*. Perhaps prompted emotionally by the near-simultaneous deaths of his mother and uncle Hosea, Roberts embarked on a course fraught with danger. His decision to publish an abolitionist journal, financially questionable under the best of circumstances, came at the very moment when the abolitionist movement was crumbling from internecine strife. Whatever the need, the timing proved inauspicious.

The only African American newspapers previously published in the United States, the chronically undersubscribed *Freedom's Journal* and its successor, *Rights of All*, had struggled for three years before collapsing in 1830. The following year, Garrison set up his *Liberator* only a stone's throw from the Roberts family home and immediately secured a loyal black readership by opening its columns to African American issues and writers. Indeed the paper depended upon blacks from across the North for subscriptions and financial contributions. Garrison's rank as the nation's most controversial abolitionist made him a still more formidable competitor. Additionally, the New York *Colored American* began publishing in 1837, putting even more pressure on the scarce resources of Northern blacks. As the national economy faltered into recession and mob violence persisted in the later 1830s, abolitionists divided over "Garrisonian" doctrines and tensions increased between black and white activists. Some African Americans, for example, questioned the

---

26. The history of the Roberts family, its connections to the Eastons, and its place in Boston's black community is treated in the introduction to Robert Roberts, *The House Servant's Directory; or, A Monitor for Private Families: Hints on the Arrangement and Performance of Servant's Work*, ed. Graham Russell Hodges (Armonk, NY, 1998), xi–xlii.

relevance of Garrisonian religious perfectionism and women's rights to their primary goals: abolishing slavery and facing down racial bigotry. Some whites in turn, resented the independent-mindedness of their African American critics.

To surmount these adversities, Roberts tried to incorporate the idea of James Easton's manual labor school into his paper, announcing that subscribers to the *Anti-Slavery Herald* would also be supporting apprenticeships for young African American printers and compositors. By adding the value of "uplift" to his appeals for subscribers, Roberts evidently expected to attract the attention of affluent abolitionists. Toward that end, he solicited personal endorsements from leading white immediatists.[27]

Details of the ensuing disaster remain unclear, but a disaster it surely was. Since no copies of the paper have survived, one can safely assume that it had a limited circulation and an extremely brief life. Judging from the response of one of Roberts's endorsers, the prominent immediatist abolitionist Amos A. Phelps, it appears that white abolitionists deemed Roberts an overtly bigoted and brazen self-promoter. After reading the paper, Phelps demanded that Roberts return his letter of endorsement. Roberts's extraordinary response to Phelps's request captures vividly the frustration, anger, humiliation, and disappointment that engulfed him as his dreams crumbled. Roberts's words also provide deep insight into the pride, determination, and conviction that had underpinned the Easton family's struggles against racial bigotry for three generations. He wrote:

> I am aware that there has been and *now is*, a combined effort on the part of certain *professed* abolitionists to muzzle, exterminate and put down the efforts of certain colored individuals effecting the welfare of the colored brethren. The truth is respecting myself, my whole soul is engaged in the cause of humanity. I am for the *improvement* among this class of people, *mental* and *physical*. The arts and sciences have never been introduced to any extent among us—therefore they are of the utmost importance. If our anti-slavery men will not subscribe to the advancement of these principles,

---

27. A brief biography of Benjamin Roberts that sheds light on his efforts to publish the *Anti-Slavery Herald* is to be found in *The Black Abolitionist Papers*, 5 vols., ed. C. Peter Ripley et al. (Chapel Hill, NC, 1985–92), 3:269–71.

but *rail out* and *protest against* them, why, we will go to the *heathen.* The principle upon which the anti-slavery cause is said to be founded (and *boasting* are not a few) *are the elevation of the free colored people here.* Now it is altogether useless to pretend to affect the welfare of the blacks in this country, unless the chains of prejudice are broken. It is of no use [to] say with the mouth we are friends of the slave and not try to encourage and assist the free colored people in raising themselves. Here is sir the *first* effort of the colored men in this country of this kind, vis. the paper *published, printed* and *edited* by colored persons in Massachusetts. Shall *this* be defeated? But it is contended that the *individual* [Roberts] who started the enterprise has not taken it up from principle—*he* don't intend what he pretends. Base misrepresentations! False accusations!—I was not aware that so many hypocrites existed in the anti-slavery society. According to what I have seen of the conduct of some, a black man would be as unsafe in their hands as those of Southern slaveholders.[28]

After this bitter remonstrance, Benjamin Roberts retreated from visible leadership for a decade. As a professional printer, however, his career continued. During this "quiet" period, one finds his printer's imprimatur on a variety of books and pamphlets, many by African American authors, documenting his unassuming but ongoing and important role in his community. His apparent quiescence in the antislavery movement raises the speculative question, in retrospect, whether the Easton legacy represented a recipe for disaster. After all, James had seen his dreams shattered with the bankruptcy of his school and Hosea had lived in despair after the mob burned his church. From this perspective, Roberts's own defeat could be seen as extending a family tradition of high-minded struggle that led to abject failure.

Roberts, nonetheless, invested far too much of himself in the Easton family past to succumb to demoralization. In 1848, he again reached for family leadership through activism by more fully embracing his grandfather's example. Indeed, his desegregation suit against the Boston school committee echoed with stories his mother had surely told him

---

28. Benjamin Franklin Roberts to Amos A. Phelps, June 19, 1838, ms. #2.0499, Antislavery Collection, Boston Public Library; reprinted in Ripley et al., *Black Abolitionist Papers*, 3:271.

about his grandfather's defiance of white bigots who sought to relegate him and his family to a separate pew. The story of the Eastons carrying their own chairs into the house of God was an irresistible example and spur to action. At the time of the first church protest, Sarah Easton was eleven years old. Now, Benjamin Roberts's daughter, also named Sarah, was barely five and had just begun school when her father initiated his lawsuit. In both instances, outraged fathers distinguished themselves in heroic public efforts to protect their children from soul-destroying segregation and racism.

Benjamin Roberts was acutely sensitive to these parallels in family history, and his justification for his lawsuit evoked the same profound anger at racial bigotry that Hosea Easton had expressed in all of his writings, that tumbled from the lips of James Easton, and that Roberts himself displayed in his reply to Amos A. Phelps. Racial segregation, wrote Roberts, was a system run by "monsters," one that bred "shame and humiliation" among the most vulnerable, causing its young victims to regard themselves as "*inferiors and outcast*" and burdening them with "naught but black despair and troubled mind."[29] These, Roberts proclaimed, were the torments that descended upon his daughter each day as she walked past nicely appointed white schools to attend a distant, inferior facility reserved for those without white skin. Like his grandfather, and like so many other African American activists in New England after 1776, Benjamin Roberts positioned himself as his family's shield against racial bigotry.

While Roberts drew on these forces of historical continuity and family memory as powerful reservoirs of personal motivation, the strategies and tactics of New England's black abolitionist movement had changed during his decade of quiescence. By 1848, the incremental approaches to "elevation" familiar to James Easton had evolved into something resembling a modern movement for unqualified legal and political equality. Beginning in the late 1830s, African American activists had detached themselves from the rapidly factionalizing white-led movement to explore new approaches under black leadership. In 1843, after an eight-year

---

29. Benjamin Roberts, "Report of the Proceedings of the Colored Citizens of Boston, on the Subject of Equal School Privileges," *Liberator*, Apr. 4, 1851; Roberts, "Our Progress in the Old Bay State."

hiatus, the National Negro Convention resumed its meetings to debate demands for racial integration and plans for strengthening independent African American institutions. Nothing better reflected these transformed circumstances than did Roberts's decision to file his lawsuit. His attempt to outlaw institutionalized bigotry in the Boston school system through the courts constituted a project vastly different in scope and substance from his grandfather's struggles to sustain a single manual labor school, or his own earlier attempt to institute apprenticeships.[30]

Roberts's team of attorneys, Robert Morris and Charles Sumner, also reflected changing times. The former, only the second licensed African American attorney in Massachusetts, bore witness to the new militancy and sophistication that had reshaped black abolitionism into a broad-based social movement. The latter, the famed antislavery politician, embodied a deepening Yankee opposition to Southern political demands for access to western territories and the unlimited power to recapture fugitive slaves. Together, Morris and Sumner embodied the emergence of a powerful new alliance between groups of black and white activists, not as philanthropists sponsoring projects of "uplift" but as a coalition of insurgents bent on ridding the "Old Bay State" of "southern influences" and legal oppression.

The state's new political culture took shape under this new coalition in the 1830s and 1840s. White abolitionists had joined African American militants—led by Bostonian Lewis Hayden—in sit-ins, boycotts, and lawsuits that challenged discrimination in public transportation. Daring leaders such as Wendell Phillips and Frederick Douglass habitually invaded segregated train cars, on their own, with African American companions, or in the company of other whites thus resisting segregation on a day-to-day basis all but inconceivable in James Easton's time. Well before Benjamin Roberts filed his lawsuit, many smaller towns and cities in Massachusetts had integrated their public school systems, thanks to abolitionists' persistence. Despite the court's ruling against Roberts

---

30. For two good overall surveys of this shift in free African American approaches to activism, see Donald Yacovone, "The Transformation of the Black Temperance Movement, 1827–1854," *Journal of the Early Republic* 8 (Fall 1988): 282–97; and C. Peter Ripley, Roy E. Finkenbine, Michael F. Hembree, and Donald Yacovone, eds., *Witnesses for Freedom: African American Voices on Race, Slavery and Emancipation* (Chapel Hill, NC, 1993), 1–17.

in 1848, the power of interracial coalition only grew stronger in the years following. Its leaders mobilized supporters across the state, and the Commonwealth's representatives in Congress publicly challenged the slave power during the 1840s and 1850s.

In particular, the new Fugitive Slave Law passed by Congress in 1850 prompted intense, even violent resistance especially in Boston. The law empowered federal marshals to enforce provisions that so manifestly trampled upon the legal rights of African American citizens that all blacks rightly feared false accusations and enslavement. The same coalition of activists that flooded the Massachusetts legislature with antisegregation petitions formed vigilance committees to protect black refugees, resist federal authorities, and harass would-be slave catchers. At election time, black and white activists could be found stirring up support for candidates pledged to overturning school segregation and the Fugitive Slave Law. Perhaps for the first time in the nation's history, politicians incorporated racial egalitarianism into their larger strategies for achieving electoral success, a trend that demonstrated the effectiveness of this Massachusetts insurgency.[31]

Powerful ties of memory that linked the struggles of the 1840s and 1850s to the "spirit of 1776" also accompanied these changes. The white abolitionists and antislavery politicians who defended fugitives and endorsed antisegregation petitions insisted that their actions upheld the same sacred principles of freedom established by their revolutionary forbears. The claim marked a critical convergence of white and black abolitionist ideology. Abolitionists such as Phillips, Edmund Quincy, and Samuel Joseph May, who had initially condemned the founding fathers as compromisers with slavery, held fervently to that belief. Simultaneously, they embraced the insurgent traditions of Lexington and Concord that they could trace to their own parents and grandparents. During the 1850s, a younger generation of white militants such as Thomas Wentworth Higginson, Theodore Parker, Charles Sumner, and John Gorham

---

31. Mabee, *Black Freedom*; Dorothy Porter Wesley, "Integration versus Separatism: William Cooper Nell's Role in the Struggle for Equality," in Donald M. Jacobs, ed., *Courage and Conscience: Black and White Abolitionists in Boston* (Bloomington, IN, 1993), 207–24.

Palfrey joined the movement, men who constantly and on good authority referred to their forebears' patriotic acts of resistance. For prominent female abolitionists such as the Weston sisters—Deborah, Caroline, and Ann Weston and Maria Weston Chapman—and Ann Greene Phillips, activism meshed with roles established by female forebears who had participated as "liberty's daughters" during the Revolution. When the magnificent orator Wendell Phillips joined William C. Nell in fundraising efforts to honor the "colored patriot" Crispus Attucks with a heroic statue, their collaboration perfectly captured how deeply black and white abolitionists now shared an empowering view of New England's revolutionary past. Having launched and then sustained their movement by attacking the legacy of the founding fathers, white abolitionists in Massachusetts now embraced the same history that resonated powerfully within Easton family traditions. "One lived in the atmosphere of the Stamp Act, the Tea Act and the Boston Massacre," Henry Adams recalled of the 1840s and 1850s. "Within Boston a boy was first an eighteenth century politician." [32]

In the final analysis, this ideological shift in the white abolitionists' understanding of New England's history allowed abolitionists of both races to come to together in the "spirit of '76." As we have seen, African American abolitionists such as the Easton and Roberts families and William C. Nell always had understood the Revolution as a struggle for racial justice. By the 1850s, many white abolitionists had come to similar conclusions. This portentous development goes farthest to explain how abolitionists of both races managed to work together with such unique effectiveness in Massachusetts during the 1840s and 1850s and why the legislature voted Benjamin Roberts so stunning a victory. To be sure, white abolitionists in Massachusetts had forgotten the system of Northern slavery that once oppressed the Eastons and countless other families. They also failed to recognize what the Eastons always had known, that

---

32. James Brewer Stewart, "Boston, Abolition, and the Atlantic World, 1820–1860," and James Oliver Horton and Lois E. Horton "Affirmations of Manhood: Black Garrisonians in Antebellum Boston," both in Jacobs, *Courage and Conscience*, 101–55; Bruce, *Origins of African American Literature*, 211–300; William H. and Jane H. Pease, "Abolitionism and Confrontation in the 1850s," *Journal of American History* 17 (1972): 117–28.

rigid categorizations of humanity into races based on skin pigmentation were pernicious human inventions, not facts of nature. These limitations would have ominous implications for the future.

But by re-imagining the legacies of the Revolution in racially egalitarian terms, the Sumners, Phillipses, Westons, and Garrisons could respond constructively to the tireless demands for justice from leaders like Benjamin Roberts and William C. Nell. Consequently, for his own part, Roberts realized the goal he had held uppermost and found so terribly difficult to achieve. Through his allegiance to the legacy of his forebears, Roberts expanded the boundaries of equality within the Commonwealth. The legislative ban on segregated schools, he believed, was "the greatest *boon* ever bestowed upon our people." Now we can appreciate more fully the deep satisfaction Roberts felt when publishing his triumphal recollections in the *New Era*, and why he chose to title them "Our Progress in the Old Bay State." We also understand why Roberts was so careful to include in his reflections a passing yet crucial reference to "James Easton, a black man, born in Middleboro."[33]

---

33. Pease and Pease, "Abolitionism and Confrontation"; James Brewer Stewart, *Wendell Phillips: Liberty's Hero* (Baton Rouge, 1986), 146–208; Henry Adams, *The Education of Henry Adams* (Boston, 1918), 29, 43; Frank O. Gatell, *John Gorham Palfrey and the New England Conscience* (Cambridge, MA, 1963), 236–88; Wendell Phillips, "Crispus Attucks," in his *Speeches, Lectures, and Letters*, 2d ser. (Boston, 1891), 69–76; Carol Williams, "Active Vigilance Is the Price of Liberty: Black Self-Defense against Fugitive Slave Recapture and Kidnapping of Free Blacks," in John R. McKivigan and Stanley Harrold, eds., *Antislavery Violence: Sectional, Racial, and Cultural Conflict in Antebellum America* (Knoxville, TN, 1999), 108–27; Ann-Marie Taylor, *Young Charles Sumner and the Legacy of the American Enlightenment* (Amherst, 2002), 284–335; Donald Yacovone, *Samuel Joseph May and the Dilemmas of the Liberal Persuasion, 1797–1871* (Philadelphia, 1991), 105–15, 155–68; Lawrence J. Friedman, *Gregarious Saints: Self and Community in American Abolitionism* (New York, 1982), 196–222; Nell, *Colored Patriots*.

William Lloyd Garrison, Wendell Phillips, and the Symmetry of Autobiography
Charisma and the Character of Abolitionist Leadership

When explaining the motivations of America's white abolitionists, many historians emphasize the importance of "grassroots" approaches. Yet, the problem of motivation can also be fruitfully investigated by considering the movement "from the top down," in this instance by comparing the biographies of William Lloyd Garrison and Wendell Phillips. By examining the lives of these two preeminent abolitionists and then by suggesting their impact on their less well-known associates, it becomes possible to understand the leadership of Garrisonian abolitionism as well as the sources of the movement's collective motivation.

In the following analysis, qualities of leadership and the biographical elements that nourished them are of central importance, particularly the roles in the lives of Phillips and Garrison of absent fathers, of dominant single mothers, of climactic moments of self-definition, and of the long-term influences of wives, marriages, and families.[1] The longevity of the Garrisonians' collective commitment to their cause must be attributed in some measure to the powerful inspiration contributed by these visible men. The sources of their personal magnetism, in turn, can be found

Originally published as "Garrison, Phillips and the Symmetry of Autobiography: Charisma and the Character of Abolitionist Leadership" in John R. McKivigan and Randall Miller, eds., *The Moment of Decision: Biographical essays on American Character and Regional Identity* (Westport, CT: Greenwood Press, 1994), 117–33. Reprinted with permission.

1. For the latest survey of the historiography of abolitionist motivation, see Richard O. Curry and Lawrence Goodheart, "'Knives in Their Heads': Passionate Self-Analysis and the Search for Identity in Recent Abolitionist Historiography," *Canadian Journal of American Studies* 13 (1983): 401–14. Among the best recent examinations of the dynamics of abolitionism from the "bottom up," see Nancy A. Hewitt, *Women's Activism and Social Change: Rochester, New York, 1822–1872* (Ithaca, 1984); and Christopher Padgett, "Hearing the Abolitionist Rank and File: The Wesleyan Methodist Schism of 1843," *Journal of the Early Republic* 12 (1992): 63–84.

in Garrison's and Phillips's lifelong responses to these intimate circumstances and influences.

No two individuals can seem to have had less in common than did Phillips and Garrison—the Beacon Hill "aristocrat" versus the nondescript commoner, the Harvard graduate versus the self-taught printer's devil, the cosmopolitan orator versus the provincial scribbler, the Calvinist intellectual versus the Christian utopian. Contemporaries puzzled over how these two could tolerate each other, let alone share so close a friendship.[2] Yet, the friendship itself suggests that these two leaders sensed their less apparent commonalities of temperament, wrought by similarities of background and experience. These shared characteristics endowed both men with qualities that continuously deepened their own commitments to leadership in abolitionism while allowing them to nurture the long-term participation of their colleagues. Lawrence Friedman has demonstrated that groups of abolitionists found refuge from a hostile world in family-like communities that clustered around dominating personalities. Some found a supportive leader in the congenial Gerrit Smith, while others were attracted to the steady evangelicalism of Lewis Tappan. Garrisonians, by contrast, responded to the charisma of Garrison and Phillips, leaders whose very natures seemed to radiate spiritual inspiration and spontaneous insight.[3]

As both Max Weber and Anthony F. C. Wallace have employed the term, charisma is a quality imputed to visionary moral leaders by their followers, especially in times of great social uncertainty, when traditional institutions and venerable moral categories seem to have lost their public support. According to both of these scholars, charismatic leaders derive their power from ambiguous historical contexts and from the perceptions of crisis on the part of their followers, not just from the innate qualities possessed by leaders themselves. If ever there was a period when traditional institutions and received wisdom no longer seemed capable of

---

2. For the most recent treatments of both of these figures, see James Brewer Stewart, *William Lloyd Garrison and the Challenge of Emancipation* (Arlington Heights, IL, 1991); James Brewer Stewart, *Wendell Phillips: Liberty's Hero* (Baton Rouge, 1986; repr., 1998). Much of the material in this chapter is drawn from these two books; subsequent documentation on Garrison and Phillips will refer the reader, wherever possible, to primary sources.

3. Lawrence J. Friedman, *Gregarious Saints: Self and Community in American Abolitionism* (New York, 1982).

supplying direction to human affairs, the early 1830s seemed just such a time. However, as Weber and Wallace also explain, charismatic leaders articulate their own intense opposition to society's perceived loss of moral anchor, not just the anxieties of their fervent supporters. They regard themselves as standing at dramatic turning points in history, empowered to articulate fundamental insights that can reverse society's plunge into chaos and inaugurate a new era of harmony based on universal truth. To express the truth with the power they feel it deserves, such leaders invent new words, ideas, and symbols in a style that is often highly personalized and contemptuous of established institutions. All this, of course, roughly parallels general characteristics that historians attribute to the rhetoric of the abolitionists. At the same time, charisma also reshapes the private lives of the leaders themselves, sending them on lifelong quests to secure moral unity between their understandings of their private worlds and their ongoing senses of public mission.[4]

In Jacksonian America, personifications of charismatic leadership seem to have multiplied, starting with "Old Hickory" himself. The "Age of Jackson" was also the age of Joseph Smith, Frances Wright, John Humphrey Noyes, and Charles G. Finney, as well as of Garrison and Phillips—whose anointees believed that their leaders evoked a heavenly new order for a nation mired in blasphemy. In this broad sense, Weber's concept of charisma and the Jacksonian world that spawned so many social visionaries seem to explain each other uncommonly well. The same observation also obtains as we consider specifics of Garrison's and Phillips's biographies.[5]

---

4. For an extended discussion of the concept of charisma, as Weber and other political theorists have developed it, see Reinhard Bendix, *Max Weber: An Intellectual Portrait* (New York, 1960); Ruth Willner, *Charismatic Leadership* (New York, 1990); Ruth Willner, *The Spellbinders: Charismatic Political Leadership* (New York, 1984); Max Weber, *Economy and Society: An Outline of Interpretive Sociology*, 2 vols. (Cambridge, 1950), 1:215–45; Anthony F. C. Wallace, "Revitalization Movements," *American Anthropologist* 58 (1956): 264–81. I am deeply indebted to Calvin Roetzel, Department of Religious Studies, and Jeff Nash, Department of Sociology, Macalester College, for their clear and patient guidance on the points in the preceding discussion regarding charisma. Three evaluations of abolitionism in terms compatible with the concept of charisma are Lewis Perry, *Radical Abolitionism: Anarchy and the Government of God in Antislavery Thought* (Ithaca, 1973); Robert M. Abzug, *Passionate Liberator: The Life of Theodore Dwight Weld* (New York, 1978); and Stanley Elkins, *Slavery: A Problem in American Institutional and Intellectual Life* (Chicago, 1959).

5. A stimulating exploration of this point that also furnished a starting point for this inquiry is Thomas Brown, "From Old Hickory to Sly Fox: The Routinization of Charisma in the Early Democratic Party," *Journal of the Early Republic* 11 (Fall 1991): 339–70.

Phillips spent his Boston childhood studying at the fashionable Latin school, while Garrison, on the streets of nearby Newburyport, sold apples and homemade candy to fend off family impoverishment. As Phillips prepared for Harvard in his parents' Beacon Hill mansion, Garrison wandered with his family to Lynn, Massachusetts, and then to Baltimore, apprenticing to first a shoemaker and next a cabinetmaker. Finally, at age twelve, he left his mother and sister in Baltimore and returned alone to Newburyport, where for the next seven years he learned the printer's trade. While the handsome Phillips—athletic, popular, and eloquent—flourished at Harvard and stayed on in Boston to begin his legal practice, the self-conscious Garrison taught himself the rudiments of literacy and published occasional articles as he served out his apprenticeship at the *Newburyport Herald*. Soon after, Garrison went on to fail in several attempts to establish himself as a political moralist and newspaper editor. Until he and Phillips finally met in 1835 or 1836, no two lives could have seemed less connected. Yet, their remarkable similarities are actually not hard to find.[6]

Garrison and Phillips both spent their formative years struggling with the legacies of vanished fathers, the exacting expectations of extraordinary mothers, and the dreams of futures that would allow them to rest secure with their disrupted pasts. Phillips's father died suddenly when his youngest son was twelve, and Garrison's father abandoned his family when his William was three. The elder Phillips had achieved a distinguished career in business, politics, and philanthropy that built on the formidable traditions of his Puritan ancestors; the elder Garrison was given to sloth and strong drink. Nevertheless, their absent fathers and the powerful, pious mothers who brought them up unaided created comparable emotional challenges for the two young boys.

For young Garrison, paternal abdication drove the remaining family into poverty and his older brother to alcoholism, sexual abusiveness, and self-exile. This shameful legacy Garrison strove both to suppress with unbending moral self-control and to transcend by frantically seeking an extraordinary measure of the world's attention. He began in adolescence to dream of a future when the American public, morally redeemed by his

---

6. Stewart, *Garrison*, 1–40; Stewart, *Phillips*, 1–35.

courageous example, would unite to honor him with power and respect. Meanwhile, Garrison's mother complicated her son's yearnings with a regime of unremitting evangelical discipline and guilt-provoking warnings against the "snares and temptations" hidden in his vaulting ambitions.[7]

As Phillips struggled with the implications of his father's death, he, like Garrison, dreamed of transforming the future. However, instead of confronting a legacy of failure, Phillips faced his family's extraordinary heritage of public service (two governorships of Massachusetts, the founding of Phillips Exeter and Andover academies, and the first mayorship of incorporated Boston, just to mention some of the highlights) that extended unbroken to earliest Puritan days. While Garrison dreamed of gaining fame for his devotion to morality, Phillips absorbed himself in Puritanism's revolutionary history and directed his fantasies into the past. He identified strongly with Oliver Cromwell, Edmund Burke, Sam Adams, and other men who seemed to Phillips to share his ancestors' ability to twist the direction of history in liberty's favor. Once installed in his law office, he remained immersed in his studies, linking his investigations quite explicitly to familial expectations by developing an elaborate genealogy of his forebears. All the while, like Garrison, he also remained quickly responsive to his dominating mother. She frequently had summoned him home from Harvard to account for himself, and after he opened his law office, she continued her demands while pushing him to slough off his seeming disinterest in advancing his worldly position.[8]

Apart from these similar patterns of uncertainty, the stories of Garrison's and Phillips's entries into abolitionism are textbook fare. Garrison, in 1829, became the editorial partner of the Quaker abolitionist Benjamin Lundy, was soon after jailed in Baltimore for libeling a slave trader, and by 1831 had returned to Boston to launch his famous *Liberator*. Phillips, six years later, had already impulsively married the militantly emancipationist Ann Terry Greene when he learned of the murder of the abolitionist

7. Frances Lloyd Garrison to William Lloyd Garrison, August 29, 1817, in Wendell Phillips Garrison and Francis Jackson Garrison, *The Life of William Lloyd Garrison as Told by His Children, 1805–1879*, 4 vols. (Boston, 1889), 1:33 (quotation). Stewart, *Garrison*, 1–40; R. Jackson Wilson, *Figures of Speech: American Writers and the Literary Marketplace from Benjamin Franklin to Emily Dickinson* (Cambridge, MA, 1989), 117–60.

8. Stewart, *Phillips*, 1–53.

editor Elijah Lovejoy by a proslavery mob in Alton, Illinois. At the meeting called in Faneuil Hall to protest this event in November 1837, Phillips suddenly rose and electrified the audience as he eulogized Lovejoy and announced his own conversion to "the cause."[9] Buried in the details of these familiar narratives were some of the dynamics that transformed dreamers into leaders and unsure young men into the charismatic builders of a revolutionary crusade. A brief contrast between the personal outlooks of America's eighteenth-century's founding fathers and those of Garrison and Phillips suggests how such dynamics might be identified.

As Douglass Adair has suggested, the men of the Revolutionary era conducted their lives with eyes fixed on posterity. Vindication, they believed, could be achieved only through the favorable verdicts of their future biographers, whom they set out to influence with elaborate displays of virtue. Garrison and Phillips, by contrast, embarked on lifelong searches to establish through their abolitionism the moral unity between their private worlds and their public missions. In place of the founding fathers' preoccupations with history, Garrison and Phillips substituted a charismatic drive to confirm for themselves that their lives cohered in dramatic moral symmetries. Vindication would come not from posthumous historical judgments but from first-hand experiences that documented to their own satisfaction their lives' moral wholeness.[10]

For an aging Garrison, in the summer of 1864, Baltimore was the most logical place to reconfirm the symmetry of his life as an abolitionist. Truly, the city was replete for Garrison with memories of his beginnings. Also, because the Republicans had invited him to the city as an honorary delegate to attend their presidential nominating convention, Baltimore offered Garrison a unique opportunity to fuse his sense of his past with the present in one grand design. Here, forty years earlier, he had prayed with his mother for the last time as she lay on her deathbed, racked by tuberculosis and by fears that her son was succumbing to godless ambition. Here, earlier still, he had assisted his mother in her work as a domestic servant by carrying slop jars while his older brother

---

9. Ibid., 36–63; Stewart, *Garrison*, 41–55.

10. Douglass Adair, "Fame and the Founding Fathers," in Trevor Colbourn, ed., *Fame and the Founding Fathers: Essays in Honor of Douglass Adair* (Chapel Hill, 1974), 3–26.

struggled with bouts of violent drunkenness. Here, finally, had been the site of Garrison's most climactic moment in the odyssey that led to his abolitionist destiny—his forty-nine-day incarceration after his conviction for libeling the Newburyport slave trader. Baltimore, to Garrison, documented a lifetime of triumphant coherence between public achievement and private morality.

When wildly applauded by the assembly that renominated Abraham Lincoln, Garrison sensed vividly his moment of vindication, informing his wife, Helen, that the tumultuous reception "gives a full endorsement of all the abolitionist 'fanaticism' with which I stood branded for all these years." After the convention adjourned, he lingered in the city, connecting his sense of fulfillment with memories of his abolitionist beginnings. He searched in vain for the old city jail in which he had served his sentence, but after being told that it had been torn down, Garrison prevailed on the city clerk to check for surviving jurors. When the clerk, who identified eight, asked Garrison whether he would like to reempanel the jury in the hope of securing a more favorable verdict, Garrison replied that he was happy with their original finding. Although deprived of the chance to read an ode to emancipation that he had inscribed on the wall of his now-demolished cell, Garrison felt satisfied that he had shaped his life with transcendent moral exactitude. As he revealed to Helen, his retrospections "have been such to gladden my heart and almost make me fear that I am at home dreaming, not in the state of Maryland."[11]

Phillips, like Garrison, set out at the end of the Civil War to confirm his sense of his lifetime's completeness, touring the North in mid-1867 and speaking to enormous audiences on the necessity of radical Reconstruction. In every city, as he reported to his wife, Ann, "mayors, congressmen, and all the leading men" eagerly sought private audiences with him. Much as had Garrison in Baltimore, the orator clearly sensed his life, and his lifetime's cause, achieving a common fulfillment. "The day dawns," he exulted. "May we be worthy to rejoice at it's [*sic*] noon."[12]

Remote Alton, Illinois, however, was not a place for attracting huge

---

11. Ibid., 187–89; William Lloyd Garrison to Helen Benson Garrison, June 8, 1864, Garrison Papers, Antislavery Collection, Boston Public Library.

12. Stewart, *Phillips*, 270–83; Wendell Phillips to Ann Phillips, April 19, 1867, Crawford Blagden Collection, Houghton Library, Harvard University; *National Anti-Slavery Standard*, April 29, 1867.

audiences and bevies of "leading men." Instead, his visit there inspired in Phillips a retrospection that took him back to Faneuil Hall in 1837, when the murder of Elijah Lovejoy had first ignited his passion for emancipation. Though this was to be his only visit there, Alton was just as freighted with symbols of moral symmetry for Phillips as was Baltimore for Garrison. Visiting Alton prompted Phillips to recall how, decades before, the terrible news of Lovejoy's murder had "scattered" his "world of dreams" by revealing so vividly the moral terrorism of slavery. Ever since, Phillips explained, the mention of Alton's name had always filled him with "an involuntary shudder," but now this visit had "broken that spell." On this "beautiful spring day," as Phillips stood high on a wooded bluff above the broad Mississippi contemplating the destruction of slavery, he finally achieved reconciliation between his sense of the present and his abolitionist past. Now, as he explained, he preferred "to think of Alton as the home of brave and true men," inspired by Lovejoy, who, in resisting mob tyranny, had "consecrated this great valley to liberty." For Phillips as for Garrison, memory and a sense of the present came together to capture the essence of a lifelong commitment. Assessing his own life as he wrote of Lovejoy's, Phillips exclaimed: "What world-wide benefactors these 'imprudent' men are—the [John] Browns, the Lovejoys, the saints and the martyrs. How prudently most men creep into nameless graves while now and then a few forget themselves into immortality!" [13]

Nearly all abolitionists indulged in self-congratulation as Union military victory finally led to slave emancipation.[14] However, in the midst of the general jubilation, Phillips's and Garrison's vivid attempts to relive their abolitionist origins remain illuminating. Above all, their actions document the enduring influences of their initial moments of commitment in prompting them to structure their lives as unfolding dramas of moral unity.

Although neither Phillips's nor Garrison's climactic moment represented a first encounter with "the cause of the slave," the events of Faneuil Hall and the Baltimore jail marked culminations of struggles by both to

---

13. *National Anti-Slavery Standard*, April 29, 1867.

14. See James M. McPherson, *The Struggle for Equality: The Abolitionists and the Negro during the Civil War and Reconstruction* (Princeton, 1964), 135ff.

address their youthful dilemmas through the medium of abolitionism. Garrison had moved back to Baltimore in 1829 to coedit *The Genius of Universal Emancipation* with Benjamin Lundy. Earlier, in Boston, Garrison had spoken strongly against slavery and had endorsed immediate emancipation. Phillips, too, was no stranger to abolitionism prior to his address in Faneuil Hall. Like Garrison, he had defied a dominating mother, specifically by suddenly proposing marriage to the abolitionist Ann Terry Greene, even as his intended lay on what all believed was her deathbed. Both men, in short, already were involving themselves in abolitionism as they attempted to address their inner turmoil.

Neither, however, seemed to be making much progress. Garrison already had bankrupted three newspapers with his editorial vehemence. Phillips, no less stymied, had lingered around the fringes of abolitionism. After his wedding to Ann, where guests gossiped that Sarah Phillips behaved "like a perfect dragon," he found his situation increasingly complicated by conflicting loyalties to mother and wife. For Phillips no less than for Garrison, abolitionism now provided a promising means for self-assertion in response to parental influences. However, for precisely this reason, it also added deeply to each man's personal tensions. Elijah Lovejoy's death and Garrison's guilty verdict suddenly impelled these impasses toward resolution.[15]

Alton and Baltimore provoked remarkably similar responses in Garrison and Phillips, because both locations embodied the nation's middle ground, the contested borderland shared by slavery and freedom that Barbara Fields, William Freehling, and other historians have described. Although Garrison experienced Baltimore first-hand while Phillips confronted Alton only in his vivid imagination, the middle ground, for both, epitomized terrifying moral opposites operating in disturbing proximity. The close interaction of slavery with freedom provoked all-encompassing responses from Garrison and Phillips that transformed dreams into visions and confusion into clarity.[16]

---

15. Stewart, *Garrison*, 28–55; Stewart, *Phillips*, 36–63; Caroline Weston to Ann Warren Weston, October 17, 1837, Weston Family Papers, Antislavery Collection, Boston Public Library.

16. Barbara Fields, *Slavery and Freedom in the Middle Ground: Maryland in the Nineteenth Century* (New Haven, 1985); William W. Freehling, *The Road to Disunion*, vol. 1, *Secessionists at Bay* (New York, 1990).

For Garrison, the provincial Yankee, Baltimore meant immersion not only in memories of family tragedy but also in jarring experiences with races and sectional cultures. He and Lundy boarded with two free African Americans, and for the first time, Garrison began sensing the precariousness of the distinction between enslavement and freedom. Moreover, day after day, he visited the local slave auction, mingled with masters, and then composed editorials condemning all that he had seen. In this manner the middle ground emphasized the gulf Garrison already sensed between his personal values and the conduct of daily life, prompting his attempt to knit his life together through a comprehensive series of actions.[17]

Francis Todd, a respected merchant from Garrison's old hometown of Newburyport, inadvertently provided the precipitating moment. In July 1829, when Todd transshipped eighty slaves from Baltimore to New Orleans, Garrison condemned Todd in a vitriolic editorial as a "MURDERER" who "should be sentenced to solitary confinement for life." He then posted a copy of this bitter attack to Ephraim Allen, the editor in Newburyport to whom Garrison had been apprenticed. Hoping to demonstrate to all in his hometown who remembered him that he had risen to unassailable moral ground, Garrison instructed Allen to publish the attack at once.

Todd aided Garrison unintentionally by filing and winning a criminal libel suit against the young editor. For forty-nine days of benign incarceration, Garrison continued to pull past and present into a tight moral focus by acting out his self-proclaimed martyrdom. To fuel the controversy in Baltimore, he wrote barbed letters to Francis Todd and the prosecuting attorney. Meanwhile, to advance his reputation in Newburyport, he goaded Ephraim Allen into commenting on the case in the *Herald*. Also, instead of paying his fine, Garrison used the last of his funds to print and mail hundreds of copies of a pamphlet in which he trumpeted his innocence. He claimed that he feared himself "in danger of being lifted up beyond measure, even in prison by excess panegyric and extraordinary sympathy," but that was exactly what Garrison sought to achieve.[18]

---

17. Stewart, *Garrison*, chap. 4.
18. Ibid.

By attracting such notoriety, Garrison believed he was now proving false his mother's warning that his search for fame would lead him one day to "starve in some garrett [*sic*] or some place that no one inhabits."[19] Confinement, instead, was winning him popular recognition for his uncompromising embrace of abolitionist principle. Self-respect and moral certitude finally had become his: "I pay no rent and am bound to make no repairs—and enjoy all the luxury of independence. I strut like the lions of the day, and of course attract a great number of visitors. . . . How do I bear up under my adversities? I answer—like the oak—like the Alps—unshakeable—storm proof. Opposition, and abuse, and slander, and prejudice and judicial tyranny are like oil to the flame of my zeal. . . . Am I to be frightened by dungeons and chains? Can they humble my spirit? . . . If need be, who would not die a martyr to such a cause?"[20]

It is not surprising that thirty-five years later, Garrison felt drawn back to Baltimore to reflect on his lifelong fidelity to this moment of illumination.

While Garrison experienced the middle ground first-hand, Phillips, in Boston, confronted it no less comprehensively in his highly developed imagination. Mob-ridden Alton, for Phillips, connoted a society debased by Southern influences, driven to bloodlust and murder, a denial of all morality that suddenly demanded his adamant opposition. For Phillips as for Garrison, the moral provocation of the middle ground stimulated a dramatic transformation from personal uncertainty to a lifetime molded around abolitionist truths. Also like Garrison, Phillips was moved to action by the behavior of one of his own prominent townsmen, the attorney general of Massachusetts, James T. Austin. For both abolitionists, self-transformation began with vehement attacks on respected local custodians of traditional authority.[21]

At the Faneuil Hall meeting, Austin delivered an impassioned defense

---

19. Frances Lloyd Garrison to William Lloyd Garrison, June 3, 1823, reprinted in Garrison and Garrison, *Life of Garrison*, 1:31.

20. For extensive documentation on Garrison's trial and imprisonment, including all of the quotations above, see Garrison and Garrison, *Life of Garrison*, 1:179–92.

21. For evidence of these images of Alton, see Wendell Phillips, "The Murder of Lovejoy," in *Speeches, Lectures, and Letters* (Boston, 1863), 2–10.

of the Alton mob. After castigating the murdered editor as a "firebrand," he equated the mob's actions to the resistance of the patriots of 1776, arguing that violence was justified in both instances to protect popular liberties. As Phillips listened, Austin seemed to be perverting the precious familial legacies of service and patriotism with which Phillips had always so deeply identified. To believe Austin, Phillips was soon to protest, "you must read our revolutionary history upside down." Even worse, from Phillips's perspective, Austin was daring to utter these falsehoods in Boston's shrine of patriotic resistance, Faneuil Hall, on whose wall hung huge portraits of Sam Adams, James Otis, and John Hancock, the leaders whom Phillips had so long yearned to emulate. As Phillips reacted to Austin's provocation, present and past began to synthesize with one another, much as they had for Garrison in Baltimore.

Phillips's rebuttal pictured Alton as a political culture run amok, cut off from New England's heritage of liberty and overrun by corruption from the nearby South. "The people there seem to have forgotten the blood-tried principles of their fathers the moment they lost sight of our New England hills," he exclaimed, acting instead like "a community staggering like a drunken man, indifferent to their rights and confused in their feelings." The town had been reduced by a pack of "drunken murderers" into "the tyranny of this many-headed monster, the mob," which only the valiant Lovejoy had found courage to resist. "The crisis had come," Phillips insisted. "It was time to assert the laws," to reassert boldly "the priceless value of the freedom of the press," just as had the patriots whose memories Austin had just impugned. "The men of the revolution went for right as secured by law," Phillips exclaimed. "The rioters of today go for their own wills, right or wrong."

Gesturing toward the portraits of Adams, Otis, and Hancock, Phillips next described his own reaction upon hearing Austin equate Lovejoy's killers with his beloved patriots. Suddenly, it became clear how completely Phillips was fusing his dramatic embrace of patriotic abolitionism with the legacies of family and his inspirational view of his own destiny. "I thought," Phillips exclaimed, "those pictured lips would have broken into voice to rebuke the recreant American—the slanderer of the dead. . . . In the sentiments he has uttered, on the soil consecrated by the prayers of Puritans and the blood of patriots, the earth should have yawned and swallowed him up." Afterward, Phillips always insisted that it had been the portraits, not the audience, to whom he had spoken.[22]

The Lovejoy of Phillips's imagination, like the imprisoned Garrison, embodied moral supremacy in the middle ground by defying slavery's licentiousness. Phillips himself, by attributing charismatic qualities to Lovejoy, likewise transformed his own self-understanding into that of the heroic leader, the role he had so associated with the obligations of his lineage and had so long dreamed of assuming. At the same time, he also claimed Ann Phillips's abolitionist vision as his own, putting to rest his conflicting loyalties to mother and wife. Now he could feel himself an extension of the heroic history with which he so strongly identified and the worthy heir of the legacies left him by his father. Phillips had begun to construct an inspiring design for living. At Lovejoy's gravesite three decades later, he would remember vividly how the news of his hero's murder had "shattered" his "world of dreams."[23]

Once personal history and public leadership finally had begun to cohere for Garrison and Phillips, the synthesis grew to encompass their most intimate levels of daily living. Their parents had influenced Garrison and Phillips to think of themselves as heroic individuals, acting with solitary force to conform the world to their wills. Their wives, by contrast, influenced them to expand their qualities of leadership around their understandings of themselves as husbands and as men. Helen Benson Garrison and Ann Greene Phillips, in completely contrasting manners, taught their husbands to foster nurturing relationships and to value collective effort.

Because the differences between Garrison's and Phillips's spouses were so striking, such assertions might at first seem impossible. Ann Greene Phillips possessed a force of personality that certainly matched that of her mother-in-law, Sarah, but Helen Benson Garrison was remarkably passive, judged against any standard. Wendell and Ann Phillips, sexually repressed and childless, lived as recluses while he nursed her through a lifetime of rheumatoid arthritis. The Garrison household, teeming with children and relatives, meanwhile became famous as "the abolitionist

---

22. Stewart, *Phillips*, 58–63.

23. *National Anti-Slavery Standard*, May 25, 1867.

hotel," always open to out-of-town guests. Wendell and Ann Phillips grew intellectually as peers and became inseparable collaborators in abolitionism. Helen Garrison, by contrast, played no active role in the workings of the crusade. During four decades of confidential philanthropy, Wendell and Ann Phillips slowly divested themselves of two enormous inheritances. The Garrisons, always in need, openly relied on friends such as the Phillipses to help meet rent and tuition payments.[24]

Yet, these obvious contrasts obscure more important similarities. Ann Phillips and Helen Garrison both led their husbands to discover comprehensive connections between their private family affairs and their leadership within abolitionism. Their relationships with their spouses enabled both men to transform indelible memories of their mothers into new symmetries between their senses of domestic fulfillment and their leadership roles in abolitionism.

Ann Phillips matched genealogies and fortunes with all the Beacon Hill aristocrats, Sarah Phillips included. She also commanded the strength and sophistication necessary to overcome her prepossessing mother-in-law, who hated her abolitionism and resented her hold on Wendell. Their choice to live reclusively, far from Beacon Hill, announced that Wendell had freed himself from his mother's day-to-day dominion and the conventions of "brahmin" society. Yet, Phillips testified to his mother's enduring influence by marrying someone so like her in temperament. Indeed, he felt no hesitation in acknowledging to Ann the power of his memories of his mother. "If there be any truth in spiritualism," he told his wife, "I think my mother may be my guardian angel—the thought of her comes to me so often and at such singular times. It ought to make me [a] better [person]. Perhaps it will." Ann, for her part, always acknowledged, apparently without resentment, that Sarah "was everything to Wendell."[25]

Soon after marrying, Wendell Phillips had to confront the terrible afflictions that suddenly overcame his spouse. Usually bedridden in a

---

24. Stewart, *Phillips*, 84–96; Stewart, *Garrison*, 75–81.

25. Wendell and Ann Phillips to Elizabeth Pease, January 31, 1846, Garrison Papers; Phillips to Ann Phillips, December 10, 1867, Crawford Blagden Collection.

semi-dark room, Ann relied on Wendell as her lifelong nurse, as well as her sole intellectual and social reference. As a result, Wendell Phillips developed a deeply nurturing side to his personality and suppressed all hint of aggression while he and Ann framed their relationship around her moment-to-moment medical and emotional needs. By turning himself into her caregiver and their home into what both jokingly termed "the hospital," the Phillipses reversed conventional gender roles with results that became apparent to colleagues in the abolitionist movement. The self-styled hero who dominated podiums and enforced Garrisonian orthodoxy was also able to develop close and enriching collaborations with some of the nation's most powerful and self-expressive activists, his own wife foremost among them.[26] Phillips soon declared woman's rights a central tenet of his abolitionism. He now explained that it was not only Elijah Lovejoy but also Ann and her feminist friends who had first "anointed" him in the cause and thanked them "for all that they have taught me." In the same vein, he attested that he drew special inspiration from female abolitionists and feminists, declaring that he had "never seen a more intelligent or cultivated audience [or] more ability guided by better taste on a [speaker's] platform" than at their meetings.[27]

Wendell Phillips, in short, ultimately interpreted his own abolitionism through powerful women such as Ann Phillips as well as through powerful male symbols such as Elijah Lovejoy. Of Ann, he was given to say to others, "A sick wife though she may be, I owe the little I am and do to her guardian spirit." To Ann herself he once wrote, slipping into the third person, "I am not worthy to button her old black shoes. She is my motive and inspiration. He owes her everything."[28] Again, in Phillips's outlook, past and present, public and private had merged into

---

26. Perusal of the files containing the correspondence between Phillips and Lydia Maria Child, Stephen S. and Abby K. Foster, Mary and George Luther Stearns, Caroline Dall, Parker and Sarah Pillsbury, Sidney and Elizabeth Neale Gay, Edmund Quincy, Lucretia and James Mott, Samuel J. May, Samuel May, Jr., and two of William Lloyd Garrison's sons—Francis Jackson Garrison and Wendell Phillips Garrison—in the Crawford Blagden Collection document this statement.

27. Wendell Phillips, "The Boston Mob," in *Speeches*, 226–27; Wendell Phillips, "Woman's Rights and Woman's Duties," in *Speeches, Lectures, and Letters,* 2nd series (New York, 1891), 110–27.

28. Wendell Phillips to Richard D. Webb, June 29, 1842, Garrison Papers; Wendell Phillips to Ann Phillips, March 24, 1867, Crawford Blagden Collection.

a symmetrical pattern of motivation and style of leadership. The solitary postures of Phillips the dominating orator now began to mesh with powerful collaborative instincts that Ann brought out in him during the course of their marriage.

Marriage also led Garrison to discover new and powerful connections between family life and abolitionism. Soon after their wedding, Garrison wrote to his "Dearest Helen": "Am I not a strange compound? In battling with the whole nation, I am as daring, as impetuous as unconquerable as a lion, but in your presence I am as gentle and as submissive as a dove." The spiritual inspiration of their wedded love, he assured her, would only lead him to battle all the more fiercely for slavery's overthrow because he could now "realize how dreadful a thing it is for lover to be torn away from lover, the husband from the wife, parents from children." [29]

Finding himself at last in the center of a loving family, Garrison began to flourish emotionally. With patient Helen he could, for the first time, let down his defenses, relax, and unguardedly respond to what he described as his "womanish" self, that is, his feelings of vulnerability and desires to give and receive emotional nurturing. His children knew him as a deeply involved, expressive father with a playful sense of humor and a genuine love for the routines of domestic life such as baking pastry and putting up jam. He so fully absorbed his in-laws into his own family that distinctions between the two groups became close to irrelevant. Further still, Garrison used the security of his new family to ease some of the pain left over from the old. When his brother James suddenly reappeared, terminally ill after more than twenty years of suffering and abusive living, Garrison took him in, lovingly nursed him through his final months, and assisted him in making his peace by helping him compose a confessional history of his life. Garrison, the solitary prophet, had become Garrison the empathetic spouse, brother, father, and colleague. As in Phillips's development, marriage and mission became fully enjoined. Of Helen, Garrison once remarked, "I did not marry her expecting that she would assume a prominent station in the anti-slavery cause, but for domestic

29. William Lloyd Garrison to Helen Benson Garrison, April 24, 1834, Oswald Garrison Villard Papers, Houghton Library, Harvard University. See also Walter Merrill, "A Passionate Attachment: William Lloyd Garrison's Courtship of Helen Eliza Benson," *New England Quarterly* 29 (1956): 116–34.

quiet and happiness."[30] Yet, that very "quiet and happiness" enabled the defiant, prophetic Garrison to exert the appealing collaborative influence that inspired so many for so many years. Garrison, like Phillips, found in his marriage some of his deepest sources of motivation and leadership.

Absent fathers, dominating mothers, dreams of heroic transcendence, provocations from the middle ground, moments of self-liberation, and emotionally nurturing marriages—syntheses of dominance with collaboration—all combined to make Garrison and Phillips embrace as life's purpose securing moral symmetry through abolitionism. The public and private experiences of both men thus generated the aura of charisma. What remains to explore is the impact over the years of such powerful styles of leadership within the Garrisonian movement as a whole.

As several historians have observed recently, the Boston-based Garrisonian wing of abolitionism, by contrast to the groups that coalesced around Gerrit Smith and Lewis Tappan, upheld the overriding value of individual self-expression. These particular Garrisonians viewed with deepest suspicion all "godless" hierarchies that suppressed the individual not only by spawning enslavement in the outside world but also by threatening their movement's liberating inner purity. Rooting out such impious distinctions led first to immediatism, then to endorsements of woman's rights, and finally to comprehensive changes in established conventions of gender. Some men within this branch of abolitionism

---

30. William Lloyd Garrison to Anna E. Benson, April 14, 1834, Garrison Papers, contains a statement to his sister-in-law on this matter that is worth quoting at length. "I feel more and more child-like as time hurries me on to the maturity of manhood. My mind is as succeptable [*sic*] as it was in my infancy—it is a fountain of tenderness. It is not unusual for men to indulge in tears; yet how frequently do I weep! Not that I am unhappy when I weep . . . exactly the reverse is true. . . . I *know* that I possess an Indian fortitude, which the fires of persecution can never subdue—a hostile world cannot move me from the path of duty—yet I am a very woman in the gentleness of my disposition." The quotation referring to Garrison's expectations in marrying Helen is found in William Lloyd Garrison to George Benson, October 5, 1838, Garrison Papers. A number of scholars have depicted Garrison as an emotionally repressive father, citing as evidence a tragedy that occurred when he fatally scalded his young son, Charles Follen Garrison. An instinctive follower of faddish "cures," Garrison attempted to treat his son with hot sitz-baths for what was feared to be rheumatic fever. Overriding the boy's cries of great pain, Garrison forced the boy to remain in the bath until he received terrible burns from which he soon died. John L. Thomas, *The Liberator: William Lloyd Garrison, a Biography* (Boston, 1965), 133–35, was the first to use this tragedy to document Garrison's repressive instincts and the general repressiveness inherent in abolitionist motivation. Another account that repeats this view is Ronald Walters, *The Antislavery Appeal: American Abolitionism after 1830* (Baltimore, 1976). By contrast, Aileen Kraditor, *Means and Ends in American Abolitionism: Garrison and His Critics on Strategy and Tactics* (New York, 1969), documents a more flexible and relaxed Garrison, a view that comports with my own impression of his temperament. A wise commentary on the problem of repressiveness is Lewis Perry, " 'We Have Had Conversation with the World': The Abolitionists and Spontaneity," *Canadian Journal of American Studies* 8 (1980): 116–33.

developed androgynous expressions of "fraternal love," involved them-selves in fundraising bazaars, and interested themselves in childrearing. Some women, meantime, joined executive committees, edited newspa-pers, gave speeches, and invented new modes of expression in material culture, popular literature, and public address. Distinctions, thus, blurred between the traditional "male" world of power politics and the "female sphere" of "domestic influence."[31] Boston Garrisonianism, in short, thrived as a spontaneous fellowship of antiauthoritarians that required charismatic leadership to give it both inspiration and order. By embody-ing in equal measure unflinching heroism and collaborative benevolence, Garrison and Phillips met these two requirements perfectly.

Phillips and Garrison never hesitated when unilaterally defining the essential beliefs of the movement as a whole. Garrison took the lead when he decreed a powerful theology of woman's rights, abstention from voting, and disunionism. Phillips soon joined Garrison in zealously guarding the movement's borders by purging those who embraced com-munitarianism, tried to lead others to the ballot box, or confused the problem of poverty with the sin of slavery. Naturally, the two developed a division of responsibility consistent with their public roles. Although Garrison promulgated the movement's religion with perfectionist for-mulations, Phillips embellished its politics with "golden eloquence" and articulated theories of agitation and justifications for overthrowing the federal union.[32] Charisma, according to Weber, marks leaders in the eyes of their followers as inspired and unquestionable lawgivers, roles that Garrison's and Phillips's most fervid supporters happily ascribed to them.

---

31. For some of the more recent studies bearing on these matters, see Donald Yacovone, *Samuel Joseph May and the Dilemma of Liberal Reform* (Philadelphia, 1991), chap. 4; Lewis Perry, *Child-hood, Marriage and Reform: Henry C. Wright* (Chicago, 1980); Hewitt, *Women's Activism and Social Change*; Lori Ginsburg, *Women and the Work of Benevolence: Morality, Politics and Class in the Nineteenth-Century United States* (New Haven, 1991), 11–132; Jean Fagin Yellin, *Women and Sisters: The Antislavery Feminists in American Culture* (New Haven, 1990), chaps. 1–4; Friedman, *Gregarious Saints*, 129–59.

32. On these points, see John L. Thomas, "Antislavery and Utopia," in Martin Duberman, ed., *The Antislavery Vanguard: New Essays on the Abolitionists* (Princeton, 1965), 240–70; Jonathan Glickstein, "'Poverty Is Not Slavery': The Abolitionists and the Labor Market," in Lewis Perry and Michael Fellman, eds., *Antislavery Reconsidered: New Perspectives on the Abolitionists* (Baton Rouge, 1979), 195–218.

While acting as lawgivers, however, Garrison and Phillips simultane-ously began to extend to their friends and coworkers their experiences of marriage, fostering an environment of openness that freed participants to follow their private visions far into public life. Strict divisions of labor began to blur, along with distinctions of race and class. As Lawrence Friedman has suggested, Garrisonians did, indeed, come to comprise a family that conducted its relationships through self-expressiveness rather than by precedent.[33] Garrison and Phillips remained intensely involved in the process, insisting upon the frank exchange of differing ideas and offering warm support to all parties. "I think Garrison has done his work wisely and well," Ann Warren Weston once confided to Phillips, so that "there might be honest differences of opinion."[34]

Garrison and Phillips reciprocated their colleagues' loyalty and at-traction with intensely emotional warmth. Coworkers began referring to "father Garrison," because, indeed, he did embody both authority and affectionate nurturing. Garrison eagerly multiplied the bonds between himself and his coworkers by constantly addressing them as his "dearest brothers and sisters." He freely opened his home to them all, wept over their griefs, laughed over their moments of happiness. Carrying these impulses further still, Garrison named all of his children after his dearest abolitionist friends and happily accepted gifts of his colleagues' money to meet his domestic expenses. For Garrison, the public and private had meshed in a synthesis sufficiently powerful to be felt by others as charisma.[35]

Although Garrison extended his actual family to encompass his friends, Phillips offered his friends instead all that his forebears had left in his care. The Phillips's home remained closed to outsiders. He and Ann had no children to name after his abolitionist comrades, and no one ever dared to call this aristocrat "father Phillips." Yet, like Garrison, Phillips equated the abolitionist movement with "family." By sharing his extraordinary wealth, his education, his indisputably privileged position

33. Friedman, *Gregarious Saints*, 43–67.

34. Ann Warren Weston to Wendell Phillips, May 16, 1846, Garrison Papers.

35. Friedman, *Gregarious Saints*, 49–57.

with his fellow abolitionists, Phillips incorporated them into the paternal heritage of responsibility he so deeply revered.[36]

Although Phillips technically refused to practice law under a proslavery constitution, he spent countless uncompensated hours as the Garrisonians' personal attorney, managing the family affairs of his closest colleagues and friends. Among his clients, besides the Garrisons, were Steven and Abby Foster, Lydia Maria Child, Henry C. Wright, and Parker and Sarah Pillsbury, all prominent but financially strapped abolitionists. When legal assistance proved insufficient, Phillips opened his bank account, creating yet another level of synthesis between the domestic affairs of the family of abolitionism and the legacies of his own.[37]

In the final analysis, however, it was Garrison, not Phillips, whose presence and leadership most fully embodied the movement throughout the decades. In the Garrison family, as Phillips freely admitted, there could be but one father. For Phillips, the dictates of moral symmetry ultimately moved him to exalt Garrison, not compete with him, through the formidable power the orator exercised as the movement's patriot hero. Phillips understood that Garrison was a truly charismatic figure whose inspired vision had opened vistas of freedom for African Americans while endowing abolitionists like him with lifetimes of transcendent purpose. "How can we ever thank him?" Phillips once asked an audience of coworkers. Because of Garrison's fearless insights, abolitionists now found it possible to defy injustice and expose hypocrisy while seeking life's most fulfilling meanings. "Life, what weariness it is," Phillips exclaimed, "with its drudgeries of education, its little cares of today, all to be lived over again, its rising, eating, lying down, only to continue the monotonous routine!" Then, describing the precious gift that he believed Garrison offered to all who followed him, Phillips concluded: "Thank God that He has inspired any one of us to awaken from wearing these dull and rotting weeds—revealed to us the joy of self-devotion—taught us how we intensify life by laying it on the altar of some great cause. . . . My friends,

---

36. See note 24.

37. Stewart, *Phillips*, 127–32.

if we never free a slave, at least we have freed ourselves in our efforts to free our brother man." [38]

It is hard to imagine a more concentrated explanation of the sources and consequences of charisma for these abolitionists, or why, for all committed Garrisonians, the "personal" was always so inextricable from the "political." It also becomes clearer why they were so tenacious in their lifetime quests to destroy slavery and discrimination. For all of them, not just for Phillips and Garrison, lifetimes inspired by visions of moral symmetry seemed always within their grasps.

---

38. *Liberator*, January 24, 1851.

Consequences

Political historians who explain the coming of the Civil War see little reason to emphasize the importance of the abolitionists. In the epochal shattering of the nation's systems of electoral politics and governance, they discern little if any influence being exerted by so small and marginalized a group. Historians of the abolitionist movement, by contrast, have claimed great credit for these crusaders for forcing the nation into the ultimate political reckoning with slavery that came with the collapse of the political system. The four essays presented here attempt to put these conflicting claims to rest by developing a greatly expanded approach to abolitionism's relationships with and impact on the sectional crisis of American politics.

Joshua Giddings, Antislavery Violence, and the Politics of Congressional Honor

To historians of the American conflict over slavery, the censure and re-election of Congressman Joshua Giddings is a familiar but important story. In 1842 Giddings defied the House of Representatives' "gag rule" by presenting resolutions that defended the right of slaves on ships in international waters to rise in bloody insurrection. After the U.S. House had voted his censure for this action, Giddings resigned his seat and appealed to his constituents in northeastern Ohio's Western Reserve. They re-elected him by a crushing majority, arming him with an explicit mandate to offer his resolutions again. This Giddings did in defiance of House rules and slaveholders' wishes, thereby opening a new phase in the politics of the sectional conflict. The days of the "gag rule" were now numbered, but the animosity created fears in the North of a "great slavepower conspiracy," which helped to hasten the sectional crisis.[1]

This well-known account, however, can also be shown to document a

---

Originally published as "Joshua R. Giddings, Antislavery Violence, and the Congressional Politics of Honor," in John R. McKivigan and Stanley Harrold, eds., *Antislavery Violence: Sectional, Racial and Cultural Conflict in Antebellum America* (Knoxville: University of Tennessee Press, 1999), 167–92. Reprinted with permission.

1. Much of the information in this essay is drawn from James Brewer Stewart, *Joshua R. Giddings and the Tactics of Radical Politics* (Cleveland: Press of Case Western Reserve Univ., 1970). For standard treatments of the "gag rule" controversy and for Giddings's role in it, see Stewart, *Joshua R. Giddings*; Leonard R. Richards, *The Life and Times of Congressman John Quincy Adams* (New York: Oxford Univ. Press, 1986); George R. Rable, "Slavery, Politics and the South: The Gag Rule as a Case Study," *Capitol Studies* 3 (Fall 1975): 69–87; James M. McPherson, "The Fight against the Gag Rule: Joshua Leavitt and Antislavery Insurgency in the Whig Party, 1839–1842," *Journal of Negro History* 48 (July 1963): 177–95; William Lee Miller, *Arguing about Slavery: The Great Battle in the United States Congress* (New York: Knopf, 1996); and Michael Kent Curtis, "The Curious History of Attempts to Suppress Antislavery Speech, Press and Petition in 1835–37," *Northwestern University Law Review* 89 (1995): 785–869.

CONSEQUENCES

more complex dynamic of sectional estrangement stimulated by debates in Congress over black Americans' right to resist and use violence. Congressman Joshua R. Giddings and his impact on the political process still take center stage, but a reconsideration of his career suggests that the "gag-rule" controversy and his censure and re-election were only parts (albeit crucial) of a much more volatile drama played out over two decades in the House of Representatives between Giddings and his slaveholding counterparts, men who embodied codes of ethical behavior deeply antagonistic to his, and who loathed beyond measure Giddings's challenging assertions not only that black people held rights to liberate and defend themselves but that white people had obligations to assist them.

Much has been written about the contrast in values between Yankees inspired by evangelical "conscience" and Southern "men of honor" driven by the need for personal dominion. Little is known, however, about the impact of these conflicting ethical systems on the nation's legislative processes, or about the responses they evoked from elected representatives concerning the relationship of violence to the political problem of slavery.[2] This essay speaks to these questions through a close examination of Giddings's political values and an assessment of his impact on the politics of Congress. From the late 1830s on, Giddings's repeated conflicts with angry Southern congressmen compromised the House's capacity to debate slavery in a spirit of civility. Long before Charles Sumner was beaten by Preston Brooks, rituals that flirted with violence had been deeply infused by Giddings and his Southern antagonists within the culture of the Congress.

---

2. See Bertram Wyatt-Brown, *Southern Honor: Ethics and Behavior in the Old South* (New York: Oxford Univ. Press, 1982); Steven M. Stowe, *Intimacy and Power in the Old South: Ritual in the Lives of Planters* (Chapel Hill: Univ. of North Carolina Press, 1987); Dickson D. Bruce Jr., *Violence and Culture in the Antebellum South* (Austin: Univ. of Texas Press, 1979); Drew G. Faust, *James Henry Hammond: A Design for Mastery* (Baton Rouge: Louisiana State Univ. Press, 1982); Edward L. Ayres, *Vengeance and Justice: Crime and Punishment in the Nineteenth-Century American South* (New York: Oxford Univ. Press, 1984); James Brewer Stewart, "A Great Talking and Eating Machine: Patriarchy, Mobilization, and the Dynamics of Nullification in South Carolina," *Civil War History* 27 (Sept. 1981): 198–220; Kenneth S. Greenberg, *Honor and Slavery . . .* (Princeton: Princeton Univ. Press, 1996). Two recent works that introduce Yankee "saints" are Robert Abzug, *Cosmos Crumbling: American Reform and the Religious Imagination* (New York: Oxford Univ. Press, 1994); and James Brewer Stewart, *Holy Warriors: The Abolitionists and American Slavery* (New York: Hill and Wang, 1996).

For more consecutive terms than any other congressman, from 1838 through 1858, Giddings brought a highly provocative version of Northern religious radicalism to the floor of the House of Representatives. As all Southern congressmen knew only too well, there was in national politics no more disturbing a "yankee saint" than he. On some topics Giddings professed an abiding hatred of violence typical of "sentimental Christian reformers" (as skeptics called them), advocating pacifism in the treatment of Indians and in the conduct of foreign policy. Yet, like some of the rhetorical warriors of the American Anti-Slavery Society (Wendell Phillips seems a fair comparison), he also emphatically defended the right of freedom-seeking slaves to shed the blood of their oppressors, commended fugitives who slew their pursuers, and lauded whites who assisted escapees.[3]

Even Giddings's defense of the supremacy of "the law" itself seemed to slaveholders' ears to invite violence, couched as it was in an evangelical pietism that appealed beyond statutes to overriding moral absolutes. Though he insisted, for example, that he upheld the master's "legal rights" of ownership and denied that he was an abolitionist, in the next breath he usually informed his slaveholding fellow congressmen that they had no "moral right" whatever to retain their human property. This lack of "moral right," in turn, made slave revolts, though technically illegal, entirely justifiable in God's sight. Especially when juxtaposed against Giddings's professions of pacifism, such statements invariably led slaveholders to charge hypocrisy and to suspect much worse.

Even as Giddings's statements endorsed violent resistance by others, his own day-to-day comportment in the House also seemed to flirt with violence. As Southern congressmen listened from their desks close by, Giddings laced his speeches on the floor of the House with images of slavery so lurid and scathing that they drew William Lloyd Garrison's applause. And when forbearance was exhausted and tempers flared, Giddings invariably responded to slaveholders' attempts to intimidate him verbally or to threaten him physically by rising and delivering bitterly disparaging comments on their "codes of chivalry." In the opinion

---

3. For a full treatment of Giddings's early career and beliefs, see Stewart, *Joshua R. Giddings*, 1–83.

of one his most acid political critics, Massachusetts Whig Robert C. Winthrop, Giddings's bellicose style seemed to put him "at war with Washington" itself.[4]

Though couched in partisanship, Winthrop's observations do suggest the origins of Giddings's personal combativeness. They also help to explain why he so quickly adopted doctrines supportive of violent slave resistance. Their roots lay in the shock and disgust Giddings experienced as he observed slavery both as practiced in the District of Columbia and as represented in the halls of Congress. Scenes he encountered on Washington's street corners during his two decades of national service seemed, from the first, to mock the convictions of the people he represented and to rip at the core of his deepest personal friendships, associations, and beliefs. Slaveholding colleagues he met during routine business seemed to behave like petty tyrants, not like republican lawmakers, and quickly he took offense at what appeared to him to be their verbal arrogance, domineering postures, and ruthlessness in working their legislative wills. Just as rapidly, his urge to express defiance and enter into combat with them began to grow.

In faraway Ohio Giddings had spoken against slavery as a matter of ethical principle and political necessity. Now, however, he sensed that a vile institution and the overbearing men who represented it were surrounding and challenging him at every turn. What he had once opposed in the abstract he now instinctively hated in fully human terms, and he wanted to see it destroyed.

Yet Giddings knew from the start that these terrible realizations had to be reconciled somehow with his genuine loyalty to the national Whig Party and to his long-sought position as a national legislator, commitments that pledged him to ally himself closely with the same slaveholding politicians he so deeply distrusted and to uphold powerful laws that protected their human property. There was simply no possibility that he could rise from his seat in the House of Representatives, demand immediate emancipation, and expect to be allowed to continue his congressional career. He could, however, compromise the deepest dictates

---

4. Robert Charles Winthrop to Nathaniel Appleton, Feb. 7, 1848, in Robert Charles Winthrop, ed., *A Memoir of Robert C. Winthrop* (Boston: Higginson and Lee, 1897), 156–57.

of his conscience and make statements falling short of abolitionism that still conveyed as much of his deeper feelings as possible. In this tension between moral imperative and political necessity lay the deepest reasons for Giddings's espousals of violence and his combative demeanor with slaveholders. At war with himself as an authentic "man of conscience," Giddings expressed his inner conflicts in his public behavior in the House of Representatives. To explain the deeper reasons for these powerful reactions, however, requires further analysis of Giddings's personality and his circumstances as a newly elected representative.

When Giddings was at home in his "abolitionized" district in Ohio's Western Reserve, his view of himself meshed perfectly with a thick local monoculture of evangelical reform. It was this congruence that made Giddings correctly regard himself as embodying his district comprehensively while in Washington rather than simply representing it in a legalistic sense. But in the city of Washington itself, Giddings faced unprecedented complexity and pluralism, not the uniform evangelical culture that so nicely defined his provincial outlook. Washington in actuality constituted an intrasectional crossroads where people from highly diverse regions met to transact the nation's business and where, more disturbingly, the institution of slavery itself seemed disconcertingly ubiquitous. This abrupt and repeating disjunction between the fixed values Giddings brought with him from his district and the morally dislocating mix of pluralism and slavery he experienced once in Washington begins to explain why endorsements of antislavery violence became so quickly interwoven with his political doctrines. It also explains why he became so willing to seek confrontation with slaveholding congressmen.

Much in Giddings's personal history just prior to his first election enhances further our understanding of his extreme initial reactions to the culture of the nation's capital. Only eighteen months before his arrival there, in mid-1837, he had wrenched himself out of a protracted crisis of identity and, at age forty-two, now clung tenaciously to the newly acquired values that had finally restored his equilibrium. Through a profound religious transformation, he had found respite from a deep depression triggered by fiscal bankruptcy, family estrangement, vocational dissatisfaction, friction with close friends, and frustrated political hopes. Though Giddings was as politically ambitious as ever and deeply dedicated to the Whig Party, his religious conversion had altered his values exhaustively and transformed his position in the Western Reserve's political culture. Once at ease in the local tavern, he now espoused strict temperance. Once a colonizationist, he now added his sponsorship to the Ashtabula County Anti-Slavery Society, originally founded by the charismatic immediate abolitionist Theodore D. Weld. Once a headline-seeking criminal attorney, he now visited his jailed former clients, supporting revivals among them and urging a religious repentance similar to his own.[5]

Now, moreover, he had also come to believe that his budding career as a legislator and his sacred new calling as a Christian believer were one. By voting as his conscience dictated, he automatically furthered God's larger plans for humanity. Early in his career he remarked privately, "I must do my political duty and leave the consequences to God," since "the wisdom of providence . . . is manifestly to be seen in any subject brought before our Congress." This idea, he further disclosed, was one upon which he "love[d] to meditate."[6] The private political musings of an authentic "man of conscience" could not have been more clearly rendered.

But as Giddings revised his sense of his life's purpose, one crucial trait remained unchanged—his feelings of debilitating depression in the absence of substantial external challenges. When denied the tension of struggling with difficult tasks, he succumbed to "hypochondria," as he called it, a physically painful lassitude that overtook him "till all was blue." His only remedy lay in finding formidable new goals toward which to strive, and this was precisely his concern as he began congressional duties. Deeply protective of his new self-understanding, eager to avoid "hypochondria," and fully imbued with the pious axioms of the Western Reserve's "culture of conscience," Giddings was predisposed, as few elected officials could have been, to resistance in the face of repeated personal encounters with the institution of slavery.[7]

For all of Washington's pronounced "southernness," however, Gid-

---

5. For Giddings's vocational crisis and its resolution, see Stewart, *Joshua R. Giddings*, 22–33.

6. Joshua R. Giddings to James A. Briggs, Apr. 29, 1843, James A. Briggs Papers, Western Reserve Historical Society, Cleveland.

7. Giddings to Laura W. Giddings, June 28, 1836, Apr. 27, 1837, Dec. 9, 1838, Joshua R. Giddings Papers, Ohio Historical Society, Columbus.

dings quickly found a small part of the city where he could find refuge from cosmopolitanism and where he felt closer to home. As in the city of Baltimore that Barbara Jeanne Fields has portrayed so well, Washington constituted a "middle ground" where elements of Northern and Southern culture interacted comprehensively. Within this admixture, infused though it was with slavery's influence, Giddings's provincial ways and reformer's outlook gave him entry into a rich though minuscule social circle. Here politicians very much like himself confirmed still further that war against slavery offered the highest challenges to a statesman of conscience (especially to one who feared "hypochondria"). Joining the handful of pious, antislavery-minded congressmen already clustered around former President John Quincy Adams, Giddings quickly and permanently attached himself to this closest approximation he could find of the culture of the Western Reserve.[8]

In seeking familiar accommodations, Giddings was hardly unusual. Nearly all congressmen came to Washington without their families and roomed together with "messmates" who shared their regional preferences. The boarding houses where congressmen roomed and ate together created a spirit of fraternal brotherhood that reinforced cultural homogeneity. Southerners hived together just as Yankees did, and congressmen habitually referred to one another by mess group affiliation, such as "Dowson's crowd" or the "Army mess," a habit that suggests the large social distances that separated these various groups. By joining a "mess" with like-minded Northerners at Mrs. Sprigg's boardinghouse and by attaching himself to Adams, Giddings, like most other representatives, instinctively reinforced his own parochialism.[9]

Adams himself inspired genuine awe in Giddings, who regarded the former President as an almost overpowering model of antislavery statesmanship—"a specimen of true greatness" who radiated "genuine republican simplicity" and devotion to the nation's highest ideals. And

---

8. Fields, *Slavery and Freedom in the Middle Ground: Maryland in the Nineteenth Century* (New York: Oxford Univ. Press, 1986); Giddings Diary, Jan. 1, 1839, Giddings Papers.

9. For a detailed description of Washington boardinghouse culture and its relationship to the national legislative process, see James Sterling Young, *The Washington Community, 1800–1828* (New York: Harcourt, Brace and World, 1966), esp. 1–109. Though Young's study ends in 1828, it is clear that his analysis also applies to the period of Giddings's Washington career, from 1839 to 1859. For documentation on this point, see n. 31.

other new friends from the House of Representative ("two Presbyterians and one Methodist") joined Giddings in observing temperance vows rather than feeling uncomfortable in Washington's "gay and social circle" of drink, cigars, and conviviality, where Giddings believed himself "allmost [*sic*] a stranger." Instead of attending soirees, they met for devotional services, and once Giddings had decided that he must bring himself to witness a local slave auction, two of his friends proved their loyalty by going along with him.[10] Lawrence J. Friedman has persuasively documented the abolitionists' efforts to build supportive "sanctuaries" of friendship that sustained their sense of moral purity as they struggled for decades to redeem a sinful nation. John Quincy Adams and his fellow boarders at Mrs. Sprigg's were to play such roles for Giddings, who soon became one of this group's leading figures.[11] Within this context, a desire to earn Adams's approval was both a natural reaction and still another incentive for abolitionism, helping to define Giddings's outlook as he walked the streets of the nation's capital and learned for himself the reality of slavery.

First, in late January 1839, he encountered a "coffle of about sixty slaves . . . chained together on their way south" being driven by "a *Being* the shape of a man . . . on horseback . . . with a huge bullwhip in his hand" who occasionally cracked it as he "chastised" laggards. As the group passed before him, Giddings, like all the other passersby, could do no more than to stand by helplessly and "to view the barbarous spectacle." By the next day, he had seen still more and had grown all the more disturbed, reporting hotly to his wife: "We have public auctions where slaves are sold right before the Capitol, and in sight of the door, And a number of slave prisons. In allmost [*sic*] every walk I take I pass some of them."[12]

Two weeks later, he again found himself part of a horrifying drama that seemed to demand his involvement, and once again he could only

---

10. Giddings Diary, Jan. 1, 1839; Giddings to Laura W. Giddings, Jan. 3, Dec. 1, Dec. 16, 1839, Jan. 1, 1840, Giddings Papers.

11. Friedman, *Gregarious Saints: Self and Community in American Abolitionism* (New York: Cambridge Univ. Press, 1982); Stewart, *Joshua R. Giddings*, chap. 4.

12. Giddings Diary, Jan. 30, 1839; Giddings to Laura W. Giddings, Jan. 31, 1839, Giddings Papers.

look on with the other spectators, feeling enraged and shamefully ineffectual: "In the evening we were alarmed by a thrilling cry of distress which continued for some minutes. It proved to be the outcry of a slave who was undergoing the chastisement of his master; and fearing that he would die in the operation, broke from him and ran. He was pursued, knocked down & pounded by the master & son till he appeared lifeless; and the spectators, interfering, were told that he was the property of his master and that he had the right to kill him if he pleased. The master and his son then took him & dragged him through the street as they would have done a dead hog to a stable and there left him." [13]

But as his next encounter with slavery indicates, Giddings could not long sustain the agonizing role of the incidental observer. Only two days later, Giddings and his two "messmates" watched a twenty-six-year-old black man being put up for auction at the Pennsylvania Avenue Slave Stand. This time, in contrast to the earlier incidents, Giddings sought out a direct encounter with slavery, perhaps in the hope that his developing reputation as an enemy of the institution might do some good. Giddings did report that when he entered the room the auctioneer "became exceedingly embarrassed . . . the moment he saw me." Yet his naive thought that an antislavery presence alone might somehow make some difference ultimately meant nothing, even despite the fact that the person being auctioned had apparently been kidnapped and should have been legally free. An exceedingly outraged Giddings empathized deeply with the pain that the captive was enduring: "as the bidders one after another raised the price of their fellowmen, his eyes followed them and the deep horror and agony of his soul was portrayed in the contortions of his countenance." [14]

Had Giddings voiced objections aloud as the price rose, his diary would surely have recounted them. For a loyal Whig and upstanding congressmen such as Giddings, however, any such heartfelt remonstrance was clearly impossible, a feckless act of political suicide. As in the incident of the slave beating, Giddings retired again in silence, a "man of

---

13. Giddings Diary, Feb. 14, 1839.
14. Ibid., Feb. 16, 1839.

conscience" as disturbed by his own inability to act as by the "horror and agony" he had witnessed. At times like these, the morally clear-cut world of the Western Reserve could hardly have seemed more remote.

Painfully conscious of the emotional distance that separated his political position in Washington from the Western Reserve culture he best understood, Giddings took quick steps to reconnect the two. He repaired to the reassuring sanctuary of Adams's drawing room and met with his antislavery "messmates," seeking their help in his plan to attack the slave trade on the floor of the House.[15] He also conveyed to his family back home in Ohio news of the terrible things he had witnessed. Though he had not been able to help the slave on the auction block, he surely could lead his children to oppose atrocities like this one. To his ten-year-old son, Grotius, he wrote moralistically of a slave girl of eighteen he had met who was "well dressed, well behaved and appears as well informed a girl as any other. But her master can sell her when he pleases. What think you, is it right?" Soon after this his elder daughter, Lura, also received fatherly interrogations that requested her moral judgments on the buying and selling of slaves. Though Giddings could never bear witness in public to his wholehearted abolitionist "conscience," he privately exercised it widely when challenging his children to meet that higher standard. That he largely succeeded with them documents the power of his displaced commitment: Lura became a feminist Garrisonian, and Grotius a devotee of John Brown; two other children also became deeply involved in antislavery politics.[16]

While Giddings explored the city, in early 1839 House proceedings opened, and debate turned quickly to a petition requesting diplomatic recognition for Haiti, the Caribbean republic born of black insurrection. This was Giddings's first chance to assess congressional discussions on slavery, and everything he heard upset and angered him: "Northern men appear afraid to come out and declare their sentiments. . . . They keep a distance from the subject." Still more tellingly, he sensed at once in slaveholders' remarks their deepest fears, those of slave violence. Though

15. Ibid., Jan. 30, 1839; Giddings to Laura W. Giddings, Feb. 1, 1831, Giddings Papers.

16. Giddings to Grotius Giddings, Dec. 29, 1839; Giddings to Lura Maria Giddings, Feb. 17, 1839, Giddings Papers; Stewart, *Joshua R. Giddings*, 50–51.

he himself flatly dismissed these fears as unfounded, he had nonetheless pinpointed perhaps the most volatile element in the ethic of Southern honor, one that a man of "conscience" might directly address to guarantee a deeply felt impact. It was "amusing and astonishing," he thought, that in "the South the general impression [of abolition] is that it is designed to create a general rebellion among the slaves & and have them cut their masters' throats." It was long past time for someone to "come forth & with plainness set forth the claims of the north."[17]

As Giddings saw the "gag rule" reenacted and the "stalwart" Adams silenced when presenting antislavery petitions, he reached a plainly distressing conclusion: in the House of Representatives, arrogant slaveholders called the tune. Everyone else bowed to their wishes when it came to matters of slavery. As Giddings judged it, slaveholders went out of their way to intimidate "diffident, taciturn and *forbearing*" Northerners with their "high and important bearing . . . their confident and bold assertion, their overbearing manners."[18] It was, to Giddings, an abhorrent style of political leadership, like nothing he had ever encountered in the Western Reserve.

As Giddings now understood the situation, the Southerners' heavy authoritarianism and his own horrifying encounters with slavery were beginning to explain one another. The House itself was being "enslaved" by haughty planters, coarsened by their power as masters, and "our Northern friends are in fact afraid of these southern Bullies"; even Adams doubted the wisdom of confronting the issue of slavery in the District of Columbia. But for Giddings, in stark contrast to his agonizing position at the slave auction, this was a situation in which he could and must speak out. To choose otherwise would be tantamount to permitting his own enslavement, and, as a consequence of his capitulation, the enslavement of his constituents as well: "we have no northern man who can boldly and forcibly declare his abhorrence of Slavery and of the slave trade. This kind of fear I have never experienced nor shall I submit to it now."[19]

---

17. Giddings Diary, Dec. 17, 1838.
18. Ibid., Dec. 14, 1838.
19. Ibid.

Now Giddings consulted with his "messmates" while mulling over the idea of demanding a House report on how many slaves in the District had committed suicide or killed their own children rather than endure further enslavement. As he prepared to speak out forcefully against the detestable scenes he had witnessed, his anger and revulsion could not have been plainer. In mid-December, he rose from his seat, delivered a stinging attack on slavery in the District, and spoke feelingly about his recent experiences: "on the beautiful avenue in front of the capitol, members of Congress, during this session, have heard the harsh voice of the auctioneer, publicly selling human beings, while they were on their way to the capitol. They also have been compelled to turn aside from their path to permit a coffle of slaves, males and females, chained to each other by their necks, to pass on their way to this National slave mart."[20] "I felt that forbearance ceased to be a virtue and my national pride was humbled," Giddings recalled after the speech. "I no longer felt myself the Representative of *Freemen* while I was compelled to remain silent and witness my country's disgrace."[21]

The politician of "conscience" now set about to discover the furthest possible limits allowed him to express publicly his hatred of slavery. Doctrines that endorsed violence and behavior that invited direct confrontation on the floor of the House were soon to become the vehicles that served this end. They also forced him to press very heavily against the restraints understandably felt by any congressman who detested slavery, but who also claimed fidelity to the Whig Party and to the Constitution.

Giddings addressed these conflicting allegiances in his own way by simply denying their existence. To the contrary, he flatly insisted that antislavery action and participation in the Whig Party amounted to the same thing. "True Whigs" must espouse the antislavery position, he decided, and "true antislavery" meant supporting the Whig Party. Citing House votes on the "gag rule," which Democrats solidly supported while Whigs split along sectional lines, Giddings concluded that

20. *Congressional Globe*, 25th Cong., 3d sess., 1839, 7, 179–81.

21. Giddings to "Dear Sir," Feb. 26, 1839, Joshua R. Giddings Miscellaneous Papers, New York Historical Society, New York.

the Democrats, on one hand, as a party, were fundamentally responsible for every proslavery measure. Whigs, on the other hand, even Southern ones, might be persuaded to condone his antislavery creeds. To this dubious assertion, however, Giddings added a second, more disturbing claim that the Whig programs of economic nationalism actually forwarded the cause of emancipation. Protective tariffs, homestead bills, national roads, and the like, he argued, would invariably disseminate wealth, knowledge, and culture throughout the nation, a process deeply "dangerous to the interests of slavery, which must ever depend on ignorance and stupidity, and is jealous of the knowledge which teaches men to know the rights that God has given him." [22]

In asserting the harmony between Whig economic ideology and antislavery, Giddings was perfectly serious, as he proved throughout most of the 1840s by voting for slaveholding Whigs to be Speaker of the House and campaigning vigorously for slaveholding presidential candidates. Yet from any critical perspective, Giddings's attempts to reconcile his conscience with his claims of Whig loyalty were obviously fraught with sectional danger. His demand that Southern Whigs accept his antislavery doctrines alienated his colleagues and defied intricate sectional understandings that actually held his party together. His assertion, moreover, that Whig programs of economic nationalism led people in the slave states to learn "the rights God has given [th]em" seemed to imply to some sensitive listeners an interest in promoting unrest among the slaves. Understandably, Giddings's version of Whig loyalty provoked suspicions among slaveholding fellow congressmen.

Reasons for suspicion became still more apparent once Giddings started to expound his constitutional doctrines. And when he began (as he generally did) by asserting that his ideas were ones that slaveholders had always agreed to, one can easily imagine how rapidly resentments compounded. As Giddings emphasized time and again, his constitutional doctrines respecting slavery were "not new, as they are as old as the Con-

---

22. Giddings's fullest expositions of antislavery constitutional theory are found in his seven essays, published under the pseudonym "Pacificus," which were originally published in the *Western Reserve Chronicle*, Nov. 8, 15, 22, 27 (quotation), 30, Dec. 6, 13, 1842. The essays are also reprinted in George W. Julian, *The Life of Joshua Giddings* (Chicago: A. A. Mc Clurg and Co., 1892).

stitution, nor are they *antislavery* for they have been, for a half a century, agreed to by the southerner."[23] When making this stunning assertion he meant, as he explained, that the "reserved powers" clause of the Tenth Amendment explicitly denied the Congress any legislative power over slavery in parts of the Union where state law already permitted it. Put another way, neither the federal government nor the citizens of the free states had the slightest constitutional obligation to the peculiar institution and were therefore free to express their opposition to it in fullest terms. With his hatred of slavery now validated by this interpretation of federal statute, Giddings could with a clear conscience swear loyalty to the Constitution, occupy his seat in the House, and begin to attack slavery on behalf of his constituents.[24]

Giddings's weapons of constitutional warfare did render full justice to his deepening sense of militancy. Since Giddings held that the federal government had no power to involve the free states with slavery, his constituents were perfectly within their rights to aid escaping slaves and to impede the fugitives' pursuers—peacefully if possible, but violently if physically threatened. And though he granted that bondpersons in the slave states could be suppressed for insurrection under federal laws of treason, they nevertheless retained their moral warrant to seize their freedom as they saw fit, and whites had every legal right to help them. But when addressing the case of slaves who did escape beyond the reach of the state slave codes, Giddings no longer qualified his endorsement of emancipatory violence. Where federal statutes alone prevailed, slaves had both constitutional law and God's justice to support them when rising in arms and slaying their oppressors. In this particular instance, Giddings stated unequivocally, the Constitution itself upheld the shedding of the masters' blood. His challenge to "southern honor" could hardly have been put more bluntly.[25]

---

23. Ibid., Nov. 30, 1839.

24. For a complete evaluation of Giddings's antislavery constitutionalism, see Stewart, *Joshua R. Giddings*, 43–49. For the Whig Party's actual relationship to the problem of slavery in both national and regional contexts, see Michael Holt, *The Political Crisis of the 1850s* (New York: John Wiley, 1978); Daniel Walker Howe, *The Political Culture of the American Whigs* (New York: Oxford Univ. Press 1979); James Brewer Stewart, "Abolitionists, Insurgents, and Partisan Politics in Northern Whiggery, 1836–1844," in Alan M. Kraut, ed., *Crusaders and Compromises: Essays on the Relationship of the Antislavery Struggle to the Antebellum Party System* (Westport, CT: Greenwood Press, 1983).

25. See Stewart, *Joshua R. Giddings*, 43–49, and citations in n. 22.

One can only suspect that this was Giddings's conscious intention, but whatever his motives, the impact of his assertions guaranteed tempers would flare. "The Federal Government has no right to interfere with our domestic institutions!" declared slaveowning politicians time and again. Heartily agreeing with these assertions of "states'-rights," Giddings invariably rose in the House and challenged his Southern colleagues to follow their own logic to its bitterest antislavery conclusions: (1) Abolish slavery in the District of Columbia; (2) Never expend a penny of national revenue to recapture fugitives or to compensate masters for the loss of their escapees; (3) Endorse the obligation of citizens in the free states to protect and arm fugitive slaves; (4) Guarantee the right of the slaves to escape beyond the reach of the Southern slave codes and, once free, to defend that freedom by killing their pursuers.

Though it took him over a year to elaborate these doctrines fully, by 1841 Giddings was fully prepared to challenge "Southern honor" on the floor of the House. He did so by specifically connecting the issue of violent resistance by escaped slaves to the current congressional debate on the ongoing war in Florida against the Seminole Indians. His provocative remarks and the slaveholding Whigs' enraged responses revealed for a moment the violence that lay just below the surface when Southern codes of "honor" and Yankee creeds of "conscience" clashed openly within the House of Representatives. A close examination of this initial incident reveals a sequence of volatile interactions between members of the House that would repeat itself throughout Giddings's long career.[26]

As Giddings spoke against appropriating federal funds for the army to prosecute this war, slaveholders discovered to their shock that he was basing his objections on a defense of the Florida maroons, an armed insurgency of slave escapees who had fled from Georgia plantations and now fought side by side with the Seminoles. As everyone listening knew well, these escapees had been maintaining a bloody resistance to re-enslavement unprecedented in cost and duration, yet here was a congressman openly taking their side during the course of ordinary legislative debate.

---

26. The entire incident, as recounted here, is documented in *Congressional Globe*, 26th Cong., 2d sess., 1840–41, 3, 157–72, and app., 346–52.

This war, Giddings insisted, had "prostituted" the U.S. Army "to the base purpose of leading an organized company of negro catchers" for Georgia slaveholders who sought the return of their "supposed property." But if, as the "gentlemen from the south who hold to a strict construction" insisted so endlessly, the federal government must never meddle with slavery, why, Giddings queried, was the army trying to re-enslave people whose freedom was clearly guaranteed by "the laws of nature and nature's God"? Indeed, Giddings added hotly, "If the negroes had quietly suffered themselves to be trailed with bloodhounds or had supinely permitted themselves to be hanged for their loss of liberty, they would have deserved the name of slaves." Expending taxpayers' dollars to subsidize the army as "man-stealers" made his constituents complicit in the "sin" and "guilt" of slavery, Giddings insisted further; the forty thousand dollars in question would be much better spent on internal improvements for the benefit of the nation as a whole rather than being used to turn the people of his district into "the purchasers of human beings." The army should withdraw, he concluded, leaving slaveholders daring enough to risk their own lives to face the maroons by themselves.

Of more than an hour's duration, the speech displayed Giddings's unusual talent as an archival researcher, filled as it was with references and quotations from War Department documents, Claims Committee reports, and clauses from Indian treaties. Over the decades, in fact, Giddings was to become so fascinated by the history of the war against the maroons that he continued his investigations and in 1858 published an impressive volume of value to scholars even today. His lifelong attraction to the subject of violent resistance seems to have engaged him intellectually as well as emotionally.[27] For the slaveholders who were listening to his speech, however, emotional responses took an altogether different form; insulted Southern honor was quick to assert its claims.

One witness to the near melee that ensued once Giddings had ended his speech wrote that "the House was nearly all the time agitated like the waves of the sea"; it was "a peaceful riot," as Giddings himself described

---

27. Joshua R. Giddings, *The Exiles of Florida: A History of the Seminole War* (Columbus, OH: Follett and Foster, 1858).

it.[28] One after another, slaveowning congressmen, all from districts close to the area of the Seminole War, rose to repulse Giddings's assaults on their honor by inflicting him with shame and intimidation. Since from their point of view Giddings had utterly breached parliamentary etiquette by assaulting their values so openly, they were wholly justified in administering their rites of humiliation. In an instant, civility evaporated as the conflict of slaveholding "pride" with evangelical "conscience" exploded on the floor of the House.

Giddings at first sat quietly as William Cooper, a Georgian, began the assault "in a very agitated manner," scorning Giddings's honesty and hotly denying that his constituents would "steal . . . Negroes from Indians." He remained silent when next Edward Black, also from Georgia, swore that had Giddings uttered his "violent, inflammatory abolition speech" in Georgia, "he would most certainly be subjected to the infliction of lynch law; . . . we would give him an elevation of which he little dreams." Black then yielded the floor to his South Carolina colleague Waddy Thompson, who concluded the day's assault by attempting to read Giddings out of the Whig Party, an enterprise in "which every Southern man should only feel as a Southern man." He next took care to insult Giddings to his face by scorning him as the "*very obscurest of the obscure*" of all congressmen.[29]

To close the proceedings with honor's requirements satisfied, Thompson took pains to have the last word. He successfully moved adjournment, which prevented Giddings from making any further reply, a humiliating conclusion for Giddings from Thompson's point of view. As the Georgian saw it, the upstart Ohio "firebrand" now stood shamefully before Congress, made mute by slaveholders' rebukes. And just to make certain that Giddings's humiliation would be deeper still, Thompson arranged for his insults to be printed verbatim and in italics in next day's *National Intelligencer*, in particular the references to Giddings as "*the very obscurest of the obscure*" of all congressmen.

By trying so elaborately to humiliate Giddings, slaveholders obviously

---

28. Joshua Leavitt to "Readers," *Emancipator*, Feb. 18, 1841; Giddings to Laura W. Giddings, Feb. 14, 1841, Giddings Papers.

29. *Congressional Globe*, 26th Cong., 2d sess., 1840–41, 3, 158–59, 165–67, 170–72, documents the exchanges quoted in the following paragraphs. See also George W. Julian, *Life of Giddings*, 92–96.

meant to break his will, not to fortify his intransigence. But Giddings had promised himself several years before never to give in to "these southern bullies," so when the House opened the next morning, he immediately rose to respond to "a matter personal to himself." Thompson's published remarks, Giddings stated, "are printed in italics and I suppose they are intended as a direct personal insult." As a matter of "personal privilege," he demanded the right to reply. Rather than submission to slaveholders' chastisements, Giddings's comportment registered defiance. Realizing this, another Georgia planter seated near Giddings, Julius Alford, suddenly lost his temper and exploded, swearing that he would "sooner spit on Giddings than listen further to his abolitionist insults."

The formal record of Giddings's response captures him vividly as he asserted his "manly courage," while spurning his tormentor's challenge: "Mr. G. said that it was related of a veteran marshal, who had grown old in the service of his country, and who had fought a hundred battles, that he happened to offend a fiery young officer, who spat in his face for the purpose of insulting him. The General, taking his handkerchief from his pocket, and wiping his face, remarked: 'If I could wash your blood from my soul as easily as I can this spittle from my face, you should not live another day.' " Killing him would be easy, Giddings was telling Alford. All that stayed his hand was a devotion to conscience that left him unafraid and contemptuous of lesser men who could never intimidate him. Alford immediately leapt to his feet, began shouting threats, and headed straight for Giddings. Onlookers quickly intercepted him and steered him back to his seat.

With Alford forcibly silenced, Giddings now commanded the field. An imposing physical presence—six feet, two inches tall, 225 pounds, an expert marksman and wrestler—he turned to his original tormenter, Waddy Thompson, and lectured him on what honor really meant: "I claim no station superior to the most humble, nor inferior to the most exalted," Giddings told the slaveholder as he dismissed Thompson's characterization that he was "*the very obscurest of the obscure.*" Men who tried to slander him, moreover, would never be able to bait him into defending his honor with force because "at the North we have a different mode of punishing insult from what exists in the South. With us," he told Thompson severely, "the man who wantonly assails another is punished by public sentiment." For the moment at least, the "man of conscience," his honor intact, stood triumphant over those who had sought to demean him.

Historians have demonstrated that competing definitions of masculinity powerfully influenced cultural norms and personal behavior throughout the antebellum era. This skirmish between Giddings and the Southern Whigs displayed one form of this male competitiveness, expressed through assertions of abolitionist "conscience" and slaveholding "honor." Among congressmen who embodied these conflicting self-understandings, angry competition for advantage on the floor of the House now became almost inevitable. Driving this process forward, moreover, was the powerful influence of the various Washington boardinghouse subcultures that were mentioned earlier.[30]

While Giddings broke bread and prayed with antislavery evangelicals like William Slade and John Mattocks of Vermont and Seth Gates from New York's "Burned-Over District," Waddy Thompson, Julius Alford, Edward Black, and Mark Cooper also lived together with other Deep South "messmates," fraternities as intensely loyal to the values of the plantation as were Giddings and his friends to their culture of religious piety. Over the next decade, at Mrs. Sprigg's boardinghouse, Giddings presided over an ever more visible antislavery brotherhood of pious temperance men with whom he could enjoy the "good company." Planters, meanwhile, grouped together in boardinghouses of their own where strong drink and religious indifference often prevailed. In legislative processes that brought together such antagonistic fraternities, it was hardly surprising that the militant Giddings and easily insulted slaveholding congressmen often drove each other toward confrontation.[31]

---

30. See n. 2 and also Mark C. Carnes and Clyde Griffin, *Meanings for Manhood: Constructions of Gender in Victorian America* (Chicago: Univ. of Chicago Press, 1990).

31. Giddings to Lura Maria Giddings, Dec. 1, 1839, Dec. 15, 1844; Giddings to Laura W. Giddings, Dec. 1, 1839 (quotation), Giddings Papers. For the evidence of the Southern boardinghouse arrangements, see Faust, *James Henry Hammond*, 166–67. Perry M. Goldman and James Sterling Young, *The United States Congressional Directories, 1789–1840* (New York: Columbia Univ. Press, 1973), which lists congressmen by boardinghouse addresses, indicates that in 1839–40 all of Giddings's Southern antagonists lived together either at Mrs. Ballard's or Dr. Jones's boardinghouses and that all their "messmates," with one exception, represented districts deep in the cotton or rice South. See 356–61. In the next session (the last reported in the *Directories*) the mix and locations changed somewhat, but the general pattern from the previous session remained. See 307–15. Throughout all this, Giddings remained at Mrs. Sprigg's with other "yankees."

Other features of life in the nation's capital further intensified these frictions. In the streets of the District of Columbia, a "pedestrian's city," congressmen met one another time and again as they traveled on foot to engage in personal business. Chance encounters and impromptu observation took place constantly, so it was easy to notice Giddings in the company of nationally prominent abolitionists like Theodore Weld and Joshua Leavitt. These same two "fanatics" could also be seen openly consulting with the Ohioan and his "messmates" just outside the House, and for a time both abolitionists became "messmates" of a sort at Mrs. Sprigg's boardinghouse. Worse still, from the planters' perspective, Giddings also felt no reluctance to be seen in public with black people or to entertain them privately, and he was justly suspected of having assisted local fugitive slaves. (Mrs. Sprigg herself was actually a slaveholder but of a highly unusual and subversive sort: she retained this status simply for the purpose of releasing anyone she managed to acquire.)[32] Little wonder that slaveholding congressmen saw Giddings, the organizer of maddening "abolitionist conspiracies," as someone who purposely inverted all social order, so they shunned him whenever they met him by chance. The snubbing upheld their honor. It also prevented the loss of tempers and perhaps worse.

The details of the specific confrontations in the House that arose from these circumstances, especially that of Giddings's censure and re-election in 1842, have been well recounted elsewhere. But in all these conflicts, Giddings and his slaveholding enemies played out a consistent ritual that followed the general pattern of the initial explosion over the Seminole War. Every incident began with Giddings adamantly defending the slaves' constitutional right to seize their own freedom, violently if necessary, his

---

32. For evidence of Mrs. Sprigg's antislavery activities, see Joshua R. Giddings to Joseph Addison Giddings, Aug. 13, 1842, Giddings Papers. In addition to this evidence, it seems inconceivable that abolitionist purists such as Theodore Weld or Joshua Leavitt would have permitted themselves to rent rooms from a serious slaveholder. For discussions of Washington, DC, as an intimate, pedestrian's city, see Young, *Washington Community*, 87–110; Constance McLaughlin Green, *Washington: Village and Capitol, 1800–1878* (Princeton: Princeton Univ. Press, 1962). For confirmation of slaveholders' street-corner snubbings of Giddings, see Julian, *Life of Giddings*, 76. A flavor of Giddings street-corner abolitionist activism is conveyed in Giddings's letter to Theodore D. Weld, Jan. 28, 1844: "We want a man to go among the people of the city, get up petitions, hold meetings, prepare the minds of the people of both Blacks and Whites." Gilbert Hobbs Barnes and Dwight L. Dumond, *The Letters of Theodore Weld, Angelina Grimké Weld and Sarah Grimké* (Washington, DC: American Historical Association, 1934), 2:990–91.

constituents' right to remain untainted by slavery's sin, and his personal right to speak the dictates of his conscience. Next, enraged slaveholders made strenuous efforts to intimidate him into silence that ranged from the famous attempt to censure him to attempts to attack him physically on the House floor. As each of these dramas finally closed, Giddings invariably stood once again to face down his adversaries. In this manner controversy over slave violence and congressmen's inability to maintain common civility became connected in one self-reinforcing process.

On a political level, Giddings welcomed and fostered these developments as "cheering signs of the times" that presaged the slaveholders' total capitulation. His expressions of optimism, however, also revealed some of the deeper satisfactions he derived from his disruptive behavior. "We are forming a phalanx that will drive slavery into the Atlantic or the Gulf of Mexico," he reported to his eldest son in 1843. The planter politicians were finally receiving their due, and the scales of justice were finally coming into balance: "Thank God I have lived to see those fellows tremble before northern influence." On a still more personal level, he drew deep exhilaration from the atmosphere of confrontation that he, his "messmates," and John Quincy Adams were creating. (Once he had opened his war against slavery his "hypochondria" seems to have vanished.) Nothing excited him more than "with my own eyes [to] see the southern slaveholders literally shake and tremble through every nerve and joint." Baiting "arrogant" planters to the limits of their patience was a challenge that Giddings relished: "I enjoyed the sport yesterday first-rate," he once confided. His reflexive personal animosity toward Southern "bullies" cannot be doubted. Slaveholding congressmen certainly sensed it.[33]

Between 1841 and 1858, when Giddings retired, slaveholding congressmen attempted to goad him into physical combat on the House floor on at least seven occasions. Sometimes the moment came suddenly, as it did in 1843 when Charles Dawson of Louisiana pushed Giddings from behind, threw him into the desks on the House floor, and reached for the bowie knife concealed beneath his coat. On another occasion, in

---

33. Giddings to Laura W. Giddings, Feb. 6, 1842, Jan. 23, 1843; Giddings to Joseph A. Giddings, June 1, 1842, Dec. 25, 1843, Jan. 7, 1844, Giddings Papers.

1845 Georgia's Edward Black interrupted Giddings while he was speaking against slavery, yelled out that the Ohioan ought to be hanged, and then charged, with cane upraised, swinging fiercely but inaccurately at Giddings's head. During the tense debates over the Wilmot Proviso in March 1849, a drunken Richard Meade of Virginia seized Giddings by the collar and, according to Giddings, "shaking his fist in my face began to threaten me." Even advancing age offered him no protection from these spontaneous outbursts, as the Mississippian Lucius Q. C. Lamar proved in 1858 when he called the sixty-three-year-old Giddings a "damned old scoundrel" and "with a countenance filled with rage" tried to attack.[34]

On other occasions, however, slaveholders attempted to enrage Giddings into making the first move, which of course he never did, by subjecting him to insult after insult. During the "Pearl Affair" in 1848 (a failed attempt to smuggle escaped slaves out of the capital in which Giddings was personally involved), proslavery rioters roamed the streets, while within the House slaveholders taunted Giddings with threats to hang him or to "deliver him bodily to the mob."[35] Edward Stanly, however, went furthest in telling the world in 1852 why slaveholders so hated Giddings by castigating him for his "disreputable habit" of associating with black people. At bottom, it was Giddings's genuine racial egalitarianism, which he practiced so visibly so consistently and on such a personal level, that disturbed planter politicians most of all: "He receives visits in his home from free negroes. He gives them money and treats them as close friends, entertaining them in his private quarters." Giddings had to be an "insane man," Stanly could only believe, the equivalent of a

34. *Congressional Globe*, 27th Cong., 3d sess., 1843, 3, 140–58; app. 194–98; Giddings to "Daughter," Feb. 13, 1843, Giddings to Laura W. Giddings, Feb. 19, 1843, Giddings Papers. *Congressional Globe*, 28th Cong., 2d sess., 1844–45, 14, 250–56; Giddings Diary, Mar. 2, 3, 4, 1849, Giddings Papers; Giddings to Lura Maria Giddings, Jan. 24, 1858, George W. Julian Papers, Indiana State Library, Indianapolis.

35. Joshua R Giddings, *A History of the Rebellion: Its Authors and Causes* (Columbus, OH: Follett and Foster, 1864), 273–77; *Congressional Globe*, 30th Cong., 1st sess., 1847–48, 17, 641, 652–59, 667–70; Giddings to Seth M. Gates, Apr. 27, 1848, Gerrit Smith-Miller Papers, Syracuse Univ. Library; Giddings to Joseph Addison Giddings, Apr. 25, 1848, Giddings to Laura W. Giddings, Apr. 20, 1848, Giddings Papers; Joshua R. Giddings, *Speeches in Congress* (New York: Negro Univ. Press, 1968), 220–49. The best scholarly treatment of the Pearl Affair is Stanley C. Harrold Jr., "The Pearl Affair: The Washington Riot of 1848," *The Records of the Columbia Historical Society* 50 (1980): 140–46.

"bad nigger" who should be hanged for "stealing and [for] slandering his neighbor."[36]

Unless he protected his "manhood" by defending himself against these attacks, every code of Southern honor marked him as a coward, and Giddings knew it. Invariably, however, he met these challenges by scorning his attackers to their faces as morally stunted people who were to be pitied, not fought with, since they were literally beneath his contempt. In short, he heaped dishonor on Southern honor itself. To Stanly he replied scornfully: "When a man decends to the vulgarities of barroom blackguards he gets lower down than a man can go. . . . I cannot follow him so far as to throw the mantle of charity over him. "And when Dawson pushed him into the desks and reached for his knife, Giddings repelled him, saying that he was a "perfectly harmless" drunkard who deserved "pity" instead of a thrashing. To his wife, however, Giddings also observed, "Had I struck him, his bowie knife would have been of little avail." The imposing, well-muscled Giddings found his assailants easy to restrain until peacemakers intervened.[37]

But while order could be patched back together, each of these incidents ruptured a bit more seriously the tissues of civility upon which peaceful deliberation depended. Viewed in this manner, Preston Brooks's assault on Charles Sumner in 1857 was a predictable next step in the rituals of attack and defiance that had so often involved Giddings for nearly two decades.

A brief comparison between Giddings's case and Sumner's is instructive at this juncture. Giddings's consistent intransigence ultimately protected him when expressing his hatred of slavery. In the midst of the uproar over the "Pearl Affair," Giddings made certain that everyone remembered this: "I will inform the gentleman that it is too late in the day to attempt to seal the lips of any northern representative. . . . I give notice to the gentleman, and to all others, that I shall say just what I think on any and every subject that comes before us. It is my intention to

---

36. *Congressional Globe*, 32d Cong., 1st sess., 1851–52, 21, 160–82, 187–96, 200; for Stanly's remarks and Giddings's response, see 531–35. Giddings to Lura Maria Giddings, Feb. 15, 1852, Joshua R. Giddings–George W. Julian Papers, Library of Congress.

37. *Congressional Globe*, 32d Cong., 1st sess., 1851–52, 21, 531–35; Giddings to Laura W. Giddings, Feb. 13, 1843, Giddings Papers; Giddings to "Daughter," Feb. 13, 1843, Giddings–Julian Papers.

call things by their right names, and to speak, so far as I am able, in such direct, plain and simple language as to be understood."[38]

In the more decorous Senate, Sumner had established no such protective boundaries before delivering his philippic on "The Crime against Kansas." Unlike Giddings, moreover, whose speeches never singled out a single individual, Sumner carefully subjected one particular fellow Senator to an elaborate pattern of insults. Thus, while Giddings no less than Sumner transgressed the etiquette of civility, they did so under different circumstances with very different consequences. The disabled Sumner became a martyr in the North and an embarrassment to moderates in the South. The untrammeled Giddings, by contrast, confirmed slaveholders' most terrifying suspicions about the insurrectionary goals of the new Republican Party.

The 1856 remarks to the House by Henley Bennett from Mississippi suggest just how profoundly unsettling Giddings's long-accumulating impact had actually been. The Republican Party stood indicted of endorsing slave insurrections, Bennett charged, and to prove it, all one needed to do was refer to Giddings's speeches in Congress. According to Bennett, Giddings had stated only two years earlier that he would welcome the day when: "The black man, armed with British bayonets and led on by British officers shall assert his freedom and wage a war of extermination against his master, when the torch of the incendiary shall light up the towns and cities of the South and blot out the last vestiges of slavery. . . . I will hail it as the dawning of the millenium."[39]

While Giddings immediately denied that he had ever "uttered such sentiments," the truth of his rebuttal rested on narrowest literalism. In the speech to which Bennett referred, Giddings actually had been protesting what he had taken to be the Pierce administration's policies to bolster slavery in Cuba. But as he had done so, he had pushed his "states' rights" theories of slavery to an extreme that made Bennett's warnings, accurate or not, perfectly understandable. The "popular sentiment [against slavery] which is now rolling on in the north" would,

---

38. Giddings, *Speeches in Congress,* 231.

39. *Congressional Globe,* 34th Cong., 3d sess., 1856–57, 34, 53–56, 78–80.

Giddings predicted, soon sweep the institution away: "When the contest shall come, . . . when the slaves shall rise in the South; when in imitation of the Cuban bondsmen the slaves shall feel that they are *men*; when they feel the stirring emotions of immortality . . . entitled to the rights that God had bestowed upon them . . . the lovers of our race will stand forth and exert the legitimate power of the Government for freedom. . . . Then we will strike off the shackles . . . and make peace by giving freedom to the slave.[40]

Soon other slaveholders began joining in with still other damning examples of Giddings's presumably insurrectionary intent. One speech in particular that Virginia's John Letcher cited before the House told slaveholders all they felt they needed to know. Giddings had delivered this speech in 1846, when supporting the annexation of all of British-held Oregon. Annexation, he had argued, would not only increase the number of free states but also would lead to a British invasion of the South and the liberation of the slaves. Though denying that he desired "servile insurrection," he nevertheless had emphasized his belief that slaveholders had already become terrorized by the "prospect of black regiments of the British West Indian Islands. Servile insurrection torments their imaginations; rapine and murder dance before their affrighted eyes." As for his own feelings about this prospect, as well as those of his constituents and the people of the North in general, Giddings could not have been clearer: "hundreds of thousands of honest and patriotic men will 'laugh at your calamity and will mock when your fear cometh.' If blood and massacre should mark the struggle for liberty of those who for ages have been oppressed and degraded, my prayer to the God of Heaven shall be that justice, *stern unyielding justice* be awarded to both master and slave."[41]

Technically speaking, Giddings had not actually advocated that the slaves rise in rebellion. Instead, as he emphasized in rebuttal to the slaveholders, he had simply described his feelings should insurrection occur. After all, as he had argued for so many years, neither Congress nor the

---

40. Ibid., 33d Cong., 1st sess., 1853–54, 33, app., 986–89.

41. Ibid., 34th Cong., 3d sess., 1856–57, 34,159–60. Here Giddings read into the record part of the actual speech he had given in 1846 during the debate over the annexation of Oregon.

Northern states had any right whatever to be involved with slavery in the South; as an upholder of the Constitution it was certainly not his place to interfere with the "peculiar institution."

Repeated yet again was the same "states' rights" distinction in support of slave violence that had so deeply angered slaveholding congressmen for so many years. As they heard Giddings explain it once more, it revolted them, just as it always had, as a piece of hypocrisy so transparent that it offended their intelligence and openly mocked their deepest values. Giddings, as slaveholders saw him, had always been a self-aware insurrectionist who dissembled by speaking constitutional nonsense. Yet, despite their most strenuous efforts to drive him into silence, for two full decades he always succeeded in having his way with them. Ever defiant and eager to traffic in violence, Joshua Giddings stood as a sustained, unavenged rebuke to Southern honor.

To conclude, it is useful to speculate on the thoughts of Giddings and his antagonists upon the occasion of the Ohioan's retirement after twenty years of continuous service. At a private reception to which all in Congress were invited in March 1859, 104 Republican senators and representatives presented to "Father Giddings" (as many Republicans now called him) a solid silver tea set that bore this inscription: "To Joshua R. Giddings as a token of his Moral Worth and Personal Integrity." Not a single Southern representative attended the event, and Giddings, one suspects, took pride in their gesture of contempt.[42]

---

42. Julian, *Life of Giddings*, 363.

The Orator and the Insurrectionist

"I regard you as providentially raised up to be the James Otis of the new revolution," wrote William Lloyd Garrison to Wendell Phillips in 1857. The year before, Thomas Wentworth Higginson had also offered him the same challenging thought: "Some prophetic character must emerge as the new crisis culminates. . . . Your life has been merely preliminary to the work that is coming for you."[1] The Kansas-Nebraska Act opened this new crisis, and in its aftermath Wendell Phillips began to fulfill this prophetic role that he too had long yearned to attain. After Stephen A. Douglas's bill became law, parties slowly collapsed, the nation lurched toward catastrophe, and Wendell Phillips secured a formidable reputation as the North's most compelling sectional orator. Through forensics, not disunionist politics, Phillips finally began gathering the national power he had always wanted, even as he forced the radical voice of abolitionism into debates that led to Civil War.

The Kansas-Nebraska Act set off a sectional footrace to the territories and triggered a disruptive train of events. Free-state and Southern settlers became locked in guerrilla combat as they struggled to control the territories. Meanwhile, former Whigs, former Democrats, and Free-Soilers endorsed the Wilmot Proviso and coalesced to form a huge new sectional party that called itself Republican. The Whig Party fragmented and the

Originally published as "The Orator and the Insurrectionist," in James Brewer Stewart, *Wendell Phillips: Liberty's Hero* (Baton Rouge: Louisiana State University Press, 1986), 177–208. Reprinted with permission.

1. William L. Garrison to Phillips, October 15, 1857, and Thomas W. Higginson to Phillips, November 18, 1856, Crawford Blagden Collection, Houghton Library, Harvard University.

Democrats began splitting along sectional lines. In the presidential election of 1856, the Republican nominee, John C. Fremont, carried eleven Northern states and received no Southern support, showing well against the Democratic winner, James Buchanan. The Republican's motto had decried "Bleeding Sumner" as well as "Bleeding Kansas," for just before the election an outraged South Carolina congressman, Preston Brooks, beat Phillips's friend senseless with a heavy cane, avenging "insults" to his family's honor uttered by Charles Sumner during a speech, "The Crime Against Kansas." The following year, the U.S. Supreme Court announced its famous *Dred Scott* decision, which seemed to guarantee slavery the right to move wherever it wished. Black people, the chief justice affirmed, had "no rights that white men were bound to respect.

Phillips denounced all these developments with a predictable mixture of distress, disdain, and self-vindication. His public appraisal of the new Republican Party rehearsed all the old themes. After all, he emphasized, most Republicans were even more conservative about the Constitution and immediate emancipation than the Free-Soilers had been. He lamented their moral shortcomings, vilified their leaders, and occasionally gave credit to the most advanced of them when they defied their party's "half-measures." Phillips also continued zealously to preach disunion, for the Kansas conflicts and the *Dred Scott* decision, he said, only reconfirmed what he had first said in 1842, that every attempt to hedge in slavery with constitutional restrictions was doomed. In 1858 he found American politics as bankrupted as they had been in 1840. "I have nothing new to say," he admitted, as he rose to address the Massachusetts Anti-Slavery Society in 1857. "You will not be surprised that at these gatherings, repeated year after year, there is very little new to be offered. We only repeat the same exposition of principle, varying it by application to the latest facts." [2]

The continuity of Phillips's behavior was equally clear when he reacted to the violence in Kansas. He showed his usual ambivalence about bloodshed, expressing the hope that the fighting presaged peaceful disunion

---

2. *Liberator*, July 10, 1857, and see Phillips's speeches reported on May 19, 1854, August 8, 1856, February 30, 1857, and May 11, 1858, for his specific views on major sectional events from 1854 through 1858.

even as he pledged a hundred dollars to a rifle fund for the free-soil guerrillas. Preston Brooks's attack on Sumner aroused in him the same wrath as had recent confrontations in Boston between abolitionists and public officials over the return of fugitive slaves to their masters. Again and again he blasted the "corrupted" leaders of Massachusetts politics from the platform. When anti-Catholic nativism surfaced in Massachusetts as the Know-Nothing Party, Phillips condemned it as yet another conspiracy of "cotton Aristocrats against Irish Catholics, slaves in the South, and the health of republicanism in the free states." To all who remembered, such words echoed his gestures to the Irish in 1842.[3]

All the while, Phillips continued as ever to sustain his fellow Garrisonians by emphasizing the overriding power of their movement and predicting its eventual triumph. He also acknowledged, however, that the Republicans now absorbed disunionist agitation far more completely than the Free-Soil Party ever had. In moments of public candor, he could even be heard lamenting that after "twenty years of incessant strife . . . the treasury is empty, the hand is tired, the toil of many years had gained but little. . . . There is no Canaan in Reform. There is no rest ahead. All is wilderness."[4] In August 1857 when Phillips made this beleaguered-sounding admission, Northern disunion certainly remained as elusive and unpopular an ideal as it had been in 1842. Nevertheless, even as he confessed his deep discouragement, Wendell Phillips had also begun to make his name as a public speaker without peer, as the matchless orator of Yankee abolitionism.

As an undergraduate, Phillips had once hailed the fast-multiplying number of books, newspapers, and pamphlets as the most important achievement of his own age, but he could never have foreseen the length to which Yankee culture would go to advance public enlightenment. As populations grew by millions, so did the literacy and sophistication of readers and audiences. By the 1850s, the North had become a hive of

---

3. Ibid., June 15, August 10, 1855. January 30, 1857, New England Emigrant Aid Society Papers, Amos Lawrence Papers, Massachusetts Historical Society, Boston; Phillips to Pease, November 9, 1856, Garrison Antislavery Papers, Boston Public Library. For more details on Phillips's activities relative to these issues, see Irving Bartlett, *Wendell Phillips: Brahmin Radical* (Boston, 1961), 188–91, 199–207.

4. *Liberator*, August 14, 1857.

reading rooms, libraries, debating societies, and civic-minded voluntary associations, which were founded, staffed, and attended by the rapidly developing business and professional classes found in many cities and towns. Meanwhile, expanding networks of roads, railways, canals, and telegraph lines meant swifter, cheaper, and wider distribution of all kinds of information. Lecturers could now venture with unprecedented speed into places unreachable years before. In publishing, too, advances in the production of cheap reading materials meant that by 1847 an up-to-date press and new stenographic techniques could turn out twenty thousand impressions an hour and disseminate a speaker's remarks just as they had been delivered. Editors, moreover, gladly filled their newspapers with densely printed multiple columns, sometimes in several installments, that reproduced to the last word even the lengthiest of speeches. Newsmen assumed, quite accurately, that subscribers made few sharp distinctions between hearing a speech and reading it (a dichotomy far more significant for readers in an age of radio and television). Instead, both activities were seen as complementary parts of one's larger interest in remaining informed. As a result, a huge reading public now formed the popular orator's second audience, participating in lectures at one remove while scanning their newspapers.

Far and away the most popular of all these new educational organizations was the lyceum movement. Before the Civil War, every lyceum was self-supporting, controlled by a local board in each town that sponsored a lecture series. Nearly every ambitious Northern community had such an organization by the 1850s, managed by its respectable bankers, attorneys, and commercial entrepreneurs, whose goal "was the mutual benefit of society." Those who joined thereby indicated their "wish to share their knowledge, and from the manner in which they associate, each may become by turns a learner and a teacher." It all amounted, most simply, to an effort to extend the goals of the public school into the larger community. Lyceum organizers promoted middle-class values among their town's citizenry, recruiting instructive speakers who would, they hoped, infuse their community with the moral direction that they feared individual families could no longer supply. Phillips, as a self-professed agitator, hailed this effort to promote self-improvement as "God's normal school for educating men, throwing upon them the grave responsibility of deciding great questions, and so lifting them to a higher level of intellectual and moral life."[5] In his assumption about social aims, although not in abolitionist ideology, he therefore supported the lyceum's ends completely. A well-run lyceum series might present in one season lectures on literature, science, philosophy, and current events, as well as humorous talks and travel accounts. A rich mixture of politicians, authors, and reformers—from Daniel Webster to Harriet Beecher Stowe—took to the circuit. National favorites included John B. Cough, the reformed alcoholic; Bayard Taylor, the brilliant travelogue lecturer; and increasingly, Wendell Phillips, who offered sectional inspiration as well as spiritually edifying entertainment.

Phillips developed a popular repertoire of noncontroversial, "elevating" topics. Audiences were eager to hear speeches titled "Chartism," "Water," "Geology," or "Street Life in Europe," but the universal favorite was "The Lost Arts," a speech Phillips repeated many hundreds of times and from which he made many thousands of dollars in fees. Read today, it seems an innocuous little talk. Phillips simply explained that most modern inventions of which people boasted so proudly had really been put to use ages before. In the realms of new discovery, in fact, there had actually been little progress for many centuries, said Phillips, reciting a string of fascinating examples. Ancient chemists and physicists, for instance, knew as much about glass, refraction of light, magnets, gunpowder, and metallurgy as any nineteenth-century scientist. Indeed, the engineers who had moved the Pelham Hotel in Boston (weight fifty thousand tons) only repeated procedures used in the sixteenth century by a handy Italian to set up a huge Egyptian obelisk in Rome. The theme justified itself easily as pure entertainment.

An audience of the time, however, would have recognized a powerful sectional message half hidden in the talk. Phillips always emphasized that these arts had been lost because privileged aristocrats had monopolized

---

5. Russel B. Nye, *Society and Culture in America, 1800–1860* (New York, 1974), 245–46; Phillips, "Scholar in a Republic," in his *Speeches, Lectures, and Letters,* 2nd series (Boston, 1891), 342. On the relationships between speech, print, and information, see Alvin W. Gouldner, *The Dialectic of Ideology and Technology: The Origins, Grammar, and Future of Ideology* (New York, 1976), 91–137; Paul E. Cochran, *Political Language and Rhetoric* (Austin, TX, 1979), 52–136. For the best treatment of the lyceum movement, consult Carl Bode, *The American Lyceum* (New York, 1956). See also John Mayfield, *The New Nation* (New York, 1982), 168–69.

them in past times. In the nineteenth century, a democratic age, people had been forced to tear aristocracy apart in order to rediscover them and apply them for the benefit of all. He then began a paean to the same belief in free inquiry and the individualistic values of self-improvement that, not so coincidentally, inspired some of the North's deepest hatred of Southern civilization. Remembering Phillips's reputation for extreme abolitionism, middle-class Yankee audiences knew exactly what he was actually driving at. "Today learning no longer hides in the convent or sleeps in the palace," he asserted. "No! She comes out into every day life and joins hands with the multitude." Astronomy dwells no more in the stars alone, but "serves navigation and helps us run boundaries." Alchemists no longer hoard the secrets of chemistry, which had now become the gift of the agronomist, "with his hands full for every farmer. . . . Our distinction lies in the liberty of the intellect and the diffusion of knowledge." Every individual, Phillips proclaimed, "has a right to know whatever may be serviceable to himself or to his fellows." For this reason, schoolhouses, town halls, lyceums, and churches—all dispensaries of democratic learning—were now the symbols of American culture, and "The care of Humanity" now constituted the nation's principal mission.[6]

Rome had once achieved all this and had yet relapsed into savagery, Phillips would warn in conclusion, asking "What is to prevent history from repeating itself? Why should our arts not be lost?" Citizens, he answered, must beware those who claim an exclusive right to knowledge or who try to keep art and science a secret from the people. Not once had Phillips mentioned either American slavery or the planter class, but not once had he departed from themes that made inherited inequality and hierarchy the mortal enemies of democratic knowledge and the programs of a free-labor civilization.

Simply by inviting Phillips to lecture, local lyceums automatically created widening opportunities for him to speak of abolition. It was a plain fact, after all, that Phillips's claims to forensic authority were as a great abolitionist, not as a hydraulic engineer, though he spoke about water, or

---

6. "The Lost Arts" is reprinted in Carlos Martyn, *Wendell Phillips: The Agitator* (New York, 1890), 533–47.

as a tale-spinner, though he also talked about lost arts. People obviously were drawn to lyceum meetings by Phillips's notoriety as "abolitionism's golden trumpet"; they wanted to measure their own beliefs about slavery against his. "The Lost Arts," though provocative entertainment, still furnished only a partial, unfulfilling exposure to the real Wendell Phillips, a Utica, New York, correspondent once complained. "Beautiful and golden as the speaker's oratory was, the audience, we think, was not satisfied," he wrote. Instead of "The Lost Arts," listeners wanted Phillips's "latest research and thoughts, lit up by the light of the latest events. . . . If a man (as Wendell Phillips) who has devoted his life to the negro question is to lecture, by all means let him lecture on the negro, or some subject akin to that."[7]

Lyceum directors, well aware of such complaints, sometimes found their meetings growing rancorous as they debated whether to permit Phillips to speak on slavery. As early as 1845, for example, the board of the Concord lyceum experienced great turmoil, including several resignations, before inviting him back to speak as an abolitionist. Phillips, in turn, manipulated these difficulties for his own ends by agreeing to lecture for no fee on slavery if the lyceum boards would also invite him to speak for pay on a noncontroversial topic. This gracious offer often relieved a divided board of the dilemma created by his notorious but popular reputation. Before proceeding directly into a lecture like "Chartism" or "The Lost Arts," Phillips would fashion an antislavery prelude, which he humorously called "The Portico."[8] He took such liberties because he knew full well that his audience came to hear him as an abolitionist, whatever his announced topic. After all, as he once shrewdly observed, people did not attend his lectures out of a sense of obligation but because they desired vicarious participation in the great events and controversies

---

7. The theoretical underpinning for much of my discussion of Phillips's rhetoric and the settings in which it took place derives partially from Erving Goffman, "The Lecture," in his *Forms of Talk* (Glencoe, IL, 1981), 162–96, and from two fine essays by Donald M. Scott, "Print and the Public Lecture," in William L. Joyce, David D. Hall, Richard D. Brown, and John B. Hench, eds., *Printing and Society in Early America* (Worcester, MA, 1983), 278–99, and "The Popular Lecture and the Creation of a Public in Mid-Nineteenth-Century America," *Journal of American History* 66 (March 1980): 791–809. See also the *Utica Herald*, reprinted in *Liberator*, April 21, 1865.

8. Bartlett, *Phillips*, 124–25; *Liberator*, February 10, 1844, March 28, 1845, December 2, 1860; Aaron Powell, *Personal Reminiscences of the Anti-Slavery and Other Reforms and Reformers* (Plainfield, NJ, 1899), 86–87; Phillips to Pease, December 30, 1842, Garrison Papers, Boston Public Library.

associated with Phillips's name. People did not say, "If I don't go, my neighbors won't do their duty. I'm sorry to waste the hour, but I must set a good example for my children." Rather, he observed, the listener hastened to the lecture hall "because his heart is there a half hour before he is. He goes because he cannot stay away. . . . He goes to share in the great struggle, and glow in the electric conflict."[9]

As sectional tensions deepened and spread, Phillips made his abolitionist tactics even more direct, adding to his list of historical topics "Toussaint L'Ouverture" and "Crispus Attucks," his great heroes of black revolution. At times, he simply loaded his talks with keen antislavery humor. In "The Lost Arts," for example, he loved to describe an ancient Syrian's beautiful steel sword as so flexible "that it could be put into a scabbard like a corkscrew, and bent every way, without breaking—like an American politician." It pleased Phillips most of all when lyceum boards simply gave in and let him talk as he wished under their formal auspices. When they did so, they became publicly associated with a sectional posture simply by attaching their organization's name to his speech. When Lee, Massachusetts, gave him his head, Phillips exulted to his wife, Ann, "The guns are spiked. . . . So the walls fall down and prejudice melts year by year—I see more and more the wide influence of the Lyceum movement in smoothing the path for other things."[10]

Phillips possessed the freedom to behave so independently because he had become a star. Following the foreigners Fanny Kemble and Jenny Lind, he was among the first generation of Americans to achieve national visibility as popular figures whom people would pay to see. The public, already aware of his reputation, wanted to find out what Wendell Phillips looked like, how he behaved, and what he "really" said. News reporters, therefore, started publishing analytical pieces on all these topics, thereby assisting all the more in the promotion of Phillips as a public personality. Before he spoke in large cities, mass-circulation newspapers carried notices that drew audiences from great distances, and people hounded

9. Phillips, "The Pulpit," in *Speeches, Lectures, and Letters*, 2nd series, 264–65.

10. Thomas Wentworth Higginson, *Wendell Phillips* (Boston, 1884), viii; Phillips to Ann Phillips, February 25, 1855, Blagden Papers.

him for autographs, artifacts that testified to a personal encounter with the famous man. The casual researcher can stumble upon Phillips's "marks" in practically every Northern historical society's autograph file, his signature commonly scrawled below his favorite slogan: "Peace, if possible—Justice at any rate!" As people entered the lecture hall, they did not expect simply to hear a man give a talk about slavery; instead, they were well prepared and eager to participate in a significant dramatic event, orchestrated by the powerful presence of Wendell Phillips. In no respect did Phillips disappoint them. His platform style was by all accounts arresting, his impact unforgettable.[11]

People often expressed great surprise at their first sight of Phillips, for his appearance greatly contradicted their expectations. He seemed not an energetic extremist but a humble, open, and friendly man. "Can this be the fiery reformer . . . ? Can this be the rank agitator. . . ? Could this easy, effortless man be Wendell Phillips?" Such exclamations echo through contemporary descriptions of Phillips's public demeanor. He projected great physical authority, to be sure, for he was full framed and athletic looking, with thinning sandy hair and a profile that grew more rugged with age. There was an "absence of vindictiveness, or even severity, though not of firmness in his appearance." He seemed the complete opposite of the flint-skinned fanatic. Instead, a "genteel man" stepped to the platform, "neatly, not foppishly dressed," his face wearing a "pleasant smile." He carried no notes and stood directly before the audience. Since he never used the podium, neither script nor props ever separated him from his listeners. He suddenly but quietly seemed to leap "at a single bound, into the middle of his subject." The "keynote to Phillips' oratory," Higginson wrote perceptively, was its conversational quality, raised "to the highest power." No other orator, in Higginson's opinion, "ever began so entirely on the plain of his average hearer. It was as if he simply repeated, in a slightly louder tone, what he had just been saying to a familiar friend at his elbow." The moment Phillips began to lecture, the psychological distance between himself and his audience collapsed almost entirely. He "held them by his very quietness,"

---

11. On audience expectation, see Goffman, "Lecture," 176–79.

according to Higginson, establishing a powerful atmosphere of intimacy with audiences of many hundreds.[12]

As Phillips developed his subject, his audiences could not doubt that they were hearing inflammatory language from an authentic extremist who aimed his words at their deeper passions. Nevertheless, by every account his delivery (so unlike Webster's) was absolutely calm. He looked, one listener recalled, "like a marble statue, cool and white, while a stream of lava issued red hot from his lips." Another witness suggested similarly that he "resembled a volcano, whose bosom nourishes inexhaustible fire . . . while all without is unruffled and unindicative of the power within." As Phillips continued speaking, his voice would grow deeper, and his sentences would begin following each other in "a long, sonorous swell, still easy and graceful, but powerful as the soft stretching of a tiger's paw." He used simple, democratic language, including slang contractions, such as "ain't," often encased in short sentences. Yet, it seemed that he never let a note of inelegance intrude as he maintained familiarity with his audiences.[13] A certain E. A. S. Smith, no prominent abolitionist or culture critic, summed up his reaction on first hearing Phillips: "I have never been so completely absorbed by a speaker. . . . He had all the ease and manner of one who is the perfect master of his subject and is confident of its truth and all the grace of a graceful man. The topics that he touched upon were all powerful, finely illustrated, and it appeared to me that they must convince every one there that they must be up and doing. His manner was so easy and every thing about his address so informal that I thought we might call it a talk rather than an address."[14]

In one way or another, all these responses suggest the crucial forensic point that goes far to explain why audiences found Phillips so captivating. He was a complete master of what Erving Goffman has called "fresh

---

12. Higginson, *Phillips*, 265–67; Andover, Mass. *Advertiser*, reprinted in *Liberator*, March 20, 1857; *New Englander Magazine*, reprinted in *Liberator*, November 5, 1860. See also Thomas W. Higginson to L. Higginson, July 9, 1845, Thomas Wentworth Higginson Papers, Houghton Library, Harvard University.

13. Lillie B. Chace Wyman, "Reminiscences of Wendell Phillips," New England Magazine 27 (February 1903): 732; *Liberator*, August 6, 1852; Martyn, *Phillips*, 493–94. For a discussion of elocution and speaking style in relation to the impact of lecturing, see Goffman, "Lecture."

14. E. A. S. Smith to Caroline Weston, n.d., Weston Papers, Antislavery Collection, Boston Public Library.

talk," the speaker's ability to appear immediately receptive to the feelings of his audience, even as he speaks with seeming authenticity of his own thoughts and emotions. The effect is one of complete spontaneity, unencumbered by physical props and rhetorical "noise" (exaggerated gestures, superficial hyperbole, or stumbling diction), which tend to heighten the audience's sense of distance from the speaker. Phillips, in other words, conveyed the impression that he was revealing his true self as he spoke, offering his listeners "a sort of common people honesty," as one reporter described it. He appeared to be a "plain, honest man that loves sincerity and the truth . . . and can tolerate no mock shows or false dignity." Another witness agreed: "He opens his heart to you as the spring buds do theirs. You never think of asking from whom he learned to do so." Thoreau had the same impression, observing that Phillips's rhetoric was unique because he was "at the same time an eloquent speaker and a righteous man." All these observations echo precisely what Phillips's college friends had said of him decades before, that he was transparent and wholly without guile.[15]

It was all arrestingly simple. Phillips seemed to stand before each individual in his audience and say honestly what was on his mind. He "forces upon his audience the belief that he is speaking exactly the convictions of his own understanding," one observer noted. Moreover, Phillips projected this impression so placidly that his most denunciatory words actually made his listeners feel serenity. (Demagogues, Phillips had always believed, inflamed the passions of mobs. Orators, by contrast, elevated audiences' interests.)[16] His words seemed like "oil on the troubled billows of the chafed sea; he rebukes the winds of strife and the waves of faction. . . . The severe front of a turncoat or tyrant present begins to relax. . . . He is the mobber of mobs." The point is crucial. Phillips's speeches have always repelled or inspired modern readers (depending on their politics) for their unabashedly extremist language. The listeners of his day likewise reacted within this range of judgment, but unless intent on harassing him, audiences never felt that Phillips was trying to

---

15. *Liberator*, March 20, 1857, December 4, 1863, March 25, 1845.

16. Phillips, "Attachment to Ancient Usages," Wendell Phillips Composition Books, Library Records, Harvard University Archives.

intimidate them or to lead them to abandon their emotional self-control. "How well he speaks," enthused another reporter, confirming this aspect of Phillips's appeal. "No waste of power. No 'bursts of eloquence.' Everything is subdued, strong, and telling. He steals upon the audience . . . and surprises them into enthusiasm." As all these qualities came together, listeners found themselves imaginatively lifted beyond the confines of the lecture hall, emotionally absorbed in Phillips's actual speech. "You heard him . . . an hour, two hours, three hours," a colleague recalled, "and were unconscious of the passage of time. . . . He had exactly the manner of an agitator. [But] it was entirely without agitation."[17] In rhetoric, as in so many parts of his life, from marriage to social ideology, self-control once again provided the basis of self-expression. This time, self-control allowed Phillips to achieve spontaneous interaction with his audiences, orchestrated in the same general way that he managed so much else, with a blending of "fire and ice." The experience, from the viewpoint of lyceum managers, was certainly worth Phillips's $250 fee.

There was much more to Phillips's rhetorical power than style, however. In successful forensics there is a point at which content and manner unite and begin to reinforce each other, endowing the orator's presentation with a compelling unity. What Phillips actually said, therefore, was just as important as his way of expressing himself, for the two elements seemed to combine in a single artistic creation. Audiences felt invited to respond to his speeches in toto, as one might to a provocative painting or piece of sculpture. One commentator, suggesting that Phillips's rhetorical artistry evoked pictures of "a beautiful damsel in *deshabille*" wrote: "His quotations, then, are ringlets rolled up in papers, and the main part of his lecture like a loose gown which now and then reveals a neck of pearl and a voluptuous bust of snowy whiteness and beautiful proportions."[18] Another observer, writing for the moderate Republican *Ohio State Journal*, also found Phillips's artistic synthesis remarkable, but chose a military rather than a sensual metaphor to describe it: "Those simple, brief sentences of which his speeches are made up, form a coat

---

17. *Liberator*, December 10, 1860, February 19, 1860; Martyn, *Phillips*, 493.

18. *New England Magazine*, reprinted in *Liberator*, October 15, 1850.

of mail so cunningly and closely wrought that no lance can pierce it." Phillips's friend and son-in-law George W. Smalley resorted to classical parallels: "There was much of the Greek in him; the sense of ordered beauty and art. . . . They were still the more evident when you heard him. . . . The symmetrical quality of mind and speech, which is almost the rarest in modern oratory and modern life."[19] A sensual maiden, chain mail, and Grecian symmetry—the diversity of imagery that Phillips's rhetoric inspired also suggests some of the deeper reasons why people flocked to hear him. By opening his rhetorical world to others, he allowed each listener to explore powerful imaginative visions of his or her own creation.

Yet the writer from the *Ohio State Journal* went on to register a warning about Phillips's speeches, which was actually a compliment of the highest order: "For the present generation, he is a most dangerous agitator. Wendell Phillips is the subtlest, stubbornest fact of the times." Continuing, this critic next touched on the most significant political element of Phillips's oratorical power. Phillips, he emphasized, had an unmatched ability to "take premises which we all grant to be true" and to "weave them into an enchantment of logic from which there is no escape." In other words, Phillips anchored the content of his rhetoric firmly in republican political axioms that few in his audience were inclined to question; no matter how extreme his doctrine, he always enunciated it in the dominant language of Northern political culture. When, for example, he propounded disunion, this analyst continued, Phillips pictured it as the essence of patriotic freedom, which left "God's natural laws to work out their own solution" in destroying tyranny. "You are hurried along by reasoning like this," the reporter complained, "and cannot make a ready answer. The more you consider it, the more mercilessly logical it appears. It strikes deep and pervades the ideas you have cherished." Still another critic, equally impressed by Phillips's republican persuasiveness, emphasized that he always "appealed to men on behalf of old and established principles. . . . His position accordingly supposes in his audience

---

19. *Ohio State Journal*, reprinted in *Liberator*, April 5, 1861; George Smalley, "Memoir of Phillips," in *Anglo-American Memoirs* (London, 1911), 141–42.

a pre-existing community of faith, a pre-existing wealth of affection for certain ideas and institutions."[20]

In the face of statements such as these, historians of the sectional conflict put their judgments in jeopardy when they dismiss the abolitionists' "hyperbole" and "rhetoric" in favor of election results plotted from computer tapes. Perhaps Phillips made only a few heart-and-soul converts to disunionism, but there surely can be no doubt, in the light of all these statements about the impact of his speaking, that he exercised a pervasive influence upon a receptive middle-class Northern popular culture, sectionalizing it in ways that had enormous political implications. In this most important sense, every one of Phillips's claims for the political efficacy of the agitator, no matter how self-serving otherwise, was grounded in firmest fact, describing surprisingly well his formidable national career as a rhetorician.

"He had many surprises in thought and diction," one contemporary recalled, trying to explain the sources of Phillips's oratorical powers.[21] The level of understatement achieved here is surely sufficient to depress any modern scholar who has carefully read the mass of Phillips's printed texts. Epigrams, analogies, parables, tall tales, teeth-grating sarcasm, torrents of personal abuse, one-liners, vignettes, candid self-revelations, historical meditations, and large thematic structures crowd the reader from every direction. By themselves, Phillips's speeches are worthy of their own book, and it would be patently untrue to suggest that any analysis of representative technique could be accomplished here without subverting the larger intentions of this biography. Yet one loose blending of elements did appear so repeatedly in Phillips's speeches that it is worth examining for a moment.

It was an endlessly flexible formulation that Phillips developed by fusing into a single evocative vision America's history, geography, economy, and moral foundations. In the many such passages that appear in his speeches, he elaborated what might be called the "moral terrain" of America's past, present, and future, while invoking every compelling

---

20. *Ohio State Journal*, reprinted in *Liberator*, April 5, 1861; *Christian Examiner*, reprinted in *Liberator*, December 4, 1863.

21. Martyn, *Phillips*, 494.

value of a dynamic, free-labor republic that imagination could supply him. It is, one hopes, better to furnish one example of this trope than to attempt any analysis. The following is part of a stenographic report by James A. Yerrington of what Phillips said on July 4, 1859, to an audience in Framingham, Massachusetts. It is not typical, except as it suggests themes that Phillips endlessly reorchestrated with varying emphases and in differing contexts during his speaking career.

It is a glorious country that God has given us, fit in every respect but one to look upon, this holiday of the Union, and seem worthy of the sun and the sky that look down upon us; for it is the people taking possession, by right, by inheritance, by worth, of the wealth, the culture, the happiness, and the achievements of the age. Show me such another! In the rotten, shiftless, poor, decrepit, bankrupt South, can you find the material that can erect a barrier against the onward and outward pressure of such a people as ours? Yes,—when the dream of the girl dams up Niagara, when the bulrush says to the Mississippi, 'Stop!' then will Carolina or Mississippi say to the potency of New England, with her three million educated, earnest, governing hearts,—say to her, in the tone of this worn-out, effete, rotten whiggery of Harvard College, 'Stop here!' (Great enthusiasm.) Why, by the vigor of such a civilization as ours, we shall take the State of Mississippi by the nape of its neck, and shake every decrepit white man out of it and give it into the hands of the slave that now tills it, and make America to represent the ideal to which our fathers consecrated it. Be worthy of this day! Create a sympathy among these toiling millions for liberty. What is it that makes us powerless? It is that your Church teaches us to look down on the black man; it is that your State teaches us, with this letter of Winthrop, that we have no duty outside the narrow circle of Massachusetts law? Here, under the blue sky of New England, we teach the doctrine, that wherever you find a man down-trodden, he is your brother; wherever you find an unjust law, you are bound to be its enemy; that Massachusetts was planted as the furnace of perpetual insurrection against tyrants, (loud applause); that this is a bastard who has stolen the name of Winthrop, (tremendous cheering)—been foisted into the cradle while his mother was out (loud laughter and applause); that the true blood of the Bradfords, the Carvers, the Endicotts and the Winthrops crops out in some fanatical abolitionist, whom the Church disowns, whom the State tramples under foot, but who will yet model both, by the potency of that truth which the elder Winthrop gave into our hands, and which we hold to-day as an example for the nation. (prolonged applause.) This is my speech for the Fourth of July.[22]

Historians have skillfully analyzed the free-labor ideology that suffuses so much of Phillips's speech, and a similar cluster of values had, from the beginning, inspired Phillips to frame his abolitionist visions. But no scholar, no matter how adroit, can ever recapture the evocative power and egalitarian universality that Phillips's rhetoric supplied to this ideology. All one can finally do is reread the printed pages and imagine what it might have been like to have actually heard the words. One must also remember that Phillips's audiences of respectable Americans, comprising commercial and business leaders and many farmers and artisans as well, did indeed come to believe strongly (as he asserted in the Fourth of July address), that Northern "wealth, culture and happiness" must triumph, even by warfare, over a "rotten, shiftless, poor, decrepit, bankrupt South." Phillips, in sum, invited his audiences to picture a glorious new era of republican freedom, supported by unvarying law, biracial egalitarianism, and a prosperous economic harmony that incorporated all classes. In so doing, he also addressed the least common denominator of Northern political belief, from which came finally the Republican Party, with its uncompromising demand for "free soil, free labor and free men."[23]

All politically literate Southerners and Northern conservatives appreciated full well the dangerously disruptive qualities of Phillips's rhetoric. From a slaveholder's perspective, Phillips might seem a potent, aggressive monstrosity, an "infernal machine set to music," as the *Richmond Enquirer* once called him. Yet Phillips could also appear as the most maddening kind of effeminate incendiary. He warred with language, after all, not pistols or heavy canes, and surrounded himself with others whom

---

22. *Liberator*, July 18, 1859. The reader is encouraged to peruse either volume of Phillips's collected speeches to learn more about what I am arguing and describing here.

23. See Eric Foner, *Free Soil, Free Labor, Free Men: The Ideology of the Republican Party before the Civil War* (New York, 1970); and Michael F. Holt, *The Political Crisis of the 1850s* (New York, 1978), for the most useful analyses of Republican political ideology in the prewar era.

white Southerners believed were as unmanly as himself—temperance advocates, pacifists, male feminists, and (of course) women. In the judgment of slaveholders, proud guardians of their own masculine positions, Phillips attacked as only a feminized coward would. "Perhaps if civil war should come," jeered the editor of the *Baltimore Patriot*, "Mr. Phillips would be surrounded by a life-guard of elderly maidens (and) protected by a rampart of whale bone and cotton wadding." Whether he was seen as effeminate or as a terrible machine, Wendell Phillips spread deep anger and fear far and wide within the planter class.[24]

Boston's conservative unionists had no easier a time of it than slaveholders from their famous local agitator. They, after all, had been forced to endure nearly four decades of unceasing Phillips invective. Plainly, they hated him, and for the best of reasons. He slandered their characters, assailed the morality of their economic endeavors, assisted their political enemies, degraded their reputations, sneered at their social pretensions, accused them of racial barbarianism, and indicted them as traitors to their city and state. They, in turn, vilified him in their presses, raised mobs against him, and packed his speeches with disrupters. In 1860 and 1861 Phillips literally risked his life, thanks to such opponents, when he walked the streets of Boston.

This unceasing local war finally became grist for the revealing newspaper satire of one "Solomon Sizzle," who quotes an unhappy textile merchant: "Wendell Phillips—I shudder with horror at the theme—I am nauseated at the remembrance that his name brings up." Phillips, the merchant complains, had turned Boston "into a reproach in our eyes and in the eyes of the world. . . . He has bruised us, he has made us sore; and the sores will not heal because he does not let them alone." Once, he recalls, the aristocrats had "spoken with authority" and had been obeyed, but now, whenever they organize a political meeting, "the very people who hear us talk go straight from us to him, to hear what he says about it, and laugh at the fun he makes of us." Finally, the merchant decides "there is nothing left to be done but to shoot Phillips." Although he fears "the noise, and the risk of hitting the wrong man" or "worst, of being hit in return," he concludes that assassination should be tried any-

---

24. *Liberator*, June 2, 1854.

way, observing that "no man will be to blame. . . . We can afford to make an example of him for the sake of peace and Union."[25] The merchant's confused solution was also Solomon Sizzle's brilliant confirmation that Phillips had developed a pervasive impact on day-to-day politics in Boston. In an entirely opposite way than his father's, Phillips had actually become a community leader as important for his own time as even the greatest of the earlier Phillipses for theirs.

How, one finally wonders, did Phillips generate such seemingly effortless rhetorical power? The answer is simply that he worked at it tirelessly. To maintain his spontaneous flow of ideas and images he disciplined himself constantly not by memorizing or outlining his remarks but by working systematically in his Commonplace Book, as he had since he first invented this system as a Harvard undergraduate. Then, Phillips had begun copying passages that he wished to retain in his memory for speeches, and by the end of his life Phillips had written over a thousand pages, certainly a testimony both to his persistence and to his accomplishments as a reader, for the range of authors he drew upon was extremely large. He had actually become something of the scholar as well as the activist that he had fantasized about in his youthful meditations on history. Dryden, Swift, Burke, Machiavelli, Sidney Smith, Arnold, Paine, Carlyle, Dumas, Fontenelle, Jefferson, Madison, George Tucker, Coleridge, Robert Browning, Tocqueville, Gibbon, Peel, Milton, Harrington, Cobden, Bright, McCauley, the *Edinburgh Review*, the *Tatler*, Emerson, John Jay Sr., and Henry Cary make up a representative list of citations over a two-year span.[26]

As Phillips assembled this rhetorical raw material in the Commonplace Book, he also developed various forms of self-therapy and intellectual play. Many of the passages he transcribed were actually descriptions of, or sayings by, other great orators with whom he felt kinship. Robert Peel, for example, attracted Phillips's admiration because, as he copied from an article, Peel was "the father of political out-of-doors agitation." Thomas Paine, by contrast, wrote libertarian doggerel that Phillips transcribed,

---

25. Ibid., May 22, 1861.

26. See generally the Phillips Commonplace Books, Boston Public Library.

first, because he agreed with it and, second, perhaps, because it rhymed almost as badly as did his own. Revealing another mood, Phillips once set down a grand historical chart that outlined the rise of freedom in Europe from A.D. 957, when the city-state of Cambrai adopted uniform taxation, through the late thirteenth century, when the king of Aragon promulgated a charter of liberties. On still other occasions, he set down passages that were clearly meant as cautionaries to himself: "It is a difficult matter to set a weak man right and it is seldom worth the trouble. But it is infinitely more difficult, when a man is intoxicated by applause, to persuade him that he is going astray."[27] No one, however, can explain how Phillips transformed these fragments, quotations, charts, and aphorisms into golden rhetoric, though clearly the process was automatic, and his persistence was richly rewarded.

Someone once asked Phillips to comment on his lecture preparations. The speaker, he replied, should always "think out" the subject with care. "Read all you can," he advised. "Fill your mind." Preparation, bluntly, meant disciplined study, but delivery required spontaneity. "Forget that you are to make a speech, or are making one," Phillips instructed, for the powerful orator must first become inspired "with the idea that you are going to strike a blow, carry out a purpose.... Having forgotten yourself, you will be likely to do your best. Be simple; be earnest."[28] His candid advice was of little use to anyone wishing to emulate him. Since his youth, the counterpoint between self-discipline and passionate self-expression revealed in this advice had given Phillips a special design for living, as well as for speaking, which no one else could possibly set out to learn. Ralph Waldo Emerson once observed that Phillips gave "no indication of his perfect eloquence in casual intercourse. How easily he wears his power, quite free, disengaged, in no wise absorbed in any care or thought of the thunderbolt he carries within."[29] It was, of course,

---

27. Ibid., 220–25. I have purposely quoted from a very few pages here, to indicate the range of Phillips's activity in the books over a few days' time. (He dated his entries sporadically at best.)

28. Joseph Cooke quoting Phillips in the *New York Independent*, February 14, 1884, reprinted in Martyn, *Phillips*, 362–63. See also Phillips to Aaron Powell, n.d., in Powell, "Reminiscences of Wendell Phillips," 86.

29. Emerson is quoted in Oswald Garrison Villard, "Wendell Phillips after Fifty Years," *American Mercury*, January 1935, 96.

quite possible to emulate Phillips's style of speaking, as many would, but never could another speaker hope to duplicate the sources of his peculiar forensic power.

By 1857, however, political revolution, not rhetorical thunderbolts, held greatest attraction for some of Phillips's abolitionist friends. For some disunionists the later 1800s had become times of terrible frustration, but to others it seemed as though substantial progress against slavery was finally taking place. One's judgment depended on one's view of that massive new antislavery enterprise, the Republican Party, which had swept into so many Northern statehouses in 1856 and had shown such strength behind John C. Fremont. It also depended very much on which part of Wendell Phillips's ambivalent view of politics one chose to emphasize. By general Garrisonian standards, all Republicans had grave shortcomings when it came to the Constitution, abolishing slavery, and treating blacks as equals. Yet William Lloyd Garrison had also begun to suspect that his years of crying in the wilderness were finally starting to be vindicated. These politicians (as Wendell Phillips had always said) must after all be claimed as the legitimate offspring of the movement that now called Garrison himself the founder. Garrison, in fact, came as close to endorsing the Republicans as possible in the 1856 elections, declaring in the *Liberator* that "if there were no moral barriers to our voting, and had we a million ballots to bestow, we should cast them all for John C. Fremont."[30] But Parker Pillsbury, the Fosters, and several others saw Republican Party growth only as a measure of the disheartening spread of proslavery constitutional compromise within the electorate. Certainly (as Wendell Phillips had always said) oath-swearing politicians like these Republicans deserved from Garrisonians not support but only sternest censure. To this faction, Garrison's warm words only indicated that he was growing soft and more eager for personal congratulation than for the slaves' freedom. "Advancing age always tends to conservatism," Abby Kelley Foster acidly observed, and Stephen S. Foster wrote vehemently to Phillips that abolitionists had always refused to be charitable toward well-intentioned politicians. Why, he demanded, should Garrison reverse

---

30. *Liberator*, quoted in the *National Anti-Slavery Standard*, October 25, 1856. See also William L. Garrison to Helen B. Garrison, February 18, 1857, Garrison Papers.

himself now? "Our business is to cry 'unclean, unclean—thief, robber, pirate, murderer'—to put the brand of Cain on every one of them." He also wondered pointedly why Phillips had made remarks supportive of Charles Sumner in a recent speech. Was Phillips, too, losing his backbone? In 1857, Foster openly attacked Garrison for displaying a pro-Republican bias, and a major schism threatened the Garrisonians' ranks.[31]

Edmund Quincy, Samuel May, Maria Weston Chapman, Deborah and Ann Warren Weston, Oliver Johnson, and the rest of the Boston clique sided at once with Garrison. Both factions began complaining to Phillips about "the impossibility of associating further" as conflicts sputtered over the next two years. By early 1858, the American Anti-Slavery Society and its state auxiliaries briefly faced open war when the Fosters and Pillsbury defied Garrison by declaring that moral suasion had failed completely. "Our people believe in a government of force," Foster emphasized, not in boycotting elections. "They wish to vote." He proposed a new abolitionist political party that would actually offer a disunion ticket at the ballot box. Higginson, always ripe for conflict, supported the Fosters while the rest of the Boston clique rallied to crush the idea. Still the Fosters persisted, hoping, in Pillsbury's words, to "build a great national party whose avowed aim shall be the overthrow of the government." By 1859 Abby Kelley Foster and Garrison had temporarily ceased communication, and she had refused to reassume her position on the Executive Committee of the American Anti-Slavery Society.[32]

These battles almost exactly foreshadowed the ideological differences that finally did split the American Anti-Slavery Society in 1865.[33] After 1857 the Fosters, Pillsbury, and many less well known abolitionists clearly equated their movement with egalitarian revolution to be accom-

---

31. Abby Foster to Phillips, June 24, 1859, Stephen and Abigail Kelly Foster Papers, American Antiquarian Society, Worcester, MA; Stephen S. Foster to Phillips, March 29, 1857, Blagden Papers.

32. *Liberator*, February 5, 1858; Pillsbury to Giddings, February 14, 1859, Giddings Papers, Ohio Historical Society, Columbus. See also Pillsbury to Phillips, July 15, 20, August 8, September 9, 1859; May to Phillips, June 10, August 6, 1859; Abby K. Foster to Phillips, July 24, 1857, all in Blagden Papers; Pillsbury to Nichol, February 17, 1859, Garrison Papers; Maria W. Chapman to Ann W. Weston, April 19, 1857, Weston Papers; Johnson to May, March 20, 1859, May Papers, Boston Public Library.

33. Lawrence J. Friedman, *Gregarious Saints: Self and Community in American Abolitionism* (New York, 1982), 255–80, discusses this final schism of 1864–65 in detail but gives these earlier conflicts little attention. Friedman's idea that Garrisonians sought prophetic vindication is, however, of great use to my discussion of this disagreement.

plished by stringent political means. They would, moreover, hold fast to these goals even after the Thirteenth Amendment had abolished chattel slavery, arguing then that true enslavement would not be crushed until the legalized power of the state abolished the masters' social authority as well. Only then would black people actually be guaranteed political freedom and equality of economic opportunity. Garrison, Quincy, and the rest, however, were already looking to a day of jubilation when slaves would be free and they themselves would be vindicated as true prophets who could stand aside in triumph.

Phillips certainly shared the Fosters' anger over the North's timorous political attitudes in the later 1800s. "We had hoped for some. . . *reaction* if Buchanan were elected and when he crushes Kansas, and steals Cuba . . . and sets up the slave trade such a reaction may come," he wrote Elizabeth Pease. "But all seems now settling down into the same old indifference. If Sumner's outrage did not rouse them, what can we expect will have an effect?" No less than the Fosters, he hated and envied the Republican stranglehold on antislavery politics. Whenever he heard that party claim antislavery supremacy, Phillips confessed in anger, "I think of the wealth of sacrifice, of the lives that have been devoted to this cause—I think of the tombs round which I have stood of those called from the struggle, [and] I say, 'In God's name beware how you peril what so much toil and so much self-devotion have purchased for us. This is holy ground that you tread!'" In addition, he showed himself wary of becoming entangled with individual Republicans, and he provoked protests from Senator Henry Wilson and Abraham Lincoln's law partner, William Herndon, for attacking their party so savagely. When Herndon came to Boston for a visit, Phillips snubbed him. Yet despite his abiding distrust of this and all parties, he nevertheless continued to claim the Republicans as direct products of Garrisonian agitation, and he opposed the Fosters' disunionist party proposal.[34]

In this way, Phillips's double vision of politics allowed him to live in

---

34. Phillips to Nichol, November 9, 1858, Garrison Papers; *Liberator*, August 14, 1857; Henry Wilson to Phillips, September 28, 1856, William Herndon to Phillips, March 9, May 12, 1857, July 2, 1858, all in Blagden Papers.

both camps of feuding Garrisonians, arbitrating between them and relying on cajolery, humor, and painstaking explanation to maintain communication between political visionaries and prophets of righteousness. Still, at times he felt forced to issue blunt warnings to the Fosters. "Your danger and Pillsbury's," he wrote Abby Foster, "is intolerance—you are leaning to sectarianism and bigotry. You incline to suspect the honesty of those you cannot at once convince to your views." [35] The breach never entirely closed, but thanks in large measure to Phillips's diplomacy, the American Anti-Slavery Society continued for several years more to maintain a semblance of unity between its saints and its radical politicians.

As they fought over the politics of disunionism, Garrisonians of all persuasions also continued as a group to reflect an increasingly accepting attitude toward sectional violence. Sims, Burns, Sumner, Kansas, and *Dred Scott*—all became symbols to them of the triumph of proslavery force since 1850 and helped justify the Fosters' contempt for moral suasion. Other names, however, became symbols of an aggressive counterthrust by antislavery forces. There was Christiana, Pennsylvania, where the slave catcher had died, and Sherman Booth, the Milwaukee abolitionist who succeeded where Higginson had failed, leading a mob that freed a captive fugitive slave. "Jerry" recalled the liberation-by-force that took place in Syracuse, and "Oberlin-Wellington" referred to a similar action in Ohio. Phillips, along with the others, made his flirtation with violence increasingly obvious. In February 1859, for example, he demanded that there be "no slave-hunting in the Old Bay State," assuring the state legislative committee before which he testified that whites were about to nullify the Fugitive Slave Law by force of arms. He also began delivering his "Crispus Attucks" and "Toussaint" speeches more and more frequently, accompanying them with predictions of insurrection and taunts at his white audiences for their "thin blooded" failure to match the courage of these black heroes. "It is a very easy thing to . . . imagine what we would have done" in Attucks's place, he declared, but "it is a very hard thing to spring out of the ranks . . . , and lift the first musket." In all these ways, Phillips both shared and spread the conviction that

---

35. Phillips to Abby K. Foster, June 10, 19, 30 (quotation), and July 20, 1859, all in Foster Papers.

every plantation had its own Toussaint, who was arming and would soon rise up.[36]

Phillips first extolled the heroic Crispus Attucks in Faneuil Hall on March 5, 1858, when abolitionists of both races gathered for a highly symbolic ceremony. It was organized by the prominent black leaders William Nell and John Rock to commemorate Attucks's death in the Boston Massacre of 1774. Space in front of the speaker's platform was decorated with some of Attucks's personal belongings, along with a wealth of other relics that attested to black heroism during the Revolution, including "a banner presented by John Hancock to a colored company called 'The Bucks of America.'" Rock and Nell invited Phillips to join them on the rostrum and participate in rituals to honor forcible resistance.[37] The setting and Phillips's words in celebration of Attucks that day accurately forecast some of the flesh-and-blood violence soon to come.

Not long thereafter, Phillips received a letter from Lysander Spooner, his old foe in debates over slavery and the Constitution during the 1840s. This time, however, insurrection, not law, was on Spooner's mind. The letter asked Phillips's endorsement for a plan to infiltrate the South with armed cadres that would join with black escapees and poor whites to set up insurgent groups in the wilderness. "I think that in five years, 500,000 men in the North would join," Spooner explained with stunning innocence, "and that nearly all the non-slave holders of the South would be with us." Finding themselves surrounded and outgunned, the planter class would then capitulate in terror, free their slaves, "and the work would be done without shedding a drop of blood," he concluded lamely.[38] Hearing the idea, most Garrisonians, even those with the most tattered nonresistance banners, recoiled, but some militant souls, Parker, Higginson, and Stephen Foster included, bid Spooner Godspeed in his plan. Even if few volunteered, these supporters hoped that knowledge of

---

36. Phillips, *No Slave-Hunting in the Old Bay State* (Boston, 1859); Phillips, "Crispus Attucks," in *Speeches, Lectures, and Letters* (Boston, 1863), 69–95. Friedman, *Gregarious Saints*, 196–222, is an excellent analysis of abolitionists' flirtation with violence.

37. *Liberator*, March 12, 1858.

38. "A Plan for the Abolition of Slavery, Addressed to Non-Slaveholders," Lysander Spooner Papers, New York Historical Society; Spooner to Phillips, July 6, 1858, Blagden Papers.

the plan would "excite terror among the slave holders." Spooner showed Phillips his plan four months before he mustered sufficient courage to circulate it more widely, and Phillips's objections to it were practical ones only. The state would certainly crush such a movement as an act of treason, he wrote Spooner, for no voluntary effort like his could ever "compete with an organized despotism like ours." But Richard J. Hinton, a visiting British journalist who was particularly fascinated by the idea of slave revolts, amplified on Phillips's reaction to Spooner's fevered inspiration. Phillips, Hinton assured Spooner, had agreed to put up cash for printing five hundred copies of a handbill explaining the plan, which were to be distributed in order to "help to spread the panic." Indeed, by December 1858, Spooner was busily mailing fresh copies. Short of actually picking up a gun, Phillips clearly was trafficking with insurrectionary violence as heavily as he could. He had experienced no bright illumination or flash of anger to bring him to this point, but by the end of this violence-filled, frustrating decade, he had, without thinking much about it, simply allowed his long-standing belief in the justice of armed resistance to assume dominance over his deep commitment to moral suasion.[39]

Phillips also knew, however, that some of his close friends were consciously sponsoring violent enterprises. Since 1857, some of his vigilance committee partners—Samuel Gridley Howe, Parker, and Higginson, as well as George L. Stearns and Franklin Sanborn—had all been holding confidential discussions with a certain John Brown. Brown was fresh from the Kansas border wars with the taint of premeditated murder on his hands, having ordered through his sons the deaths of six unarmed settlers there. Phillips had first met Brown in the home of Theodore Parker, where he had listened as this magnetic holy warrior had debated nonresistance with William Lloyd Garrison. Whenever Garrison had appealed to the pacifism of the Savior, Brown had countered with bloody

---

39. Francis Jackson to Spooner, December 3, 1858; Stephen S. Foster to Spooner, January 1, 1859; Thomas W. Higginson to Spooner, November 30, 1858; Parker to Spooner, November 30, 1858; Phillips to Spooner, July 16, 1858; Richard J. Hinton to Spooner, n.d. [1858], all in Spooner Papers, Boston Public Library. Friedman, *Gregarious Saints*, 196–222, is an effective treatment of the counterpoint between violence and moral suasion in abolitionist attitudes. So is Bertram Wyatt-Brown, "Willam Lloyd Garrison and Antislavery Unity: A Reappraisal," *Civil War History* 13 (March 1967): 5–24; and esp. Jeffrey Rossbach, *Ambivalent Conspirators: John Brown, the Secret Six, and a Theory of Slave Violence* (Philadelphia, 1982).

prophecies from Jeremiah. Soon Brown had become most familiar in abolitionist circles, drumming up funds for his Kansas campaigns from Free-Soil politicians as well as Christian perfectionists. Brown was now talking warmly with Higginson, Parker, Stearns, Sanborn, and Howe, as well as with the New York philanthropist Gerrit Smith, about fomenting black insurrection in the South. They gave him cash and encouragement, and they asked few specific questions. Finally, on October 16, 1859, Brown and a band of eighteen descended on Harper's Ferry, seized the federal arsenal, took hostages, and waited for the slaves to rise. Two days later, Brown lay in prison seriously wounded, his brigade having been routed by troops under the command of Colonel Robert E. Lee. Waves of vengeful anger swept through the plantation South.

Brown was indeed a personality of unfathomable personal power. Yet his raid was no more a supreme act of his personal will than it was the predictable result of the abolitionists' half articulated desire for a righteous triumph by blood sacrifice, which Phillips and many others had indisputably helped to foster. Certainly it had been Phillips, far more than anyone else, who had given compelling rhetorical witness to the widely accepted prophecy that slaves would soon strike for freedom by themselves. The *Boston Post*, a moderate Republican newspaper, put this truth succinctly: "John Brown may be a lunatic, [but if he is,] then one-fourth of the people of Massachusetts are madmen."[40] There was never a doubt that the orator had prepared the way for the insurrectionist. Within two weeks of his capture, Brown was arraigned, tried, and hanged for treason, as abolitionists and Yankee intellectuals sang paeans to his courage and inspiration.

Phillips was surprised not at all by the first news of Brown's attack. Back in 1857 he had given Brown a contribution, and years after the raid he told a friend that he was aware Brown "was working in such ways." Phillips had remained studiously uninformed of Brown's specific plans, however, even as close friends like Higginson, Parker, and Stearns became directly involved. He wrote to Brown to refuse an invitation, for

---

40. *Boston Post*, quoted in C. Vann Woodward, "John Brown's Private War," in his *The Burden of Southern History* (Baton Rouge, 1960), 48.

example, in the fall of 1859, a date confirmed by his reference in the letter to a relapse in his own health that he claimed had occurred in August of that year. Actually, it was Ann who was ill, but clearly Phillips did not wish to make her condition his stated reason for declining to attend a meeting with Brown and some of his Harper's Ferry supporters. Nevertheless, the moment the news broke that Brown had been captured, conspirator Franklin Sanborn, obviously assuming Phillips's foreknowledge of the raid, beseeched the orator for legal opinions and news. Phillips then plunged actively into discussions of guerrilla conspiracies, concocting a wild plan to free Brown by kidnapping the governor of Virginia and then working out an exchange of prisoners.[41]

Obviously Phillips had been caught up in John Brown's general course of action well before Harper's Ferry and, like so many others, had become greatly enamored of him as an individual. For years Phillips had paid homage only to violent men and deeds, while counseling law and order. When he had been pressed toward resistance by the most excruciating circumstances, as in the Sims and Burns cases, he had not been able to bring himself to call for mobs or guns. Now, however, after several ensuing years of slave power victory, John Brown had acted for him, just as Elijah Lovejoy had once acted for him many years before. As in 1837 Phillips felt a deep sense of release from tensions and frustrations that he had been forced to control for so long. At once, after the fact, Phillips began to participate vicariously in the Harper's Ferry raid, offering lyrical praise and acts of devotion to his new hero–saint, John Brown.

Phillips now developed an intense concern for the welfare of Brown's family, who lived a hardscrabble rural existence in remote North Elba, New York. To help them, Phillips arranged fundraising meetings, and as he did so, he also gathered up memorabilia that had belonged to the "great old man." A Virginia slaveholder unwittingly did Phillips a great favor in this respect, sending him a lock of Brown's hair, which the orator rejoiced over as a great treasure. He was greatly disappointed to learn

---

41. Bartlett, *Phillips*, 419 n .6; Wyman, "Reminiscences of Wendell Phillips," 728; Phillips to John Brown, [1859] (photocopy), Frank Stanley [Franklin Sanborn] to Phillips, October [?], November 7, October 22, 1859, all in Blagden Papers.

that a friend, J. Miller McKim, "had not *given*, only *lent*, the envelope on which Brown marked his route" to Harper's Ferry. McKim did give him a pike used by Brown's son Oliver, and Phillips made it into an object of veneration, as he did a daguerreotype of Brown's wife "taken from Oliver Brown's breast after he was shot." With Ann's enthusiastic approval, Phillips made an even more personal gesture of honor to Brown, for he embarked on a pilgrimage to North Elba to witness the funeral of his insurrectionist hero. Traveling to Philadelphia he met Mrs. Brown and her husband's casket. With McKim he then accompanied her on the long trip back to the bleak hills of eastern upstate New York.[42]

His time with Brown's family moved Phillips deeply. "If you could have seen those young widows and children, in that rude roof on the hills, so serenely meeting and accepting their part in the martyrdom, as good and grand in their places as the old man in his," Phillips exclaimed to Ralph Waldo Emerson a short time afterward. The spiritual wholeness Phillips attributed to Brown's family seemed to confirm their patriarch's stunning moral completeness, "showing what a grand whole his life was to have bred such." When others suggested that Brown's body should be put on tour as a means for fanning popular indignation, Phillips initially approved but quickly changed his mind when Brown's widow protested. Instead, he presided over a small family service in Brown's little house. The casket rested on the kitchen table, and Phillips stood next to it, surrounded by a few friends and four grieving widows—Mrs. John Brown, the widows of Oliver and Watson Brown, and the widow of another fallen warrior, William Thompson. Phillips, in his eulogy, insisted that John Brown had not failed at Harper's Ferry, that he had actually dealt slavery its fatal blow. "John Brown has loosened the roots of the slave system,—it only breathes, it does not live—hereafter." Americans would surely consecrate themselves afresh to the great cause precisely because Brown had given all, Phillips assured the company. "Only lips fresh from such a vow have the right to mingle their words with your tears." As the

---

42. *Liberator*, December 9, 1859; "A Slaveholder" to Phillips, November 22, December 19, 1859, Phillips to Ann Phillips, n.d. [1859], December 5, 1859, all in Blagden Papers; Phillips to Ralph Waldo Emerson, December [?], 1859, in Ralph Waldo Emerson Papers, Houghton Library, Harvard University; Phillips to McKim, April 7, 1860, May–McKim Papers, Cornell University Library, Ithaca, NY; *New York Tribune*, reprinted in *Liberator*, December 16, 1859.

casket was lowered into the grave, a black family from a farm nearby sang several of John Brown's favorite hymns."[43]

"I am so sad about poor Brown," Ann Phillips wrote Wendell in November 1859. "My heart aches for him. . . . I hope you talk about Brown whenever you get the chance." He needed no such encouragement. Even as the news of Harper's Ferry began to spread, Phillips burst forth with waves of rhetorical inspiration on the subject of his newfound hero. He set off immediately on tour, speaking in New York City and as far west as Cleveland before returning to Philadelphia. When he was not spreading the mythology of John Brown himself, he was arranging for others to do so, besieging Emerson, for example, with pleas to speak at John Brown memorial meetings. "You know what a vein and stratum of the public you can tap," he wrote, "far out of the range of our bore."[44]

Most important was the personal tribute Phillips paid his hero in a series of extraordinary speeches. Only once before, when Lovejoy's death had first driven him to action, had Phillips felt himself so deeply involved in someone else's heroic gesture. Lovejoy's act had opened a new era in Phillips's life, lifting him beyond vocational crisis into the great crusades against slavery. Now, in Brown, Phillips sensed the same moment of liberation for the entire nation and for himself as well, for Brown, as Phillips saw him, possessed superhuman qualities. In his apotheosis of Brown, Phillips once again recapitulated the same all-pervasive interplay of order and passion that had long ago shaped the inmost parts of his own life and thought. Brown had become for him a figure who had transfigured the national experience by the exercise of inner power. Harper's Ferry, Phillips therefore announced, had closed a corrupted era in American history, for Brown had released enormous forces, which were creating a pure new republican order that fulfilled the nation's oldest promises of liberty and fostered the spread of freedom as never before. "Why this is a decent country to live in now," Phillips rhapsodized.[45]

---

43. Phillips to Emerson, December [?], 1859, Emerson Papers; Phillips to Ann Phillips, December 5, 1859, Blagden Papers; *New York Tribune*, reprinted in *Liberator*, December 16, 1859; Phillips, "The Burial of John Brown," in *Speeches, Lectures, and Letters*, 289–94.

44. Ann Phillips to Phillips, December 1, 1860, Blagden Papers; Phillips to Emerson, January 11, 1860 (quotation), December 12, and [?], 1859, Emerson Papers.

45. Phillips, "Harper's Ferry," in his *Speeches*, 274.

Whenever he spoke on Brown, Phillips made one crucial point. Although the "lesson of the hour," he always declared, was insurrection, Brown himself most certainly had been no bringer of social chaos. Obeying his abiding devotion to order, Phillips embraced Brown's violent actions by sincerely denying all possibility that the "Old Puritan" had played a subversive role. To charge him thus, Phillips insisted, was a "great mistake," for the forces he had unleashed at Harper's Ferry were anything but disruptive. Instead, Phillips insisted, they had put an end to a most turbulently immoral society. This, according to Phillips, was the essence of Brown's genius, for he had struck out boldly to suppress forever the chaotic tyranny of slavery. Anarchic Virginia, long in a state of "chronic insurrection," contained "no basis of a government," Phillips held, for she was peopled by a "barbarous horde who gag each other, imprison women for teaching children to read, abolish marriage, condemn half their women to prostitution and devote themselves to the breeding of human beings for sale." Into this pit of licentiousness had marched Brown, the bringer of civilization, armed with God's warrant to enforce iron-handed control. "He stood as a representative of law, of government, of right, of justice of religion," Phillips declared, and therefore only the opposite could be said of Brown's captors, depraved slaveholders characterized by Phillips as "a mob of murderers who gathered about him, and sought to wreak vengeance by taking his life." What Phillips had long ago praised in Lovejoy and before that in Burke, he now attributed to Brown with even greater force. Here was a man so wholly self-disciplined that he could act completely from self-will, forcibly bringing order where chaos had once reigned. "John Brown," Phillips exclaimed in triumph, "is the impersonator of God's law, moulding a better future, and setting it for an example."[46]

It is important to notice that Brown's rhetorical image, as Phillips constructed it, sharply contrasted with the version of Webster he had created in the early 1800s. Brown, according to Phillips, derived his vital inspiration from the traditions that the impotent Webster had forfeited

46. Ibid., 271–72; Phillips, "The Puritan Principle and John Brown," in his *Speeches*, 2nd series., 308.

to pursue selfish gain. Brown, in contrast to Webster, had marched into battle as the primal exemplification of oldest Anglo-Saxon freedoms, reclaiming traditions of liberty that stretched back to the England of "two hundred years ago," when the bold Cromwell had beheaded a king and had mustered a New Model Army in defense of freedom. An "impulsive, enthusiastic aspiration . . . which obeys ideas . . . , with *action*" was the Puritan principle that Phillips believed had given Brown his animating strength; Brown was a "regular Cromwellian, dug up from two centuries" ago. Like the old opponents of Stuart tyranny, he had defied the state to defend liberty. Centuries ago "Puritanism went up and down England" and "tore off the semblance of law to reveal despotism," Phillips declared, as his emotional distance from the past collapsed almost entirely. "John Brown has done the same for us today," not "hesitating to ask what the majority thought" but striking boldly, inspired by the "great idea of crushing tyrannical power."[47]

As Phillips repeated these themes from platforms across New England and the Midwest, he fused his autobiography and rich historical imagination with his rendering of his subject. In Webster, he had discovered a hateful personal symbol whom he had rhetorically reduced to impotency. Brown, by contrast, seemed to him a towering embodiment of all the elements that the orator himself believed were giving emotional richness, spiritual harmony, personal vitality, and ideological coherence to his own life. Self-control and spontaneous expression, together with a powerful supportive vision of the past, had always supplied Phillips with inspired designs for living. Now, in his view of Brown he discovered a transcendent figure who united these elements, achieving a complete reconciliation of submission with liberation, restraint with passion, and tradition with revolt. "Prudence, skill, courage, thrift, knowledge of his time, knowledge of his opponents [and] undaunted daring"—these were the traits that Phillips saw fused in Brown's character. In addition, the Brown family was whole-mindedly devoted to their patriarch's cause; he was "girded about by his household." This family solidarity confirmed all elements of the vital symmetry. Brown's was no "spasmodic" act of

---

47. Phillips, "Puritan Principle," 295–300.

simple passion, Phillips insisted, but the "flowering of sixty years," the supreme expression that endowed his life with perfect wholeness. "Everything about him grouped itself harmoniously," Phillips exclaimed, "like the planets and the sun."[48]

Phillips certainly appreciated that he and Brown were hardly identical people. Yet in this realization he identified with the "Old Man" all the more, for Brown, after all, had mastered manly action as well as talk, and Phillips knew full well that he would never be able to duplicate that mastery. Brown, as Phillips saw him, had achieved unmatchable levels of spiritual liberation and primal masculine energy. "The very easy thing [is] to say; the difficult is to do," Phillips admitted. For decades he had called from the speaker's platform for people to trample on the law; Brown had simply marched southward, gun in hand, achieving eloquence in his deeds that no mere speaker could ever match. Brown, therefore, had shown the American people a "true manhood" that Phillips could only admire; he had stilled the chaos of slavery and faced death "with two hundred thousand broken fetters in his hands."[49]

As enraged planters escalated threats of secession, Wendell Phillips continued to talk. His principal themes, following his characterization of Brown, urged his listeners toward a final accounting with slavery. Disunion was now inevitable, he declared; it would bring either race war or the planters' terrified capitulation. Blanching at such doctrines, the Republican Party's leaders counseled moderation and rallied voters to the standard of Abraham Lincoln. Yet to slaveholders' well-educated ears, the Republicans' message in the 1860 election and Phillips's urgings to violence sounded awfully much alike. Both Phillips and Lincoln, after all, demanded an America where slavery could expand no further. Both, moreover, envisioned a nation of "free people," economically self-sufficient and spiritually self-disciplined, whose creative energy would expand republican liberty from ocean to ocean. Both, in the final analysis, accused a morally barbaric, economically benighted slave power of

---

48. Ibid., 303; Phillips, "Harper's Ferry," 274.
49. Phillips, "Burial of John Brown," 291–93; Phillips, "Puritan Principle," 296, 302.

stifling and corrupting the creative energy of American free labor. By 1860 much of the same broad counterpoint of order with liberation that had enriched Wendell Phillips's portrayals of John Brown had begun to inspire the fighting of the Civil War.[50]

---

50. Foner, *Free Soil*, 1–72; Major L. Wilson, *Space, Time, and Freedom: The Quest for Nationality and the Irrepressible Conflict, 1815–1860* (Westport, CT, 1974), 120–47, 178–200; Richard H. Sewell, *Ballots for Freedom: Antislavery Politics, 1837–1861* (New York, 1976), which is the best narrative analysis of its subject, and a sensitive explanation of the relationships between racism, egalitarianism, and sectionalism in Yankee political culture. Richard Slotkin, *The Fatal Environment: The Myth of the Frontier in the Age of Industrialization, 1800–1890* (New York, 1985), 227–78, explores the relationships between sexual metaphors (like those Phillips used in reference to John Brown), racism, and class antagonisms as these bore on the larger political conflict over slavery.

The New Haven Negro College and the
Dynamics of Race in New England, 1776–1870

In 1831, a group of black and white abolitionists embarked on a path-breaking experiment: they would establish an academic institution devoted to educating young African Americans, and, most unprecedented, it would be funded by philanthropists of both races. Modeling their scheme on the manual labor schools already popular in Germany and England, the planners adopted a curriculum designed to help students "cultivate habits of personal industry and obtain a useful mechanical or agricultural occupation, while pursuing classical studies." Organizers expected to attract talented candidates from all parts of the North, and they focused as well on the British West Indies, whose "respectable" free colored families might be persuaded to choose the school for their sons. For their innovative institution, the founders chose a prime location in the city of New Haven, twenty acres close by Yale College, whose presumably benevolent faculty would offer instruction at nominal cost. Supporters as well as detractors soon began referring to the proposed institution as the "Negro College."[1]

The plan for the college was unveiled in Philadelphia on June 11,

Originally published as "The New Haven Negro College and the Meanings of Race in New England, 1776–1870," *New England Quarterly* 76 (September 2003): 323–55. Reprinted with permission.

1. For a general history of the origins of the Negro College project, see Howard Holman Bell, ed., *Minutes of the Proceedings of the National Negro Conventions* (1831; repr., New York: Arno Press, 1969), 6; Bell, *Survey of the Negro Convention Movement, 1830–1861* (New York: Arno Press, 1969); Bertram Wyatt-Brown, *Lewis Tappan and the Evangelical War against Slavery* (Cleveland: Press of Case Western Reserve University, 1969), 87–91; and James Brewer Stewart, *William Lloyd Garrison and the Challenge of Emancipation* (Arlington Heights, IL: Harlan Davidson, 1991), 57–74. Several letters Garrison and Simeon Jocelyn exchanged on the Negro College project are in the collections of the Connecticut Historical Society, Hartford.

1831, at the First Annual Convention of the Free People of Color by three freshly minted white abolitionists: Arthur Tappan, an affluent New York merchant; William Lloyd Garrison, militant editor of a new, Boston-based abolitionist newspaper, the *Liberator*; and Simeon Jocelyn, a minister who served the African American parishioners of New Haven's Dixwell Congregational Church. The convention representatives who rose to applaud the idea included the wealthy Philadelphia entrepreneur James Forten; Bishop Richard Allen, the free states' most prominent African American cleric; and Samuel E. Cornish, editor of the nation's first African American newspaper, *Freedom's Journal*. Forten, Allen, and Cornish, the North's most visible activists of color, had led their communities with distinction for decades.

The energized delegates adjourned to drum up subscriptions for the Negro College. Never before in the nation's history had racial activists worked together so closely and enthusiastically on a project of such ambitious scope and in an alliance that brought together young and old, black and white. Arthur Tappan pledged an initial gift of one thousand dollars, and, joined by his equally wealthy brother Lewis, promised to match additional gifts up to a total of twenty thousand dollars. To facilitate his firsthand involvement, Tappan bought a house in New Haven just after the convention adjourned. Simeon Jocelyn, a proud booster for his city, confidently asserted that "the literary and scientific character of New-Haven renders it a very desirable place for the location of the College."[2]

Jocelyn's optimism, however, proved woefully misplaced. In late August 1831, only a week after he praised the municipality, news of Nat Turner's bloody slave insurrection in Virginia hit the North, just as New Havenites were convening their town meeting to consider the Negro College. In recent years, white New Havenites had grown increasingly distrustful of "vagabond Negroes." As ever greater numbers of African Americans entered the city, residents accused them of undermining moral order and undercutting the white labor market. In the midst of these national and local racial crises, townsmen voted 700 to 4 to

---

2. Simeon Jocelyn, quoted in Robert Austin Warner, *New Haven Negroes: A Social History* (New Haven: Yale University Press, 1940), 54.

condemn the college proposal and, moreover, to resist it "by every legal means."

Some quickly foreswore legalities and formed themselves into an angry mob. They stoned Arthur Tappan's house, yelled obscenities at passing blacks, and then moved into New Haven's colored community ("New Liberia," as detractors liked to call it) for two nights of mayhem. The mob vandalized several black-owned establishments and assaulted the white patrons present; when the marauders finally dispersed, several dwellings occupied by African Americans had been damaged. Yale's officialdom, whom the abolitionists had naïvely failed to consult before announcing their plans, expressed regret over the rioting but also voiced hostility toward the Negro College. Not a single professor joined Jocelyn and Roger Sherman Baldwin, a New Haven attorney, to argue in its favor. With the sole exception of Ezra Stiles Ely, Connecticut's Congregational clergy were equally unresponsive. With brutal clarity, white New Havenites delivered their all-but-unanimous opinion that they simply would not tolerate a large number of young colored men, sponsored by militant abolitionists, congregating in their midst.[3]

A venture begun so hopefully thus ended in angry defeat. Abolitionists deplored white New Havenites' failure to overcome their prejudices, and white New Havenites condemned abolitionists' inability to grasp the practical limits of reform. Despite the short and bleak history of New Haven's Negro College, the episode offers some telling perspectives on historical questions germane to the history of race in New England. One might wonder, for example, why veteran black leaders James Forten, Richard Allen, and Samuel E. Cornish so eagerly joined forces with the Tappan brothers, William Lloyd Garrison, and Simeon Jocelyn, all inexperienced white idealists. On the other hand, why did the white citizens of New Haven so easily set aside their own compelling social and economic differences to mount a united front against the Negro College? And finally, in what ways did the controversy surrounding the Negro College serve as a critical point of departure as these activists and contending social groups struggled over issues of skin color during the next

---

3. A narrative of Yale's and New Haven's responses to the Negro College project is found in ibid., 50–55.

three decades? By addressing these questions, we can understand more fully just how differently and complexly black and white New Englanders approached the problem of race during the antebellum decades.

The Politics of Race in Postrevolutionary America

For free black activists like James Forten, the path to the 1831 Convention of the Free People of Color, and thence to New Haven, proceeded directly from the American Revolution. In that earlier struggle, Forten and his associates claimed, "colored" patriot combatants (that is, anyone with dark skin: Indians and people of "mixed blood" as well as African Americans) had secured the right of citizenship for all men, including those of color. Seeking to reconfirm that right, African American leaders advocated sobriety, thrift, piety, hard work, and education, and they exhorted free people of color to "uplift" themselves to attain high levels of "respectability."[4]

From the 1790s on, the ideology of uplift and respectability proved an effective strategy for developing strong communities of color in Northern cities as adherents carefully husbanded resources and invested them for the common good. The handsome brick churches, well-attended schools, active Masonic lodges, and earnest temperance groups arising from these investments served to advance free African Americans' claims to equality. To live respectably was to elevate oneself to parity with even the most elite whites and to claim the authority to criticize slaveholders, racial bigots, and the lower orders in general. Moreover, insofar as the black community exemplified virtue, it exposed as grossly prejudicial whites' tendency to implicate all people of color in the behavior of a "degraded" few. Finally, the respectable head of household could proudly assert his manhood by displaying strength of character and protecting his home and family from attacks by the racially prejudiced—a right and a

---

4. The multiethnicity of New England history is only beginning to be understood. See, e.g., Joanne Pope Melish, "The Narragansett Indians: A Nineteenth-Century History of Racial Extinction" (paper presented at the Annual Meeting of the Society of Historians of the Early Republic, Buffalo, NY, July 2000); Gloria Main, *Peoples of a Spacious Land: Families and Culture in Colonial New England* (Cambridge: Harvard University Press, 2001); Joanne Pope Melish, *Disowning Slavery: Gradual Emancipation and "Race" in New England, 1780–1860* (Ithaca: Cornell University Press, 1998), 122–29; and Jack D. Forbes, *Africans and Indians* (Champaign-Urbana: University of Illinois Press, 1993), 51–66.

responsibility categorically denied to Southern slaves. To "colored Americans," "uplift" and "respectability," which embraced all these meanings, bespoke powerful abolitionist values. It is therefore little wonder that men like Forten and Cornish hailed the prospect of establishing the Negro College in New Haven and scorned proposals by the American Colonization Society that free blacks abandon their claims to citizenship and "return" to their "homeland" halfway around the globe.

Founded in 1816 by prominent white ministers, politicians, and philanthropists from both North and South, the American Colonization Society severely compromised African American activists' quest for equality. In New Haven its members set themselves adamantly against the establishment of the Negro College. At the heart of the colonizationists' project was a conviction that Northern free blacks, considered to be "turbulent" and "degraded," and Southern slaves, potential runaways and insurrectionists, both threatened to undermine the new nation's fragile stability. Securing full voting and civil rights for people of color in the socially segregated and politically discriminatory free states was simply unthinkable given this logic. However, the "benevolent" resettlement of free black volunteers in the West African colony of Liberia held great promise. To leading black activists, on the other hand, the society represented a far-flung conspiracy among powerful white "respectables" to drive black Americans into exile, a charge they persistently leveled throughout the antebellum period.[5]

In the South, of course, a "free" society had long been grounded in a heavily enforced white supremacy. The racial tensions that emerged in the North during the 1820s, however, had a different origin and so posed new perils for the black struggle to achieve equality by affirming respectability. In Northern cities like New Haven, industrialization forced a rapid transition from artisan work to wage labor, which, in turn, attracted unprecedented numbers of immigrants from the British Isles. When encountering the traumas of acculturation, these newly arrived

---

5. Three excellent analyses of free African American community development and activist ideology are Patrick Rael, *Black Identity and Black Protest in the Antebellum North* (Chapel Hill: University of North Carolina Press, 2002); James Oliver Horton and Lois Horton, *In Hope of Liberty: Culture, Community, and Protest among Northern Free Blacks* (New York: Oxford University Press, 1997); and Richard H Newman, *Fighting Slavery in the Early Republic, 1790–1835* (Chapel Hill: University of North Carolina Press, 2002). These three works support this paragraph and the two preceding it.

English and Irish workers saw in the skin color of their black neighbors unwelcome competition in a tightening labor market and, still more important, a mirror of their own diminishing ability to shape their futures as independent men. Fearing personal "enslavement" to the bosses who dictated their wages, immigrant workers joined the native born when claiming themselves to be white, the irreducible hallmark of full citizenship, and then "asserting" their citizenship in acts of aggression against free blacks.[6]

Most whites attributed the "turbulence" and "degradation" stirred by this mounting social unrest not to increasingly bigoted immigrant and nativist workers but to the African Americans who were becoming their victims. Imposing a racial tyranny that at every turn met respectable colored Americans' struggles for equality with repression, white mobs attacked urban black communities with increasing impunity and ferocity. The most vicious of these events was the Cincinnati race riot of 1829. Returning to black neighborhoods on three successive nights, armed mobs reduced homes and churches to rubble, left several people dead, and sent more than six hundred African Americans fleeing into exile, some settling permanently in Canada.

As less disastrous incidents disrupted other major cities—Hartford, Boston, Philadelphia, and New York among them—state legislatures across the North opened the franchise to all white men while simultaneously enacting prejudicial laws that all but stripped free people of color of what remained of their citizenship. "Black codes" restricted the civil rights of people of color, and voting requirements blocked their access to the ballot box. Newspapers, barrooms, and theaters suddenly teemed with racist cartoons and slurs, a trend in popular culture that closely mirrored the dominant ideology of the nation's emergent two-party political system as it courted a much expanded white, male electorate. Rousing unprecedented numbers of voters with speeches, parades, and barbecues, the Democratic and Whig parties offered sharply contrasting approaches to any number of fiscal and public policy issues, but when it came to

---

6. These developments are explained in depth in David Roediger, *The Wages of Whiteness: Race and the Making of the American Working Class* (New York: Verso, 1997). For an expansive explanation of the cultural roots of white supremacy and racial identities in New England, see Melish, *Disowning Slavery*.

supporting slavery and preaching white supremacy, their differences were never more than superficial. Slaveholders held positions of great influence in both parties, and the federal Constitution's three-fifths clause gave planters a magnified presence in the House of Representatives. Northern bankers and businesses increasingly invested in slavery, while industrialists founded textile mills throughout New England that turned slave-produced cotton into fabric that clothed millions. By the 1830s, enslaved humans were, second only to land, the nation's largest capital investment.[7] In the light of these circumstances, the white supremacist biases both of political parties and of elite groups throughout the free states are easy to explain. So are white New Havenites' rejection of the proposed Negro College and Northern black activists' enthusiasm for it.

When Simeon Jocelyn, William Lloyd Garrison, and Arthur and Lewis Tappan first pledged themselves to the idea at the 1831 convention, the black delegates who also warmly endorsed it had just survived a decade of aspirations blasted, claims denied, and communities besieged. Yet here, quite suddenly, even providentially, were earnest white philanthropists who denounced colonization, not recommended it, who solicited African Americans' opinions, not sneered at them, who offered interracial collaboration, not mob violence, and who, above all, believed deeply in the efficacy of racial uplift and declared dark-skinned people to be their equals. Viewed in this context, the alliance struck in 1831 between black and white activists on behalf of the New Haven Negro College marked a truly revolutionary turn in the history of race relations in the United States.

What brought these extraordinary white reformers to the Convention of the Free People of Color and thence to New Haven? It was not, as it was for Forten and other black activists, the legacy of the Revolution but instead the power of religious enthusiasm translated into a revolutionary demand for immediate slave emancipation. Inspired by evangelical

7. The fullest overview of racist violence and discrimination in the early 1800s remains Leon Litwack, *North of Slavery: The Negro in the Free States, 1790–1860* (New York: Oxford University Press, 1961). See also John M. Werner, "Race Riots in the Age of Jackson, 1824–1849" (Ph.D. diss., University of Indiana, 1973). For the political and economic position of slavery in the early republic, see John Ashworth, *Commerce and Compromise, 1820–1850,* vol. 1 of his *Slavery, Capitalism, and Politics in the Antebellum Republic* (Cambridge: Cambridge University Press, 1995); and Leonard L. Richards, *The Slave Power in American Politics* (Baton Rouge: Louisiana State University Press, 2000).

revivalists' belief that each individual could freely choose to renounce sin, strive for personal holiness, and then, once saved, bring God's truth to the unredeemed, Garrison, Tappan, Jocelyn, and other young enthusiasts discovered in slaveholding the most God-defying sin of all. In what other system, they asked, were the defenseless more brazenly exploited? For those who thought slaveholders benevolent caretakers, let the facts speak for themselves. In no place was sexual wantonness more rampant than on the plantation, where debauched masters forced themselves on their helpless female slaves. In no place was brutality more thoroughly inflicted than in Southern fields, where masters and overseers freely applied their whips. In no place was impiety more deliberately fostered than in Southern slave quarters, where men, women, and children were denied the ability to read the Bible. The remedy for all these terrible evils was "immediate" emancipation pressed urgently with earnest exhortation on the slumbering consciences of all white Americans, slaveholders and nonslaveholders alike.

Although the nation's most powerful institutions and elite groups were tightly aligned in support of slavery and Northern political culture was suffused as never before with white bigotry, young white abolitionists nonetheless saw their battle over slavery as divinely guaranteed. And as the drama of emancipation played out toward its inevitable, glorious end, Christian duty compelled them to combat white supremacy in the North ("colorphobia," they called it) as vigorously as slavery in the South. Such bigotry, they argued, blinded Northerners to the most obvious truth of all—that God had created all of his people to be equal. At the center of this logic of equality, however, was a crucial assumption: that along with the common humanity that all people shared, the Almighty had also divided his children into distinct races, in this particular instance, into black and white. White abolitionists therefore never questioned the very idea of race, their own included. Instead, they devoted themselves, self-perceived whites, to securing equality for an unjustly oppressed and therefore "degraded" race of blacks.[8]

---

8. For a broad overview of the rise of immediate abolitionism and the ideology underpinning it, see James Brewer Stewart, *Holy Warriors: The Abolitionists and American Slavery* (New York: Hill & Wang, 1996), and for a nuanced analysis of cultural and religious trends surrounding immediatism, see Robert W. Abzug, *Cosmos Crumbling: American Reform and the Religious Imagination* (New

Veteran activists of color such as Samuel E. Cornish and James Forten did not share white abolitionists' optimism or their instinct to sort people into races. Long and bitter trials with racial tyranny confounded expectations of a quick victory and turned racial categorizations into pernicious fictions. Yet black activists felt compelled for a number of reasons to make common cause with Garrison, Tappan, and Jocelyn on behalf of the Negro College. Here, after all, were whites whose condemnations of slavery and colonization expressed everything black leaders had longed to say but could not for fear of being branded as insurrectionists and suppressed. The mysterious death of David Walker in 1831, following the publication of his militant *Appeal* in 1829, all too convincingly confirmed that fear.[9] In addition, these white reformers shared colored activists' cherished moral values of racial uplift—piety, thrift, sobriety, education, and self-improvement. Most important of all, white abolitionists were eager to contribute their cash as well as their energy and to encourage black participation in all aspects of an ambitious project on behalf of equality. Therefore Forten, Allen, and the rest happily joined Garrison, the Tappan brothers, and Jocelyn in laying plans and raising funds for the New Haven Negro College, the most visionary interracial project yet attempted in the nation's history.

For this reason alone, the brief, unfortunate history of the Negro College should not be understood as a lesson in failed idealism or as an opportunity lost. Instead, it can be properly regarded as a crucial point of departure. As Louis Masur has argued about so many other events of 1831, the attempt to found the Negro College in New Haven that year had powerful repercussions that spread throughout the antebellum era.[10] As individuals who had first been involved in the Negro College controversy acted out their prejudices, ideals, and convictions in New England's next three decades of struggle over questions of race and social justice, they set the terms for larger, ongoing controversies over the

York: Oxford University Press, 1994). Bruce Dain, *A Hideous Monster of the Mind: American Race Theory in the Early Republic* (Cambridge: Harvard University Press, 2002), offers the fullest explication of racial thinking in the antebellum era.

9. Peter P. Hinks, ed., *David Walker's Appeal to the Colored Citizens of the World* (University Park: Pennsylvania State University Press, 2000).

10. Louis P. Masur, *1831: Year of Eclipse* (New York: Hill & Wang, 2001).

meanings of skin color and the challenges of equality, conflicts that in the North did not resolve neatly into polarities of black and white. The lives of these individuals—some exemplary, some not—have significance for our understanding of the region's continuing struggles over race and can help set the terms of our ongoing discussions of the meanings of race in this country.

The New Haven Negro College: Narratives of Engagement

The New Haven Rioters

It seems fair to conclude that those who took to the streets in opposition to the Negro College had little cause to regret their actions at the time and even less reason to do so as years went by. Indeed, as we can extrapolate from the findings of Paul Gilje and Leonard L. Richards, who have studied nineteenth-century mobs, the 1831 New Haven rioters neither invented white violence against blacks nor exceeded white norms for lower-class public behavior. Unlike the bloodlust let loose on Cincinnati's black community the year before or New York's three years later, restraint characterized the attack in New Haven, as it did in most Northern race riots of the period. That rampaging whites had not resorted to arson or killed anyone was, however, small comfort to terrified and demoralized African Americans.

Riots swept across the free states in the 1830s, flared anew after the compromise of 1850, and rose again in the aftermath of John Brown's 1859 raid on Harpers Ferry. Each cycle of violence reasserted the dominant culture's conviction that, in the "free" states, an overbearing majority of whites upheld two biologically incontestable and sharply exclusive modes of racialized existence, the black self-evidently inferior to the white. Critical foreign visitors such as Alexis de Tocqueville, Harriet Martineau, William Abdy, and George Thompson easily glimpsed the troubling lesson to be drawn from these successive waves of violence, writing bitterly that whites in the antebellum North built their democracy by molesting and intimidating their darker-skinned neighbors.[11] As I discuss later, a

---

11. Leonard L. Richards, *"Gentlemen of Property and Standing": Antiabolitionist Mobs in Jacksonian America* (New York: Oxford University Press, 1970); Gilje, *The Road to Mobocracy: Popular Disorder in New York City, 1763–1834* (Bloomington: University of Indiana Press, 1996).

certain Hosea Easton also came to just these conclusions. An activist who traced his mixed ancestry to Indian, African, and English origins, Easton saw his life destroyed by people much like the New Haven rioters who treated him as just another "nigger."

White Moderate Leonard Bacon

The demise of the Negro College project left the Reverend Leonard Bacon so profoundly torn over issues of race and social justice that only with the onset of the Civil War was he able to resolve his ambivalence. Precisely the sort of benevolent "Christian gentleman" whom abolitionists expected would give weight to the Negro College proposal, Bacon was a longstanding New Havenite, a Yale stalwart, and a luminary of Connecticut Congregationalism. He publicly deplored slavery and lamented the dreadful treatment of free people of color. In the mid-1820s, Bacon had become active in the Negro Improvement Society, an association of benevolent whites headquartered in Philadelphia. In New Haven, the society took credit for hiring Simeon Jocelyn to pastor the Dixwell Church, as well as for establishing a library, a Sabbath school, a savings bank, a temperance society, and academies for both children and adults in the black community. But as Hugh Davis's fine biography makes clear, Bacon's devotion to colonization compromised his otherwise impressive commitment to racial uplift. As he himself declared in 1828, attempts to "produce a general and thorough amelioration of the character and condition of the free people of color" would inevitably be essentially "fruitless."[12]

Numerous white abolitionists-in-the-making—Garrison, the Tappans, and Jocelyn among them—had once held views akin to Bacon's. In the early 1830s, however, as a means of sealing their commitment to immediatism, they vociferously attacked colonization as a sop to conscience that strengthened slavery all the more. For any number of personal and ideological reasons, Bacon could not make so radical a transition. By temperament, he was a moderate. Two of his closest friends,

---

12. The treatment of Leonard Bacon developed in the next several paragraphs and the quotations accompanying it are drawn from Hugh Davis, *Leonard Bacon: New England Reformer and Antislavery Moderate* (Baton Rouge: Louisiana State University Press, 1998), 65–91.

Yale College luminaries Benjamin Silliman and Nathaniel Taylor, were dedicated colonizationists. Several pillars of Bacon's Center Church were colonizationists who cultivated mercantile interests that were entwined with Southern markets. Moreover, in Bacon's opinion, immediatism was unsupported by Scripture, subversive of denominational unity, and un-charitable to planters of "good conscience," who deserved compassion and Christian fellowship.

Genuinely disturbed by racial injustice but constrained by both in-ternal and external forces of conservatism, Bacon reacted to the Negro College controversy by condemning both the rioters and the aboli-tionists. He felt "mortification and sorrow" that New Havenites had "rushed together to blot out this first ray of hope for the blacks," and he deplored the behavior of the mob. Still, he believed that Garrison and his kind "would smile to see conflagration, rapine and extermina-tion sweeping with tornado-fury over half the land," and he thought that the college proposal had been rightly rejected. Only "discreet men" like himself—certainly not Garrisonians—were qualified to direct the educations of "their colored brethren" away from the "spirit of wrath and insurrection." Set in the immediate context of Nat Turner's uprising, Bacon's remark suggests that by lumping into one violence-prone race both New England's free people of color and the Africa-descended slaves of the South, he, like the rioters, sorted the nation into black inferiors and white superiors.

Bacon's uncomfortable ambivalence over the Negro College question continued to afflict him in subsequent years. During the 1840s, he al-ternated between reaching out to those he called "good slaveholders," those he hoped might solve the problem of slavery, and campaigning vigorously to preserve western territories as "free soil." In the 1850s, however, Bacon finally concluded that the "slave power" was a perilous conspiracy, and he abandoned his search for "good slaveholders."

Never again did he promote colonization; instead, he advocated re-sisting the Fugitive Slave Law and putting rifles in the hands of Kansas free-soilers. In 1859 he praised John Brown for his raid on Harpers Ferry. By 1862, wartime exigencies and his long-held belief that African Americans could be uplifted persuaded him to support emancipation and to call for political equality between blacks and whites. In 1863 he favored black enlistment, and by 1866 he championed black male suffrage (within Connecticut as well as nationally) and education and civil rights for freedpeople. Bacon's family may have influenced the evolution of his thought. Two of his children moved south at the end of the war, and for several years they taught freedpeople at the Hampton Institute, a school whose goals were reminiscent of the proposed New Haven Negro College.

Leonard Bacon had long been hampered in his attempts to assist free people of color by his conflicting desire to conserve the social order. Only when sectional crisis and civil war destroyed that order did he finally find himself free to advocate equality between blacks and whites, just as did other moderates who joined the Republican Party out of fear of the "slave power" and who, during the war, found themselves compelled by the same logic of equality. In the absence of people with histories like Bacon's, the war that brought about emancipation and the peace that ultimately led to black Reconstruction would be difficult to imagine and harder still to account for. So would the overwhelming conviction throughout the North that the destinies of two sharply distinguished races defined the politics of the sectional conflict.

White Radical William Lloyd Garrison

At the time of the Negro College controversy, no white person in the North had closer ties to free people of color than William Lloyd Garrison. Free blacks with whom he had lived in Baltimore had schooled him in anticolonizationism, the harsh truths of racial tyranny, and the values of racial uplift. He drew inspiration from religious services in colored churches, and he delighted in speaking before colored audiences. Free blacks welcomed him in turn, inviting him into their homes and dominating the subscription list for his new venture, the *Liberator*. Without their crucial support, the newspaper would have quickly failed, a fact Garrison fully appreciated as he opened the *Liberator*'s pages to writers of color, a practice unprecedented in the history of American journalism. The New Haven debacle, however, had permanently negative consequences for Garrison's close relationship with darker-skinned activists and his direct involvement in their causes. By the end of the 1830s, Garrison had established himself as abolitionism's most creative ideologist, but never again would he collaborate as closely with dark-skinned associates as he had during the Negro College controversy.[13]

As a prime mover in the Negro College scheme, Garrison threw himself wholeheartedly into fundraising, issuing appeals in the *Liberator* and making numerous personal appearances. When the project collapsed, no one was more deeply shocked and angered than he. Bitterly he observed that "the Christian people of New Haven behave no better than they do in South Carolina." Distressed but undaunted, Garrison next championed the ill-fated cause of Prudence Crandall, whose attempts to open a school for "colored girls" in Canterbury, Connecticut, in 1833 were thwarted by opponents much like those who had blocked the Negro College. At the same time, however, the white abolitionist movement and Garrison's role in it were expanding rapidly. In 1833 the American Anti-Slavery Society was founded. That same year, the British government legislated the abolition of slavery throughout its West Indian colonies. Garrison, who now saw himself as the most prominent representative of a budding national movement, felt charged with the responsibility of introducing American antislavery to British abolitionists, the most powerful and successful crusaders of all.

Garrison lacked resources for overseas travel, and so he embarked on a creative fundraising campaign. In a March 1833 *Liberator*, he announced that he would visit England as a special agent of the New England Anti-Slavery Society, a regional affiliate of the American Anti-Slavery Society. His goal, he declared, was to raise funds from British abolitionists to support the establishment of a "manual labor school" for colored youth, and so he appealed directly to free people of color to support his travel. Promising to revivify the dream that had given rise to the New Haven Negro College proposal, Garrison launched a six-week American city tour that brought him before black audiences. They received him warmly and gave generously, over six hundred dollars in total. Garrison's reflections on the tour, conveyed in a letter printed in the *Liberator*, are laced with self-congratulation and paternalism.

---

13. My treatment of William Lloyd Garrison is drawn from Stewart, *Garrison and the Challenge of Emancipation*; and Henry Mayer, *All on Fire: William Lloyd Garrison and the Abolition of Slavery* (New York: Oxford University Press, 2000).

The highest interest and the most intense feelings were felt and exhibited by the audience. They wept freely—they clustered around me in throngs, each one eager to receive the pressure of my hand and implore Heaven's choicest blessings upon my head. You cannot imagine the scene, and my pen is wholly inadequate to describe it. As I stood before them, and reflected that this might be the last time that I should behold them together on earth—the last time that I should be permitted to administer advice and consolation to their minds—the last time I should have the opportunity to pour out my gratitude before them for their numerous manifestations of confidence in my integrity, and appreciation of my humble service in their cause.[14]

Once in England, Garrison apparently forgot about fundraising and devoted himself to the far more rewarding tasks of ingratiating himself with England's elite abolitionists and denouncing the American Colonization Society. The role of supplicant, evidently, did not square with Garrison's understanding of his position as the leader of the American abolitionist movement. There are no records of income solicited during Garrison's England trip, but there is clear evidence that he overran his budget and was obliged to borrow two hundred dollars for his return passage from the black activist Nathaniel Paul, who was also touring England to raise money for a manual labor school for blacks to be sited in Lower Canada. From beginning to end, funds earmarked for the benefit of people of color had been spent instead for the benefit of William Lloyd Garrison's reputation.[15]

To be clear: Garrison was no hypocrite. Neither was his paternalism remotely comparable to the profound bigotry that infected most white Americans. Yet by 1834, the "blackest" white activist in the United States had come to regard himself as a cosmopolitan and global visionary, closer in outlook to aristocratic British abolitionists than to the ordinary people of color who had helped launch his career. In subsequent decades,

---

14. Stewart, *Garrison and the Challenge of Emancipation*, 63.

15. Intent on presenting Garrison's understanding of problems of race as invariably grounded in clear moral insight, Mayer (*All on Fire*, 127–87) fails to consider Garrison's misuse of his black supporters' funds or what that matter might imply about his approach to interracial abolitionism. Garrison's finances during his trip to England are detailed by John L. Thomas in his *The Liberator, William Lloyd Garrison: A Biography* (Boston: Little, Brown, 1963), 163, 175–76.

black leaders less deferential than James Forten or Richard Allen—men like Frederick Douglass, James McCune Smith, and Henry Highland Garnet—openly rebelled against Garrison's heavy-handedness and moralistic abstractions. As blacks in his home city of Boston shouldered the day-to-day burdens of agitation, Garrison offered supportive publicity and occasional editorials but devoted the vast majority of his attention to the more personally congenial work of proclaiming disunion, condemning church and political leaders, and preaching religious perfectionism. As Bruce Dain has demonstrated, the unreflective Garrison believed deeply in the principle of racial equality but never questioned his primary assumption that the world was divided into two distinct races, one clearly in need of the ongoing patronage of the other. For all their other differences, then, Garrison and Bacon shared the view that Southern slaves and Northern free people of color together constituted one unitary black race.[16]

In 1865, with the Thirteenth Amendment's dissolution of slavery, Garrison shocked many of his closest colleagues by announcing that their crusade had ended in victory and that abolitionists should dismantle their organizations. Freedpeoples' civil and political rights, he insisted, were not the proper concerns of abolitionists, a view Douglass, Wendell Phillips, Elizabeth Cady Stanton, and many others considered unthinkable. Perhaps it is too much to suggest that Garrison's abrupt departure from abolitionism in 1865, just as the day-to-day business of empowering freed communities in the South was beginning in earnest, had its roots three decades earlier in the aftermath of the Negro College controversy. But perhaps it is not. In either case, in the long run, the more radical egalitarian turned out to be not Garrison but his old antagonist Leonard Bacon, the former colonizationist who supported black Reconstruction.[17]

---

16. Dain, *Hideous Monster of the Mind*, 48–55.

17. For the basic works on which I base my generalization, see Eric Foner, *Free Soil, Free Labor, Free Men: The Ideology of the Republican Party before the Civil War* (New York: Oxford University Press, 1970); Richard H. Sewell, *Ballots for Freedom: Antislavery Politics and the Coming of the Civil War* (New York: Oxford University Press, 1983); and James M. McPherson, *The Struggle for Equality: The Abolitionists and the Negro in the Civil War and Reconstruction* (Princeton: Princeton University Press, 1964).

White Benefactor Lewis Tappan

For Lewis Tappan, the New Haven debacle inaugurated an expansive abolitionist career during which he perpetuated, as Garrison could not, the promise of the Negro College. Underscoring the contrasting personalities and circumstances of the two men, Bertram Wyatt-Brown's superb biography of Tappan helps us understand their differing commitments. Tappan enjoyed vast wealth and a secure social position, whereas Garrison had suffered poverty and for a lifetime battled to be heard. Tappan, the canny merchant, had ample bureaucratic skills and excelled at institution building; Garrison, the intransigent ideologue, had difficulty managing even his personal affairs and delighted not in building organizations but in criticizing them. While Garrison stood on principle, Tappan pursued practical solutions. Among his abolitionist ventures were the American Missionary Association, the Liberty Party, and most important for our purposes, Oneida Institute and Oberlin College. Essential to both institutions was the mission of uplifting young black men, but the manner in which that goal was to be effected paradoxically confirmed both the power of racial tyranny and the promise of interracial collaboration.[18]

Founded by and sustained with gifts from Tappan and his brother Arthur, the Oneida Institute and Oberlin College differed significantly from the New Haven venture. Oberlin and Oneida admitted only small numbers of people of color. While the vast majority of students at both institutions were white, however, they were from families predisposed to supporting reform; indeed, Tappan himself sent his sons to Oneida. Such arrangements were certainly less ambitious and less threatening than the all-black student body of the proposed New Haven Negro College. It was also no accident that Oberlin and Oneida were located in isolated rural settings in Ohio and New York, respectively, far from the racial, ethnic, and class struggles of the urbanized North. While the Negro College was to be funded in large part with grassroots contributions generated by an interracial alliance, Oberlin and Oneida were sustained by white philanthropy and by the tuition of those capable of paying it. In short, black education at Oneida and Oberlin relied on elitist funding, escapist locations, and careful restriction of the number of students of

---

18. Wyatt-Brown, *Lewis Tappan*, informs this paragraph and the two that follow.

color admitted. Even as they turned white altruism and black activism in conservative directions, however, the ventures could not stave off strenuous racist opposition and, in the case of Oneida Institute, ultimately bankruptcy. The institute folded in 1843, having survived for less than a decade.[19]

Despite such disappointments, one must nevertheless concede the wisdom of Lewis Tappan's pragmatism. Oberlin and Oneida did uplift a significant number of African American graduates, men whose vital leadership energized black abolitionism from 1840 onward. Rather than elevating the race in general, as those who sponsored the Negro College had hoped to do, Oberlin and Oneida empowered a rising elite, a group of men including John Mercer Langston, John B. Vashon, Henry Highland Garnet, Alexander Crummell, Amos Beman, Jermaine Lougen, and William Howard Day. Tappan had gained a valuable lesson from the failure of the New Haven experiment, and he worked imaginatively to renew its promise by modifying its design and moderating its goals. In so doing he opened pathways to leadership for a new generation of dark-skinned abolitionists who found themselves prepared, as Leonard Bacon was but William Lloyd Garrison was not, to face the extraordinary challenges of emancipation and Reconstruction.

Black Victim Hosea Easton

Hosea Easton was among the delegates at the Convention of the Free People of Color who applauded the establishment of a manual labor school in New Haven. Once the project had been approved, he hastened home to Boston to begin raising funds. His obvious enthusiasm arose from deeply engrained experiences and poignant memories that freighted the Negro College project with intense personal meaning. For Easton, the Negro College was destined to revive the "uplifting" vision of his father, James Easton, a pioneer black educator in his own right.[20]

---

19. For details of the histories of both colleges, see Robert Samuel Fletcher, *A History of Oberlin College from the Foundation through the Civil War* (Oberlin, OH: Oberlin College Press, 1943); and Milton Sernett, *Abolition's Axe: Beriah Green, the Oneida Institute, and the Black Freedom Struggle* (Syracuse: Syracuse University Press, 1997).

20. My treatment of James and Hosea Easton is drawn from George R. Price and James Brewer Stewart, *To Heal the Scourge of Prejudice: The Life and Writings of Hosea Easton* (Amherst: University of Massachusetts Press, 1999), 1–47; and Dain, *Hideous Monster of the Mind*, which insightfully

CONSEQUENCES

As an extension of his successful family business, an iron foundry (located just outside Boston in Bridgewater, Massachusetts), James Easton
had established a manual labor school for African American youth, the
first such institution of its kind, in the mid-1810s. At the Good Samaritan Society—the name James gave to his school—twenty or so students
divided their time between academic study and vocational training in
smithing, farming, and shoemaking. In his teens at the time, Hosea had
studied along with them. Stern moral codes and "rigid economy" were
"enforced with surprising assiduity," Hosea recalled, and "ardent spirits
found no place in the establishment." Despite its success and the "many
thousands of dollars" invested by James and his partners, the school collapsed in the late 1820s. To Hosea, his father's magnificent creation—
indeed his father himself—had been destroyed by white racial tyranny.

James Easton died in Boston in 1830, the year before Hosea traveled
to Philadelphia and learned of the New Haven Negro College project.
His bitter recollections of the demise of his father's "noble" experiment
suggest how the grieving Hosea must have responded to the mob that
tore through New Haven's black community only a year later: "By reason
of the repeated surges of the tide of prejudice, the establishment, like
a ship in a boisterous hurricane at sea, went beneath the waves, richly
laden, well manned, well managed, and all sunk to rise no more. . . . It
fell, and with it fell the hearts of several of its undertakers in despair, and
their bodies into their graves." [21]

In 1831, Hosea Easton lamented the defeat of the Negro College as
both a defilement of his father's legacy and an affront to America's creeds
and aspirations, for which his father had fought. Once again, white racial tyranny had betrayed the promise of the American Revolution and
stripped free people of color of their citizenship and dignity.

James Easton chose to denominate himself a man of color—as did
many other indigenous, mixed, and Africa-descended patriots in revo-

discusses Hosea Easton's antiracial thinking on race without, however, considering the influence of
his multiethnic heritage.

21. See Hosea Easton, *Treatise on the Intellectual Character, and the Civil and Political Condition of
the Colored People of the U. States and the Prejudice Exercised toward Them: With a Sermon on the Duty
of the Church toward Them* (Boston: Isaac Knapp, 1837), reprinted in Price and Stewart's *To Heal the
Scourge of Prejudice*, 63–123 (quotation, 9), and *Minutes of the Annual Meeting of the New England
Anti-Slavery Society* (Boston: Garnson and Knapp, 1832), 6, 10.

lutionary New England—when he served in the siege of Dorchester Heights and at the fall of Fort Ticonderoga. Easton's bloodlines were English, African, and Wampanoag, and that mixed heritage deeply affected his world view and that of his offspring. James and his children were closely associated with the famous mixed-blood shipping entrepreneur Paul Cuffee; James's son Caleb married into a prominent white family in Bridgewater; other branches of the Easton family elected to remain attached to Wampanoag and Narragansett communities; and still others, including James and Hosea, preferred the designation "colored," a term they took to mean multiethnic, not black or African. By every measure of their experience, discrete racial categories of "black," "red," and "white" made absolutely no sense to the Eastons. As his subsequent actions made abundantly clear, moreover, James Easton had fought in the American Revolution to equalize opportunities for all men, whatever their color.[22]

Following the Revolution, James Easton emphatically demonstrated that he despised discrimination and would resist it whenever he encountered it. Once, in 1796, when white parishioners decreed that their colored co-religionists must accept segregation, Easton, his wife, four sons, and two daughters sat in the aisle and refused to move. The impasse continued for several Sundays until church officials revoked the Eastons' membership. At another church, Easton purchased a family pew in the whites-only section from a sympathetic congregant. When angry church members tarred the pew, the Eastons returned weekly, carrying their own chairs, until once again they were expunged from the church rolls. In all, records indicate at least six such incidents during the early 1800s, and perhaps there were others.

Young Hosea Easton learned early and quite dramatically that it was no easy matter to uphold family honor by defying racial tyranny, but still

---

22. George Price, "James Easton: Forgotten Abolitionist 'Giant,'" in Michael Morrison, ed., *The Human Tradition in Antebellum America* (Wilmington, DE: Scholarly Resources, 2000), 147–63. Evidence for James Easton's antiracist understanding of the term "colored," though indirect, is strongly confirmed by Hosea, *Treatise*, which begins, "I conclude it is a settled point with the wisest of the age that no constitutional difference exists in the children of men which can be established by hereditary laws. If the proposition be granted, it will follow, that whatever differences exist, are casual or accidental. The variety of color in the human [*sic*] species, is the result of the same laws which variegate the whole creation. The same species of flower is variegated with innumerable colors, yet the species is the same, possessing the same general qualities, undergoing no intrinsic changes from these accidental causes. So it is with the human species" (Price and Stewart, *To Heal the Scourge of Prejudice*, 67).

it must be done. It likewise became abundantly clear to him that the very classification of dark-skinned people as "black" and light-skinned people as "white" did terrible violence to history, to human dignity, and to his own lived experience. In sharp contrast to other leading figures in the New Haven Negro College debacle—urban rioters, Leonard Bacon, William Lloyd Garrison, and Lewis Tappan—Hosea Easton was a living embodiment of the complications to which the idea of race gives rise if simplistic, falsifying polarities are set aside. Given his heritage and circumstances, he had no choice but to reject the very idea that God had divided his people into races.

In January 1834, Hosea Easton was called to minister to the Talcott Street Congregational Church in Hartford, Connecticut, a city in which racial tensions ran unusually high. As soon as he arrived, Easton tried to raise funds for a "colored uplift" organization, the Hartford Literary and Religious Institution, but white mobsters attacked one of his parishioners and, after three days of rioting punctuated by gunfire from a black resister, several families were left homeless.[23] From then on, Easton and his congregants lived in terror of their white neighbors. Street-corner harassment was constant, and in three years mobs overran the neighborhood on three occasions. In June 1835, hecklers provoked a black resister to take up arms. Three days of looting and arson ensued, and neither the constables nor the state militia could save black neighborhoods from devastation. The English visitor Edward Abdy remarked that never before in all his travels had he encountered such brutality as he witnessed in Hartford: "Throughout the Union there is, perhaps, no city, containing the same amount of population, where blacks meet more contumely and unkindness than in this place. Some of them told me that it was hardly safe to be out on the streets alone at night. . . . To pelt them with stones and cry out "nigger!, nigger! as they pass, seems to be the pass-time of the place."[24]

Then, in 1836, Easton's church burned to the ground. Although the cause of the fire remained unexplained, Easton had no doubt about its

<hr />

23. See *Emancipator*, February 17, 1835; and Price and Stewart, *To Heal the Scourge of Prejudice*, 22.

24. Edward Abdy, *Journal of Residence and Tour of the United States of North America, April 1833 October 1834*, 3 vols. (London, 1835), 3:206–7.

origins. Soon afterward, he registered in his writings just how personally devastating the episode had been for him. In 1837, just before he died at age forty-one, he published his angry and deeply pessimistic *Treatise on the Intellectual Character, and the Civil and Political Condition of the Colored People of the U[nited] States*, a fifty-eight-page pamphlet in which he asserted, in part, that white prejudice was so intractable that people of color would never be able to overcome it; indeed, it had already reduced once highly civilized African peoples to inferiors incapable of helping themselves. While arguing strenuously that differences in skin color were but superficial "accidents," variations found throughout one single human race, Easton also demanded that those who called themselves white take full responsibility for the horrors they had perpetrated and act with deepest Christian charity to redress them.[25] In his final thoughts on his lifelong struggles against racial tyranny, Easton could do no more than issue a plea based on the same parable of the Good Samaritan that had once inspired the name of his father's school. Yet it was a plea he knew would be ignored. In the aftermath of the Negro College controversy, his father's example and his multiethnic heritage could not sustain an agonized Hosea Easton.

Colored Vindicators Benjamin Franklin Roberts and William Nell
Benjamin Franklin Roberts, James Easton's grandson, responded very differently to his family's traditions than had his uncle Hosea. Whereas Hosea Easton died believing himself a failure, his nephew ultimately took satisfaction from and pride in his struggles against white tyranny. Roberts's lifelong collaborator in black activism, William Nell, shared those feelings, both for himself and for his friend. Thanks largely to their leadership, the Massachusetts state legislature outlawed school segregation throughout the commonwealth in 1855. It was a victory over white supremacy of an order neither James nor Hosea Easton could have ever imagined. It was, for Roberts and Nell, moreover, a victory of egalitarian principle over the invidious concept of race itself.[26]

---

25. Easton, *Treatise*, 113–21.

26. The treatment of Benjamin Franklin Roberts I develop here is drawn from James Brewer Stewart and George R. Price, "The Roberts Case, the Easton Family, and the Dynamics of the Abolitionist Movement in Massachusetts, 1776–1870," *Massachusetts Historical Review* 4 (2002): 89–115.

Benjamin Roberts was nineteen years of age during the New Haven Negro College controversy. In earlier years, he had spent considerable time in his grandfather's manual labor school, which he described in a memoir many years later.[27] Though not directly involved in the New Haven controversy, Roberts was certainly familiar with its history when setting out to redeem his family's honor and egalitarian principles by crusading for school desegregation. Like Roberts, Nell was well into young adulthood in 1831, and the black Bostonians who had attempted to support the New Haven venture could be found among his colleagues. While still a young man, Nell had committed himself to the goal of documenting the history of people of "color" (his term) in the United States, and he ultimately gained well-deserved recognition as the nation's first pioneering scholar in that hitherto unexplored field. As Nell understood it, the Massachusetts school rights struggle extended the historic promise of equality for which patriots of color such as James Easton had fought. Indeed, Easton was an exemplary figure for Nell, and he set out to learn as much as he could about him from grandson Benjamin Roberts, information Nell then recounted extensively in his published writings.

To say that William Nell and Benjamin Roberts had common interests risks understatement. Only a short walk separated their homes in Boston's West End, and during the 1830s and 1840s both men pursued the printer's trade, Roberts by maintaining an independent press and Nell by assisting Garrison in the publication of the *Liberator*. The Roberts and Nell families were also allies in the many uplift projects sponsored by African Americans in 1820s Boston. Nell's parents counted as a close associate the extraordinary black protest pamphleteer David Walker. Benjamin Roberts's mother, Sarah Easton, was James Easton's elder daughter and, like her husband, Robert Roberts, a notable Boston

---

Information on William Nell is drawn from Dorothy Porter Wesley, "Integration versus Separation: William Cooper Nell's Role in the Struggle for Equality," in *Courage and Conscience: Black and White Abolitionists in Boston*, ed. Donald M. Jacobs (Bloomington: Indiana University Press, 1993), 207–24; Robert P. Smith, "William Cooper Nell: Crusading Black Abolitionist," *Journal of Negro History* 55 (July 1970): 182–99; and Patrick T. J. Browne, "'To Defend Mr. Garrison': William Cooper Nell and the Personal Politics of Antislavery," *New England Quarterly* 70 (September 1997): 415–42.

27. Benjamin Roberts, "Our Progress in the Old Bay State," *New Era*, March 31, 1870.

activist. During the 1820s, Sarah and Robert Roberts had, along with her brothers Hosea and Joshua Easton, as well as William Nell's father, strenuously opposed the American Colonization Society. All became charter members of the Massachusetts General Colored Association, founded in 1826 to resist colonization and promote African American advancement. The descendants of James Easton and the family of William Nell also fostered activism within their church, Boston's First Independent (African) Baptist Church, which welcomed white abolitionists like Garrison and donated funds to support his trip to England.[28] In short, William Nell and Benjamin Roberts were being drawn together in the 1820s and 1830s by powerful relationships, associations, and traditions rooted in Boston's colored community that, in turn, cultivated in both men a hatred of racial discrimination, resentment for the personal wounds that prejudice had inflicted upon them, and a compelling interest to seize positions of leadership against white bigotry.

In 1838—the year following that in which his mother, Sarah, and his uncle Hosea suddenly died—Benjamin Roberts struck boldly to become the next "James Easton" by announcing that he would publish a new abolitionist newspaper, the *Anti-Slavery Herald*, the only U.S. newspaper at that time to be edited by an African American. Drawing on his family's legacy of activism, especially the example of his grandfather's manual labor school, Roberts proposed to offer apprenticeships for young African Americans in his print shop. Before he could publish even one issue of the paper, however, the prominent abolitionist Amos A. Phelps charged Roberts with deception and self-promotion. Roberts exploded with anger and frustration in a letter to Phelps as he generalized the conflict beyond the personal into more fundamental tensions circulating among blacks and whites within the abolitionist movement.

> I am aware that there has been and *now is*, a combined effort on the part of certain *professed* abolitionists to muzzle, exterminate and put down the efforts of certain colored individuals effecting the welfare of the colored brethren [*sic*]. The truth is respecting myself, my whole soul is engaged

---

28. Wesley, "Integration versus Separation," 208–10; Robert Roberts, *The House Servant's Directory*, ed. Graham Russell Hodges (Armonk, NY: M. E. Sharpe, 1998), xi–xlii.

in the cause of humanity, I am for the *improvement* among this class of people, *mental and physical*. The arts and sciences have never been introduced to any extent among us—therefore they are of utmost importance. If our anti-slavery men will not subscribe to the advancement of these principles, but *rail out* and *protest against* them, why we will go *heathen*. The principle upon which the anti-slavery cause is said to be founded (and *boasting* are not a few) *are the elevation of the free colored people here*. Now it is altogether useless to pretend to affect the welfare of blacks in this country, unless the chains of prejudice are broken. It is of no use [to] say with the mouth that we are friends of the slave and not try to encourage and assist the free colored people in raising themselves. Here, sir, is the *first* effort of the colored men of this country of this kind, vis, the paper *published, printed* and *edited* by colored persons in Massachusetts. Shall this be defeated? But it is contended that the *individual* [Roberts] who started the enterprise has not taken it up from principle—*he* don't intend what he pretends. Base misrepresentations! False accusations!—I was not aware that so many hypocrites existed in the antislavery society. According to what I have seen of the conduct of some, a black man would be as unsafe in their hands as those of Southern slave holders.[29]

Roberts continued to pursue his printing business, occasionally publishing books and pamphlets by black activists, but after sending his bitter remonstrance to Phelps, Roberts retreated from visible leadership in the black community for a decade.

Like his friend Benjamin Franklin Roberts, William Nell also suffered bracing humiliations at the hands of white bigots. In 1823, when Nell was thirteen years of age, Boston mayor Harrison Gray Otis announced that the school committee had decided that Nell, two other young black students, and several whites would receive that year's awards for outstanding scholarship. School officials presented the white students with the customary silver medals bearing the likeness of Benjamin Franklin, but they handed Nell and the other black students letters authorizing them to obtain free copies of a biography of Franklin from a local book-

---

29. Benjamin Franklin Roberts to Amos A. Phelps, June 19, 1838, ms. #2.0499, Antislavery Collection, Boston Public Library; reprinted in Peter Ripley et al., *The Black Abolitionist Papers*, 5 vols. (Chapel Hill: University of North Carolina Press, 1985–92), 3:269–71.

store. The presumption, evidently, was that the young African Americans were ignorant of Franklin's accomplishments and so would not have fully appreciated the medal. Compounding the affront, the school committee excluded the black scholars from that evening's recognition dinner in Faneuil Hall. Furious, Nell gained access to the event by passing himself off as one of the black waiters serving the meal. Recognizing Nell, one of the white students proclaimed, "William! You ought to be up here with the other boys!" That evening, Nell recalled many years later, he vowed "that God help me I would do my best to hasten the day when the color of skin would be no barrier to equal school rights." It was a pledge that placed him squarely in the traditions of the Easton family, as well as those of his own upbringing.[30]

William Nell took humiliation as a goad to lifelong activism. As he entered his twenties in the mid-1830s, Nell began organizing vigilance committees to aid fugitive slaves and promoting and participating in racially integrated associations designed to foster African American self-improvement. Battling segregation in Massachusetts at the same time, he led a successful crusade to force the Eastern Railroad to abandon whites-only train cars. Once, when denied access to the dress circle at a performance of *Don Giovanni*, Nell became so enraged that ushers called for police assistance and forcibly ejected him from the opera house. Nell's rejection of segregation—indeed of the very concept that races were essentially distinct—was uncompromising. Churches serving exclusively black congregations drew his criticism no less than schools that discriminated on behalf of white students. When, in 1848, his friend Benjamin Roberts decided to reenter the fray and bring a desegregation suit against the Boston School Committee, Nell was eager to do all he could to advance the cause.[31]

Roberts acted on behalf of his five-year-old daughter, Sarah (named after her grandmother Sarah Easton Roberts), who was being forced to walk past five fine, whites-only elementary schools before arriving at the shabby facility reserved for blacks. The history of *Roberts v. Boston School*

---

30. Nell, quoted in Wesley, "Integration versus Separation," 210.

31. See ibid.; Browne, "To Defend Mr. Garrison"; and Donald M. Jacobs, "William Lloyd Garrison's *Liberator* and Boston's Blacks, 1830–1865," *New England Quarterly* 44 (June 1971): 259–77.

Committee has been ably recounted elsewhere, and so it suffices here to recall that Roberts's team of attorneys, the white Charles Sumner and black Robert Morris, saw the case go against them. In finding for the defendants, Justice Lemuel Shaw elucidated justifications for segregation identical to those set out by the U.S. Supreme Court in *Plessy v. Ferguson* nearly half a century later. Undeterred, Roberts, Nell, and a host of other leading black and white abolitionists, William Lloyd Garrison prominent among them, mobilized a statewide petition campaign directed toward the Massachusetts General Court. In 1855, after five years of arduous canvassing and agitation led more publicly by Nell than by Roberts, the legislature handed the abolitionists a stunning victory by outlawing segregated public education throughout the Commonwealth.[32]

A traditional reading of Roberts and Nell's success considers them to be the fortunate beneficiaries of circumstances far beyond their control. By the later 1840s, the political culture of Massachusetts had altered significantly in their favor. Prominent political figures such as Charles Francis Adams, Charles Allen, John Gorham Palfrey, Henry Wilson, and Charles Sumner voiced, as did Leonard Bacon, increasingly emphatic opposition to slaveholders' demands for unlimited access to western territories and to their runaway slaves. Deeply earnest, such politicians were now insisting that Massachusetts' colored citizens must be protected from "slave-catchers" and from the malevolent influence of slavery and caste oppression. Not radical abolitionists to be sure, men like Charles Sumner were, however, now willing to join Garrison, Wendell Phillips, and other powerful white immediatists in the state in extending their opposition to the "slave power" to include supporting an antisegregation campaign led by Massachusetts's free people of color. In short, one could argue that the impact in Massachusetts of the national political crisis over slavery secured Roberts and Nell's victory.[33]

---

32. For the fullest treatment of interracial coalition-building around school desegregation in Massachusetts and for the Roberts case itself, see Carleton Mabee, *The Non-Violent Abolitionists* (New York: Oxford University Press, 1970); Donald M. Jacobs, "The Nineteenth-Century Struggle over School Desegregation in Boston," *Journal of Negro Education* 39 (1970): 78–95; and Leonard Levy and Harlan B. Phillips, "The Roberts Case: Source of 'Separate but Equal' Doctrine," *American Historical Review* 62 (October 1950): 510–18.

33. See Jane H. Pease and William H. Pease, "Abolitionism and Confrontation in the 1850s," *Journal of American History* 17 (January 1972): 117–28; Carol Williams, "Active Vigilance Is the Price of Liberty: Black Self-Defense against Fugitive Slave Recapture and Kidnapping of Free Blacks," in

Certainly that was the view of those attending the celebratory gathering of black and white abolitionists at the Southac Street Church. More important, though, in everyone's mind was the leadership of William Nell. When master of ceremonies Wendell Phillips presented Nell with a gold watch and offered resolutions of thanks to him, the long, loud applause surely softened the resentments Nell had carried for better than twenty years. Phillips, who had himself written and spoken eloquently against school segregation, proceeded to credit Nell fully for creating the interracial coalition that had secured the victory: "We are greatly indebted to this young man we have met to honor; if Nell had not been the nucleus, there would have been no cause; if he had not gone up to the legislature, no one would have gone." [34]

While the importance of interracial coalition-building cannot be denied, Roberts and Nell's campaign would have been doomed from the outset had it not been rooted in New England's rich tradition of colored activism. Imperatives first established in James Easton's time and nurtured over three generations of struggle came as close as they ever would to being realized in the antebellum era in Massachusetts's decision in favor of school desegregation. Building on the limited successes of their forebears, black activists had become quite sophisticated in their approaches. Employing the law and politics in ways not possible in James Easton's day, they had shifted away from earlier attempts to promote incremental uplift through schooling and apprenticeships and adopted methods—attorneys, sustained petition campaigns, and interracial coalition building—that have characterized modern civil rights movements.

Undergirding all their means to achieve justice, from the postrevolutionary through the antebellum eras, was the colored community's same reflexive unwillingness to defer to white bigotry and to the supposed reality of race. The significance of the Negro College controversy, then, is not confined to the streets of New Haven in 1831, for over the

---

John R. McKivigan and Stanley Harold, eds., *Antislavery Violence: Sectional and Regional Conflict in Antebellum America* (Knoxville: University of Tennessee Press, 1999), 108–27; and Anne-Marie Taylor, *Young Charles Sumner and the Legacy of the American Enlightenment* (Amherst: University of Massachusetts Press, 2002).

34. Phillips is quoted and the occasion is described by Wesley in "Integration versus Separation," 213.

years, it continued to affect the thoughts and actions of those who had been involved as well as those whose lives the participants had touched. The central meaning of the controversy resides in the narratives of racial struggle (some of which have been traced here; others, like Simeon Jocelyn's ongoing service to his New Haven black congregation, have not) that began with the American Revolution and extended, uninterrupted, across the antebellum decades.

William Nell understood the matter precisely thus. In addition to battling segregation, he sought to recover American history as a multiethnic striving for racial equality that had its origins in the American Revolution. In 1855, the year that marked his victory for Massachusetts school desegregation, Nell's extraordinary *Colored Patriots of the American Revolution*, a work surveying all thirteen colonies, also appeared. The intellect whites had once acknowledged only to demean now shone forth in a pathbreaking history, one that has been consulted by historians ever since. Nell's detailed account of the Eastons, the period's most informative source on the family, treats the indigenous peoples like those from whom the Eastons were in part descended and who, like James Easton, had rallied to the patriot cause. Not only did Nell's magisterial study honor Benjamin Roberts and the Easton family, in other words, but it bespoke as well the author's devotion to an antiracist vision of the nation's history.[35]

Benjamin Roberts also understood the victory against school segregation as an extension of activist traditions he could trace back through his family to the Revolution. In 1870 he wrote an essay on the history of people of color in Massachusetts entitled "Our Progress in the Old Bay State," which appeared in the nationally circulated *New Era*, a newspaper edited by lifelong abolitionists. Roberts began by celebrating the egalitarian achievements of illustrious "colored patriots"—men like his grandfather, whom he named—who had responded as one people to the cause of independence. Roberts then chronicled the decline into racial tyranny that had defined the commonwealth from the 1820s into

---

35. William Cooper Nell, *Colored Patriots of the American Revolution* (Boston, 1855), 32–33, 67–71.

the 1850s, which, of course, had touched him personally. "Colorphobia deprived us of our common schools and many other privileges: we
were assailed in the streets . . . and it was a dark day for all of us." But
finally, thanks to the unremitting efforts of abolitionists, racial tyranny
had at last been put to rest. The legislative ban on segregation, he concluded, "was the greatest boon ever bestowed upon our people": "Our
children do not feel as their predecessors felt a thousand times when
passing the school house as *inferiors and outcasts.* To them, new ideas are
opened . . . and it will not be many years ere the full results will find our
successors in the full possession of positions of honor and emolument
and amply competent to cope with the most distinguished citizens of our
community. . . . Who among us can refrain from giving vent to highest
exhultation [*sic*] these remarkable events?"[36]

Even lacking the benefit of hindsight, one might question Roberts's
optimism. As we know all too well, Boston betrayed its promise and
became one of the North's most segregated, most racially polarized
cities. Still, Roberts's victory was real, and it was a crowning achievement in a long record of activism by New England's people of color. In
this context, and as both Nell and Roberts would have maintained, the
abortive 1831 New Haven Negro College project represented not failure
but, instead, a moment of crisis and regeneration in an extended, un-
avoidable struggle to achieve a level of equality that recognized only one
race, the human. Of all the conflicting narratives that emerged from the
unfortunate collapse of the college proposal, those presented by Nell and
Roberts recommend themselves as the most comprehensive, the most
instructive, and ultimately the most uplifting as well.

Acknowledgments

I wish to thank my insightful friend and generous critic John Stauffer
for suggestions that have improved this essay immeasurably. So have
the comments of John Howe, Lisa Norling, Jean O'Brien-Kehoe, Russ
Menard, and Kirsten Fischer of the University of Minnesota's History

---

36. Benjamin Roberts, "Our Progress in the Old Bay State," *New Era*, March 31, 1870, 415–92.

Workshop. Hilary Moss of Brandeis University graciously introduced me to her research on New Haven and provided invaluable information on James Easton. Special thanks to Lynn Rhoads, whose wise and gifted editing has improved this essay in ever so many ways. Over the years my steadfast friend and co-author George Price has generously shared with me his invaluable work on the Easton family. Without his collaboration, this essay would not have been possible.

Reconsidering the Abolitionists in an Age of Fundamentalist Politics

The era we refer to as the "Jacksonian Era" or the "Era of the Market Revolution" can just as accurately be termed the "Era of Bible Politics." As we know, people in the antebellum era quarreled incessantly over whether their nation ought to be refashioned as a "Christian Republic." Should the lives of Americans and the mandates of their institutions accord with sacred scripture? If your answer was yes, then (depending on chronology) mail on Sunday, the existence of Mormonism, and the issuance of liquor licenses must be prohibited. Masons must abolish their lodges. Catholic conspiracies must be exposed. Those complicit with chattel slavery must embrace "immediate emancipation" or the promise of colonization.

If you lived in the North, if these injunctions repelled you, and if you feared for the continuing separation of church and state, the Democratic Party beckoned. If these injunctions reinforced your conviction that Christian principles secured the nation's freedom, you likely favored the Whigs. But whichever your choice, the restless evangelicalism that continuously thrust these issues into politics was easy to identify. Like it or not, evangelicalism entwined itself in politics because of the activism it empowered, the morally engaged laity it inspired, the energetic voluntary associations it underwrote, and the bitter contention it provoked over its vision of a godly republic. And during the 1830s, throughout the North,

Originally published as "Reconsidering the Abolitionists in an Age of Fundamentalist Politics," *Journal of the Early Republic* 26 (Spring 2006): 3–31. Reprinted with permission.

it became clear that many evangelicals "voted as they prayed, and prayed as they voted."[1]

Consider for a moment our own time. As historians, what do we make of antebellum religious activists while today membership in fundamentalist churches mushrooms and evangelical voters help reelect a self-proclaimed "born again" President? Politicians with 90 percent positive ratings from the Christian Coalition shape policy on subjects ranging from stem-cell research to foreign affairs. With a fervor matching the civil rights movement of the 1960s, antiabortion crusaders declare themselves the "new abolitionists." And while public education retrenches, Bible-based academies flourish. If you embrace these developments, the Republican Party beckons. If they repel you, you're either a Democrat or you're "alienated" or you're both. In any case, our age of "Bible politics" is a time if ever there was one when historians ought to "take religion seriously."

The balance of this essay builds on this point by suggesting how our current turn to "Bible politics" might allow us to develop clearer understandings of the political role of religious activism in the antebellum era. Today's activists of the religious right exercise political agency by addressing what they identify as the most compelling moral questions of our time. For whatever reasons, millions of voters and many influential politicians respond favorably and politics itself is changed. Candidates are elected and laws are passed. The proof of having exercised political agency is in these tangible political results.

Since slavery generated so many of the most compelling moral questions of the antebellum age, one might then ask this question: What

---

1. In developing the theme of praying and voting, I am indebted to the starting point provided in John R. McKivigan, "Vote as You Pray and Pray as You Vote: Church-Oriented Abolitionism and Antislavery Politics," in Alan Kraut, ed., *Crusaders and Compromisers: Essays on the Relationship of the Antislavery Struggle to the Antebellum Party System* (Westport, CT: Greenwood, 1983), 179–204. On relationships between political issues and Yankee evangelical piety, see Bertram Wyatt-Brown, "Prelude to Abolitionism: Sabbatarian Politics and the Rise of the Second Party System," *Journal of American History* 58 (Sept. 1971): 316–41; Paul Johnson, *A Shopkeeper's Millennium: Society and Revivals in Rochester, New York, 1815–1837* (New York: Hill & Wang, 1978); Paul Goodman, *Towards a Christian Republic: Antimasonry and the Great Transition in New England, 1826–1836* (New York: Oxford University Press, 1988); Harry Watson, *Liberty and Power: The Politics of Jacksonian America* (New York: Hill & Wang, 1990) 55–57, 178–79, 180–82, 222–23; and Robert H. Abzug, *Cosmos Crumbling: American Reform and the Religious Imagination* (New York: Oxford University Press, 1994), 30–128.

political leverage, if any, did the abolitionist movement exercise as the nation moved closer to Civil War?

Political history yields largely negative answers. Historians do grant that slaveholders overreacted to the abolitionists by defending their institution. But this seems the opposite of agency. The goal of the abolitionists, after all, was to see slavery eliminated, not more strenuously defended. Historians who weigh the importance of nativism, temperance, and Free-Soil republicanism in the political realignment of the 1850s cite no reasons to emphasize the importance of the abolitionists. Historians of ideology who distinguish between racist politicians opposed to an expanding "slave power" and egalitarian reformers seeking an end to slavery do highlight the abolitionists, but only to underline their political marginality. For these scholars, Abraham Lincoln's denial of slavery's constitutional right to expand with new territories, not Fredrick Douglass's calls for emancipation, defined the Republicans' position. There are, to be sure, historians who continue to follow Gilbert Hobbs Barnes's notion of abolitionism's "broadening impulse" by tracing antislavery politics in the 1840s and 1850s to immediatist origins. But even these scholars leave the abolitionists as a movement behind as their examinations move into the mid-1840s when most of the Liberty Party merged with the Free-Soilers.[2]

Are the many scholars who are creating today's renaissance in abolitionist studies concerned about their subjects' apparent irrelevance to political historians? Does it matter to them that no one representing the North in the halls of power seemed to have been responding directly to the abolitionists? Apparently not.

Instead, these scholars explain abolitionist agency without reference

---

2. Michael F. Holt, *The Political Crisis of the 1850s* (New York: Wiley, 1978); John Ashworth, *Slavery, Capitalism, and Politics in the Antebellum Republic*, vol. 1, *Commerce and Compromise, 1820–1850* (Cambridge: Cambridge University Press, 1995); David Potter, *The Impending Crisis, 1848–1861* (New York: Harper & Row, 1976); Eric Foner, *Free Soil, Free Labor, Free Men: The Ideology of the Republican Party before the Civil War* (New York: Columbia University Press, 1970); Nicole Etcheson, *Bleeding Kansas: Contested Liberty in the Civil War Era* (Lawrence: University of Kansas Press, 2004); Lary Gara, "Slavery and the 'Slave Power': A Crucial Distinction," *Civil War History* 15 (Mar. 1969): 4–18; Gilbert Hobbs Barnes, *The Antislavery Impulse, 1830–1844* (New York: Appleton-Century, 1936), 191–97; Merton Dillon, *The Abolitionists: The Growth of a Dissenting Minority* (DeKalb: Northern Illinois University Press, 1974); Richard H. Sewell, *Ballots for Freedom: Antislavery Politics in the United States, 1837–1860* (New York: Oxford University Press, 1976).

to a demonstrable capacity to shape formal politics. This disinterest in tangible political results would hardly satisfy the Christian Coalition. Yet it does lead historians of the abolitionists to emphasize two other forms of agency, each important in its own right. Agency constitutes, first, the personally empowering insights, motivations, and self-understandings that abolitionists drew from participation in their visionary causes. It involves, second, the crucial ideological process of projecting dissenting convictions directly into an otherwise racist and proslavery "public sphere."

As a result, our current renaissance of abolitionist scholarship has deeply illuminated the movement's beliefs, strategies, tactics, and cultural productions. But it has not demonstrated its wider political impact. It has brilliantly charted the work of its contending factions, and the ideas, arguments, and projects of its African American and female participants, but it has not explained how their interventions might actually have changed Northern politics.[3]

In short, we seem to be left with these questions: What did all that agitation finally amount to in direct political terms within the free states—all those speeches, conventions, novels, narratives, newspapers, petitions, woodcuts, banners, and handbills? Did those in power representing the North and the voters who put them there take the abolitionists seriously enough to respond with something other than hostile indifference?

Abolitionist scholarship usually answers yes, but only by claiming in the most general way that the movement must have made a difference—somehow. But when political historians press these questions by asking for specifics, their findings render an unambiguous no. The indexes of Michael Morrison's and William Gienapp's recent accounts of sectional

---

3. Claims made in this paragraph and the two preceding it are reflected in several outstanding studies of abolitionism. See, for example, Patrick Rael, *Black Identity and Black Protest in the Antebellum North* (Chapel Hill: University of North Carolina Press, 2002); Julie Roy Jeffrey, *The Great Silent Army of Abolitionism: Ordinary Women in the Antislavery Movement* (Chapel Hill: University of North Carolina Press, 1998); James Oliver Horton and Lois Horton, *In Hope of Liberty: Culture, Community, and Protest among Northern Free Blacks, 1700–1860* (New York: Oxford University Press, 1996); Richard S. Newman, *The Transformation of American Abolitionism: Fighting Slavery in the Early Republic* (Chapel Hill: University of North Carolina Press, 2002); Lawrence J. Friedman, *Gregarious Saints: Self and Community in Abolitionism, 1830–1870* (Cambridge: Cambridge University Press, 1982); and Jean Fagan-Yellin, *Women and Sisters: The Abolitionist Feminists and American Culture* (New Haven: Yale University Press, 1989).

politics and the coming of the Civil War contain no entries for the abolitionists. Michael Holt's twelve-hundred-plus-page *Rise and Fall of the American Whig Party* gives equal attention in its index to the subject of "redistricting in Alabama" as it does to the "abolitionist movement."[4]

The point is not that either abolitionist studies or political history is "right" or "wrong." Instead it is to observe that the two fields have lost contact with each other. To read in them simultaneously is to slip back and forth between alternate universes. So it seems worthwhile to work against historiographical fragmentation by considering the moral challenge of abolitionism as one that extended directly into Northern politics. The remainder of this essay returns to the theme of "Bible Politics" and to the opportunity that our fundamentalist-driven moment gives us to take religion seriously. Along the way we may discover that abolitionists did exercise important agency in two-party politics within the free states but that they did so in ways that have eluded historians and bear little resemblance to today's "born-again" activists.

It is crucial to establish just how radically different the abolitionists were from most of today's conservative evangelicals. From the 1830s on, most black and white abolitionists developed a postmillennial vision of their Christian lives and duties. As they understood him, Christ is a closely abiding earthly presence with all who receive him, and he invites us to work with him to bring the world into harmony with God's designs—freeing the South's slaves, for instance.[5]

Today, in sharpest contrast, Protestant fundamentalists typically embrace premillennialism. In this vision, Christ will return to reign as prophesied only after the world has undergone terrible tribulation—the rule of the antichrist and the redemptive separation of the saved from the damned. In the meantime, Christians must live out in politics their conformity to literalist understandings of scripture. They must oppose

---

4. Michael A. Morrison, *Slavery and the American West: The Eclipse of Manifest Destiny and the Coming of the Civil War* (Chapel Hill: University of North Carolina Press, 1997); William Gienapp, *The Origins of the Republican Party, 1852–1856* (New York: Oxford University Press, 1987); Michael F. Holt, *The Rise and Fall of the American Whig Party: Jacksonian Politics and the Onset of the Civil War* (New York: Oxford University Press, 1999), 1203.

5. Abzug, *Cosmos Crumbling*, 11–56; David Brion Davis, *Slavery and Human Progress* (New York: Oxford University Press, 1984), 107–53, 231–59.

gay rights, abortion, evolution, and so forth while advocating the world over for who share their creeds.[6]

Both visions contain compelling critiques of society's ills. Both express encompassing desires to endow life with sacred meanings and redemptive experiences. Both convey energizing calls for individual activism. Both make fervent appeals to an angry God. Both place the highest premium on moral suasion to convert others. But these similarities, which are common to many religious movements besides evangelical Protestantism, end here.

The abolitionist vision offers extraordinarily hopeful views of our capacities to steer the future toward God's intended goals. Therefore, as we have always known, the movement was profoundly antiauthoritarian. In Robert Abzug's aptly borrowed phrase from Max Weber, its practitioners were "religious virtuosos." They shattered religious orthodoxies time and again by improvising still more expansive ways of enacting God's will in everyday life.[7]

By contrast, contemporary fundamentalists can seem profoundly pessimistic to those outside their circle. In their own hearts and minds, however, theirs too is a faith of unconquerable hope. Though there is nothing we sin-plagued people can do to arrest the future's spiral into perdition, redemption will prevail with Christ's Second Coming. In the meantime, biblically sanctioned literalism determines the conduct of the saved in families, in churches, in the workplace, in voluntary associations, and in one's political choices. Highly motivated religious activists abound. Spiritual originality does not. Obedience rules, not "virtuosity." Authority inspires, not spontaneity.[8]

Only in the lower South can one find an antebellum parallel to today's politicized form of religious authoritarianism. As Stephanie McCurry

---

6. Ernest Sandeen, *The Roots of Fundamentalism: British and American Millenarianism, 1800–1930* (Chicago: University of Chicago Press, 1970), 103–269. Bruce David Forbes and Jeanne Halgren Kilde, *Rapture, Revelation, and the End Times: Exploring the "Left Behind" Series* (New York: Palgrave Macmillan, 2004) documents and analyzes the pervasive influence of premillenialism in contemporary religious culture.

7. Abzug, *Cosmos Crumbling*, 31–33.

8. Sandeen, *Roots of Fundamentalism*, 233–69; John McArthur, *Hard to Believe: The High Cost and Infinite Value of Following Jesus* (Chicago: Moody Press, 2002), is representative of a large number of contemporary titles by fundamentalist ministers and social activists stressing these themes. See generally the published writings of James Dobson, Pat Robertson, and Gary Bauer for other examples.

and Christine Heyrman have both demonstrated, the explosion of evangelical revivalism that swept through that region on the eve of the Civil War affirmed as sacred the patriarchal prerogatives of white yeomen and planters to rule over their "dependents." Its demands were for the continuing subjugation of slaves and women and for secession, not for generalized Christian liberation. Its methods included seizing control of state and local politics and encouraging the forcible silencing of dissenters. The gulf between this variety of evangelical politics and the kind espoused by the abolitionists could hardly be wider.[9]

This summary, then, makes two suggestions. First, contemporary fundamentalists ought to think again, hard, before claiming the abolitionists as their historical ancestors. Standards of historical accuracy confirm such claims as specious. Second, today's religious right finds political agency a straightforward exercise. For abolitionists it was not. Obedient to established authority, fundamentalist activists today embrace prevailing governance in order to conform it to God's will by mobilizing voters, winning elections, discouraging dissent, and passing laws.

Abolitionist "virtuosos," by contrast, felt driven to question the legitimacy of conventional politics itself and to encourage freedom of conscience. Why? In general, it was because politics seemed to these anti-institutional Christians to be mired in unholy coercion and expedience. But more specifically it was also because abolitionists concluded in the later 1830s that governance on all levels was uniformly hostile to their crusade.

For this basic reason, the political consequences of the abolitionists' demand for abolishing slavery and of equivalent demands today (say, outlawing abortion) are stunningly unalike. Antiabortion activists automatically generate immense political partisanship in response to their agitation. This is precisely what today's parties thrive on in order to compete against each other, build centers of power, and forward legislative agendas. As "pro-choice" Democrats contend against "anti-choice" Republicans, political agency multiplies with rallies, campaign contribu-

---

9. Stephanie McCurry, *Masters of Small Worlds: Yeoman Households, Gender Relations, and the Political Culture of the Antebellum South Carolina Low Country* (New York: Oxford University Press, 1995); Christine Leigh Heyrman, *Southern Cross: The Beginnings of the Bible Belt* (New York: Oxford University Press, 1997), 117–261.

tions, blogs, electronic petitions, and voting. Women and people of color in all parts of the country participate on all sides.

By contrast, in the antebellum free states, women and black abolitionists utterly defied prevailing norms simply by participating in their own movement. Meanwhile, the movement itself demanded the instant liberation of the nation's second largest capital investment—three million enslaved members of a despised race. Little wonder that so exceptionally subversive a crusade did not prompt competitive divisions pro and con between national parties. Instead it generated enormous opposition from nearly all sectors of white society. The dismal results were measured in the 1830s by gag rules passed, mailbags ransacked, printing presses vandalized, suspected slave rebels executed, "colored schools" mobbed, Northern black neighborhoods reduced to ashes, and abolitionists denounced from pulpits.[10]

In the meantime, what of that influential sector of the Northern electorate that was voting as it prayed and praying as it voted throughout the 1830s? As Richard Carwardine and Daniel Walker Howe have shown, these evangelical voters held religious and social values that gave them much in common with the abolitionists. Both groups entertained postmillennial visions that fired their activism and directed their voluntary associations. Both charged Masons, Catholics, liquor distillers, wildcat bankers, and Indian removers as well as slaveholders with sponsoring immorality. Both relied heavily on "female influence" and the day-to-day work of women to forward their religious causes.[11]

So great were the commonalities between these two groups that the abolitionists at first expected these Northern evangelicals to flock to their crusade. But for all their piety, these were not religious virtuosos. When it came to politics, they prized well-organized moral renovation, not

---

10. For abolitionism's spiritual and intellectual opposition to institutional authority, consult Lewis Perry, *Radical Abolitionism: Anarchy and the Government of God in Antislavery Thought* (Ithaca: Cornell University Press, 1973). For a sense of the obvious contrasts to be drawn between the political circumstances of evangelical activists today and those of the abolitionist movement, see James Brewer Stewart, "The Emergence of Racial Modernity and the Rise of the White North, 1790–1840," *Journal of the Early Republic* 18 (Summer 1998): 181–217, 233–36.

11. Richard J. Carwardine, *Evangelicals and Politics in Antebellum America* (Knoxville: University of Tennessee Press, 1997); Daniel Walker Howe, *The Political Culture of the American Whigs* (Chicago: University of Chicago Press, 1979); Daniel Walker Howe, "The Evangelical Movement and Political Culture in the North during the Second Party System," *Journal of American History* 77 (Mar. 1991): 1216–39.

the impulse of moral revolution. Their opposition to slavery led them to colonization, or to tortured hand wringing, not to immediatism. Their devotion to scripture left them appalled by Garrisonian heresies and willing to expel abolitionists from their churches. Sharing much with the abolitionists culturally but fearful of immediatism, they headed in droves into the Whigs, the party that appealed to their full range of moral and spiritual concerns.[12]

By 1840, their migration was complete. Many Northern evangelical voters now fused their opposition to slavery with a still broader opposition to everything for which the secular Jacksonians were alleged to have stood. While log cabins and hard cider attracted workaday laborers and artisans, Whig "Bible politics" spoke powerfully to spiritually "uplifted" Northerners who voted as they prayed and prayed as they voted. Reflecting on this trend, the Oberlin immediatist Henry B. Stanton reported ruefully during the elections of 1840: "49/50ths of our friends are determined to wade to their armpits in molten lava to drive Van Buren from power." Without any apparent sense of inconsistency, such evangelicals rallied behind the slaveholding William Henry Harrison for President in 1840, not the abolitionist candidate James G. Birney, who received a scant seven thousand votes.[13]

Meanwhile, as the 1840s opened, the abolitionists were adopting new political approaches of their own. Responding to the wholesale repression of their crusade, they concluded that the white South was impervious to "conversion." As a result, they divided into several factions that disagreed over how to transform governance in what they now condemned as a profoundly un-Christian nation, North no less than South. Female activists emulated the Grimke sisters by participating in "promiscuous assemblies." They also addressed politicians directly through petitions

12. Model portraits of this Whig persuasion are developed in Hugh Davis, *Leonard Bacon: New England Reformer and Antislavery Moderate* (Baton Rouge: Louisiana State University Press, 1998); and William C. McLoughlin, *The Meaning of Henry Ward Beecher: An Essay on the Shifting Values of Mid-Victorian America* (New York: Harper & Row, 1970). See also George M. Marsden, *The Evangelical Mind and the New School Presbyterian Experience: A Case Study of Thought and Theology in Nineteenth Century America* (New Haven: Yale University Press, 1970); and Howe, *Political Culture*, 1–42, 69–122.

13. Henry Brewster Stanton to James G. Birney, Mar. 21, 1839, in Dwight L. Dumond, ed., *The Letters of James Gillespie Birney, 1831–1851*, 2 vols. (New York: Appleton-Century-Crofts, 1938), 1:531–32.

and published appeals. Some linked God's will and slave emancipation with women's rights. Seeking the "moral revolutionizing" of politics, Garrison and other nonresistants leveled novel religious arguments against participation in secular government itself, voting included. Still others saw in the Liberty Party the prospect of fulfilling God's will at the ballot box. Black activists revivified their own independent movements and organizations. Through all these varied approaches, abolitionists now began acting as political as well as religious virtuosos. This, in turn began involving them with the Northern Whig Party.[14]

To understand how this process unfolded, let us once more contrast antebellum "Bible politics" with "Bible politics" today. Two points stand out. First, today's conservative evangelicals become active Republicans in order to bend the party to their demands. Back in the 1830s and 1840s, abolitionists could not have cared less about controlling any political party, Whigs included. Instead, as "passionate outsiders" (to borrow John Stauffer's felicitous term), they worked to morally transform the entire political system to accord with Christ's teachings, not turn themselves into an existing party's electoral "base." Once more, the differences between an Angelina Grimke and, say, a Pat Robertson could hardly be clearer.[15]

Second, and just as important, the antebellum Whig Party and today's Republican Party display entirely different structures. As a result, their responses to religious activism could not be less alike. Republicans today satisfy their evangelical "base" by demanding virtual unanimity on questions such as abortion and gay rights. Conformity defines spiritual sanctity and political loyalty. Whigs, in starkest contrast, agreed to disagree about slavery during the 1840s. A decentralized party structure encouraged precisely such regional variation. In the South, Whigs spoke as slavery's avid protectors. In the free states they criticized slavery, advocated "Northern rights," and sometimes defended the abolitionists. Why? Because this was a highly effective way for Whigs to win elections in both sections by espousing economic nationalism while presenting

14. For a broad overview of these developments, see James Brewer Stewart, *Holy Warriors: The Abolitionists and American Slavery* (New York: Hill & Wang, 1996), 75–96.

15. John Stauffer, *Black Hearts of Men: The Radical Abolitionists and the Transformation of Race* (Cambridge: Harvard University Press, 2002), 15–16, 69–70, 96–97.

their party as a compelling regional alternative to the Democrats on slavery questions. "From its birth," Michael Holt reminds us, "the Whig party could and did survive a fundamental division on the slavery question." Similarly, a post–World War II Democratic Party bent on preserving New Deal liberalism found room for segregationists such as Richard Russell and for African American militants like Adam Clayton Powell.[16]

As the 1840s opened, the political situation confronting the abolitionists looked something like this. Agreeing across the Mason-Dixon Line to disagree about slavery, pious Whigs fastened on the Democrats as their crucial negative reference group—a "Bible politician's" rogues' gallery of liquor peddlers, gamblers, Catholics, antievangelicals, freethinkers, Indian killers, duelists, slave drivers, stock-jobbers, and so forth. In the free states, however, there was also a significant "affirmative reference group" for Whigs to interact with as they battled the Democrats—the abolitionists.

Affinities originated in the evangelical religious culture shared by both groups. Affinities blossomed in the "Bible politics" constituencies for whose attentions both groups competed. Northern Whigs knew that victory over the Democrats depended on retaining the support of these important evangelical voters, especially when the possibility of Texas annexation and war with Mexico raised the issue of slavery's expansion. Whatever their convictions regarding the "sin of slavery," Northern Whig leaders feared that abolitionist opposition would work to the advantage of the Democrats by drawing their evangelical supporters away to the Liberty Party in 1844 and to the Free-Soil Party in 1848. Firm ideological distinctions between Whigs and abolitionists began to blur as often as they sharpened as they battled against each other for the support of Northern evangelicals. As Stanley Elkins correctly explained so long ago, antislavery Whigs were now becoming not the abolitionists' formal converts but instead their ideologically more moderate "fellow travelers."[17]

---

16. Quotation from Holt, *Political Crisis of the 1850s*, 30. See also William J. Cooper Jr., *The South and the Politics of Slavery, 1828–1856* (Baton Rouge: Louisiana State University Press, 1978).

17. Alan Kraut, "Partisanship and Principles: The Liberty Party in Antebellum Political Culture," in Kraut, *Crusaders and Compromisers*, 71–100; Louis S. Gerteis, *Morality and Utility in Antislavery Reform* (Chapel Hill: University of North Carolina Press, 1987), 86–129; James Brewer Stewart, *Joshua R. Giddings and the Tactics of Radical Politics* (Cleveland: Press of Case Western Reserve University, 1970), 84–122; Stephen E. Maizlish, *The Triumph of Sectionalism: The Transformation of*

Beautifully crafted state and regional studies show exactly where these Whig–abolitionist codependencies flourished. Together these locations constituted a Northern "Bible Belt" where abolitionist political agency rooted itself—Ohio's Western Reserve and Firelands districts, New York State's Burned-Over District, Indiana's "Burned District," Lower Michigan's southeastern and central counties, Massachusetts's western counties and coastal towns, districts in Vermont within the Connecticut River Valley, and small towns scattered across southern Maine, regions far removed from major urban centers such as New York City, Philadelphia, and Boston where the proslavery "cotton" wing of the Northern Whig Party predominated. Together they constituted a broad band of deep evangelical belief, vibrant social activism, and "conscience" Whig loyalty that spanned the free states from the Atlantic to the Mississippi.

In all of these places, canals, turnpikes, toll roads, and waterborne shipping fostered booming cash crop agriculture, small town commercial enterprise, and expanding urban markets. Proliferating newspapers created sophisticated networks of communication that insured citizens' heightened involvement in national affairs. So did large concentrations of public schools, private academies, and voluntary associations led by women as well as by men. In short, the social and economic character of these regions harmonized perfectly with Whig promises of internal improvements, high tariffs, reliable banking, evangelical values, and "moral uplift." Voters in these strongholds of piety exercised a potent influence over the fate of the party at election time, and Whig politicians did all they could to energize this vital evangelical "base."[18]

Ohio Politics, 1844–1856 (Kent, OH: Kent State University Press, 1983); Joseph G. Rayback, *Free Soil: The Election of 1848* (Lexington: University of Kentucky Press, 1970), 201–59; Reinhard Johnson, "The Liberty Party, 1840–1848: Antislavery Third Party Politics in the United States" (unpublished manuscript in the author's possession), chaps. 2–6; Fredrick Blue, *The Free Soilers: Third Party Politics, 1848–1854* (Urbana: University of Illinois Press, 1973); Stanley Elkins, *Slavery: A Problem in American Institutional and Intellectual Life* (Chicago: University of Chicago Press, 1963), 185–89.

18. This paragraph and the one preceding it are developed from Whitney Cross, *The Burned-Over District: A Social and Intellectual History of Enthusiastic Religion in Western New York* (Ithaca: Cornell University Press, 1950); John L. Brooke, *The Heart of the Commonwealth: Social and Political Culture in Worcester, Massachusetts, 1713–1861* (New York: Oxford University Press, 1989); Ronald Formisano, *The Transformation of Political Culture: Massachusetts Parties, 1790s–1840s* (New York: Oxford University Press, 1983); Johnson, *Shopkeeper's Millennium*; John W. Quist, *Restless Visionaries: The Social Roots of Antebellum Reform in Alabama and Michigan* (Baton Rouge: Louisiana State University Press, 1998); David M. Ludlum, *Social Ferment in Vermont, 1791–1850* (New York: Columbia University Press, 1939); Randolph A. Roth, *The Democratic Dilemma: Religion, Reform*

In this context "Bible Belt" Whigs and abolitionists became increasingly involved with one another once "religious virtuosos" turned their hands to local politics. Here, politically, is where all those speeches, conventions, narratives, newspapers, petitions, woodcuts, racial "uplift" projects, banners, and handbills had their greatest significance. Here also is where black and female abolitionist activists exercised their most immediate political impact. Maintaining annual cycles of repeating activism, abolitionists created rich local environments of radical opposition to slavery that no Whig politician in the North's "Bible Belt" could safely ignore.

While Whigs rolled up majorities, charismatic Garrisonian "headliners" like Abby Kelley Foster and Wendell Phillips energized the "faithful" by keynoting annual meetings, condemning voting, and calling Whig politicians to account. Liberty Party activists founded newspapers and recruited competitive candidates. They built alliances with evangelical congregations involving women as well as men. They perfected strategies designed to draw off Whig supporters. Abolitionist women developed their roles further still when supplying day-to-day leadership in a multiplying succession of meetings, fairs, reading groups, and petition drives. Blacks redefined the politics of race by challenging discrimination, fugitive slave laws, and the moral standing of overbearing whites—overbearing white abolitionists and politicians included. As abolitionist politics intensified and local Whigs prepared for the next elections, the two groups treated each other as codependents so often do when quarreling over shared values and living space—that is, with a volatile mixture of enablement and abuse.[19]

---

and the Social Order in the Connecticut River Valley of Vermont, 1791–1850 (New York,: Cabridge University Press, 1987); Patrick Riddleberger, *George Washington Julian: A Study in Nineteenth Century Politics and Reform* (Indianapolis: Indiana Historical Bureau, 1966), 1–45; Donald Martin Bluestone, "Steamboats, Sewing Machines, and Bibles: The Roots of Antislavery in Illinois and the Old Northwest" (Ph.D. diss., University of Wisconsin, Madison, 1973); Stewart, *Joshua R. Giddings.*

19. One develops a clear sense of these political dynamics by reading widely in local antislavery newspapers, in a variety of regional and local studies of abolitionism, and in biographies of individual abolitionists. Titles cited in the preceding footnote are all pertinent in this respect. In addition, valuable and representative works include Douglas M. Strong, *Perfectionist Politics: Abolitionism and the Religious Tensions of American Democracy* (Syracuse: Syracuse University Press, 1999); Deborah Bingham Van Broekhoven, *The Devotion of These Women: Rhode Island in the Antislavery Network* (Amherst: University of Massachusetts Press, 2002); Nancy Hewitt, *Women's Activism and Social Change: Rochester, New York, 1822–1872* (Ithaca: Cornell University Press, 1984); Stacey M. Robertson, *Parker Pillsbury: Radical Abolitionists, Male Feminist* (Ithaca: Cornell University Press,

On the enabling side of the equation the two groups applied the "fellow traveler principle" in the 1840s to collaborate on a number of abolitionist-initiated campaigns. A listing of these reveals just how often Northern Whigs acted openly as the abolitionists' allies. In Massachusetts, "conscience" Whigs supported the struggles of black and white activists that overturned antimiscegenation laws, school segregation, and segregation of public transportation. In New York State, Ohio, Pennsylvania, and Michigan, Whigs campaigned in favor of personal liberty laws, and for unsuccessful efforts by African American abolitionists to repeal restrictions on black male suffrage. (Little wonder that enfranchised African Americans voted overwhelmingly Whig!) And in the U.S. Congress, it was Whig representatives from "Bible Belt" districts who most persistently put forward antislavery petitions (including those from women and blacks)—who most disruptively protested against the gag rule, the internal slave trade, and slavery in the District of Columbia, and who most stridently protested against slavery's expansion.[20]

On the abusive end of this relationship each side exploited the other shamelessly in order to amplify the political impact of its opposition to slavery. Abolitionists of every persuasion excoriated Whigs as hypocrites for supporting slaveholding candidates. They called on voters to distain this "slave-ridden" party. Vote instead for true "Bible politics," they urged, that is, for the Liberty Party. Or, insisted the Garrisonians, do not vote at all. Whigs had reasons aplenty for replying harshly as they sought to prevent critical defections to antislavery third parties. They took strong antislavery positions and appealed that pious voters reject "one idea-ed abolitionism" as a gross impracticality. They lashed out against third-party activists as tools of the slave-ridden Jacksonians. But

2000), esp. 63–91; Stewart, *Joshua R. Giddings*; Milton Sernett, *North Star Country: Upstate New York and the Crusade for African American Freedom* (Syracuse: Syracuse University Press, 2002); Bertram Wyatt-Brown, *Lewis Tappan and the Evangelical War against Slavery* (Cleveland: Press of Case Western Reserve University, 1969), 269–327; Bruce Laurie *Beyond Garrison: Antislavery and Social Reform* (Cambridge: Cambridge University Press, 2005).

20. For a general overview of these trends and tendencies, consult Stewart, *Holy Warriors*, chaps. 5 and 6 and their accompanying bibliography. For specifics, see Jane H. and William H. Pease, *They Who Would Be Free: Blacks' Search for Freedom, 1830–1861* (New York: Athenaeum, 1974), 173–205.

whatever the indictment, whoever the target, abolitionists expanded their political agency whenever they inspired Northern Whigs to campaign with heightened urgency against slavery.[21]

The extent to which Northern Whigs engaged in this "fellow traveling" out of high moral conviction rather than cold calculation can never be measured. Clearly there was mixture of both. William H. Seward, who knew the "Burned-Over District" as well as anyone, sensed the vitality of moral principles when writing of proposals for Texas annexation. "The reckless folly of the Administration and the unprincipled adoption of it by our opponents have loosed our tongue stays," he concluded. "Slavery is henceforth and forever one of the elements of political action in the republic. The ground the public mind has traveled cannot be retraced."[22]

The thoughts of one high-ranking Whig politician, however, make plain that calculation should never be underestimated. In the heat of the 1844 presidential campaign, this strategist, James A. Briggs, chair of the Ohio Whig Central Committee, advised as follows in a confidential letter: Congressman Joshua Giddings from the Western Reserve portion of the "Bible Belt" must be supported in his reelection bid and encouraged to speak his full mind on questions of slavery when campaigning across the state for Henry Clay. This, Briggs well knew, was the same Giddings who defended the rights of slaves to rise against their masters, who ferociously defied the gag rule, whose daughters counted themselves as Garrisonian feminists, who openly aided fugitives, and who rose in the House at the slightest provocation to condemn slaveholding as a moral abomination. "It would give us the abolitionist vote of the district," Briggs explained, "and exert a good influence throughout the state by out trumping the [abolitionist] third party ultras. . . . Whigs make no sacrifice of principle or measure as Mr. G. is a Whig . . . who will do us most good on the stump."[23]

As Briggs's remarks make clear, dedicated abolitionists active in the

---

21. These electoral tactics are particularly well discussed in Sewell, *Ballots for Freedom*, 80–201.

22. William Seward to Edward A. Stanbury, Sept. 2, 1844, quoted in Glyndon Van Deusen, *William Henry Seward* (New York: Oxford University Press, 1967), 103.

23. James A. Briggs to Oran Follett, July 26, 1843, Oran Follett Papers, Cincinnati Historical Society, Cincinnati.

Whigs' evangelical base were now exerting a substantial influence on his party. This, by any measure, amounted to political agency. But it is equally obvious that the strategy-conscious Briggs harbored no worries. As he saw it, unleashing the "firebrand" Giddings and others like him would neither divide his party along North–South lines nor jeopardize the institution of slavery.

To explain his confidence we need only recall the Whigs' continuing agreement to disagree about slavery issues. In 1844, Whigs both North and South had skirted the issue of slavery's expansion by opposing further territorial acquisitions. In 1848 Southern Whigs claimed that Zachary Taylor despised the Wilmot Proviso. If elected, he would successfully oppose it. Northern Whigs guaranteed that the moment that Congress passed the Proviso, Taylor would sign it.[24]

The strategy that Briggs was recommending had important consequences for his party. In the short term, the more abolitionists engaged Northern Whigs as "fellow travelers" and competed against them at the polls, the more deeply defined by antislavery the Northern Whigs themselves became. The more intensely Northern Whigs promoted antislavery to their evangelical base, the more effectively they campaigned against the Democrats. Throughout the 1840s, the vast majority of free-state evangelicals remained convinced that the Whig Party represented the full range of their moral concerns—concerns about temperance, banking, land policy, Catholicism, and immigration, just as always—but also their increasingly deep and urgent concern about slavery's place in the nation's future.

In this manner, Northern Whigs presented their party to evangelicals as a bulwark of antislavery. It was a strategy that helped elect General Taylor while also yielding impressive state-level victories. As Jonathan Earle makes clear, the Free-Soil Party in 1848 triumphed more often in districts dominated by antislavery Democrats hostile to "Bible politics" than in the evangelical Whig "Bible Belt" where abolitionism flourished. To outward appearances, the antislavery stimulus supplied by the abolitionists actually helped to make the Whig Party stronger. Little wonder

---

24. Holt, *Political Crisis of the 1850s*, 63.

that immediatists so bitterly criticized the Whigs for stealing their audiences and watering down their doctrines.[25]

Yet the Whig's short-term strength led to deeper weakness. Scholars disagree about exactly what led to the party's collapse, but most do agree that the Whig Party faltered in the 1850 once it abruptly broke faith with its Northern constituents on the many issues it had always championed. Slavery questions ranked high among these. When raw sectional conflict in Washington over slavery's expansion finally undermined the party's agreement to disagree across the Mason-Dixon Line, Northern Whig leaders implicated themselves in the 1850 compromises. To the dismay of their Northern evangelical constituents, "doughfaced" Whigs now spoke for a party that suddenly supported a harsh new Fugitive Slave Law, the suppression of abolitionist agitation, the possibility of slavery's extension into the Nevada Territories, and an end to all political discussions of slavery.

It amounted to a wrenching reversal of field. A decade of abolitionist agitation had led many evangelical Northern Whigs to expect unshakeable antislavery from their party—that was certainly what party leaders had encouraged them to believe. In the disturbing aftermath of the compromises, the lingering impact of abolitionist political agency could now be felt as alarming numbers of disillusioned Northern Whigs stayed home on election days.[26]

Powerful issues in addition to the party's shifting stance on slavery explain the Whigs' slow demise in the early 1850s. The Northern Whig retreat from antislavery and the continuing impact of abolitionist political agency can only be partially credited with these results. As several historians have emphasized, Whigs suddenly began looking strikingly like Democrats on other crucial issues in addition to slavery. A wave of German immigrants representing a huge new pool of uncommitted voters induced Whig leaders to suppress their traditional opposition to alcohol, immigrants, and Catholics. A booming economy took the edge

---

25. Jonathan H. Earle, *Jacksonian Antislavery and the Politics of Free Soil, 1824–1854* (Chapel Hill: University of North Carolina Press, 2004), 169–80.

26. Gienapp, *Origins of the Republican Party*, 1–67; Holt, *Political Crisis of the 1850s*, 101–38.

off traditional Whig issues such as tariff and banking reform. Many voters now discerned "not a dime's worth of difference" between Whigs and Democrats on any of the familiar issues. In the view of many evangelical Northerners the "turncoat" Whigs had betrayed them, not just on the slavery question, but on every moral issue for which the party had always stood.[27]

As David Brion Davis and Leonard L. Richards have demonstrated, fears of conspiratorial subversion had always played powerful roles in shaping antebellum political ideologies. Now, in the early 1850s, these fears coalesced into a potent antiparty spirit. Northern evangelicals spurned Whig Winfield Scott as President in 1852 while warning of unholy plotting that heavily implicated the "slave power" as well as Catholics, immigrants, and liquor dealers. Now that slavery questions had been banished by the two political parties, even a vote for the much-diminished Free-Soilers was no longer a viable vote of conscience. Instead, it was a vote wasted. In 1844 and 1848, there had been clear antislavery options that had promised tangible political consequences to those who "voted as they prayed"—a choice between the Whigs and a competing third party. By 1852, however, all such options had vanished. The political outlets through which "Bible Belt" evangelicals had always addressed the problem of slavery had now abruptly closed. In their place arose volatile feelings of antiparty frustration and mounting desires to express building resentment. Little wonder that the new Fugitive Slave Law proved all but unenforceable in "Bible Belt" centers of Whig and abolitionist "codependency."[28]

All of which goes far to explain why *Uncle Tom's Cabin* attracted far more notice in 1852 than did the Whig presidential candidate Winfield Scott. Harriet Beecher Stowe captured perfectly the full indictment of slavery developed by Northern evangelicals over more than a decade. The book also offered an imaginative outlet for those who could no

---

27. Holt, *Political Crisis of the 1850s*, 101–38; Holt, *Rise and Fall of the American Whig Party*, 553–801.

28. David Brion Davis, *The Slave Power Conspiracy and the Paranoid Style* (Baton Rouge: Louisiana State University Press, 1969); Leonard L. Richards, *The Slave Power: The Free North and Southern Domination, 1780–1860* (Baton Rouge: Louisiana State University Press, 2000). Carwardine, *Evangelicals and Politics*, 199–234, gives a rich account of Northern evangelicals' political alienation in the early 1850s.

longer "vote as they prayed." Hers was a masterpiece of literary "fellow traveling." Quite likely Michael Holt is correct when concluding that after 1850 "most Americans" considered the question of slavery's extension as "permanently settled" and that they "expected never to have to confront that divisive question again." If so, the popularity of Stowe's novel makes clear that many in the North found this expectation deeply disturbing and looked beyond voting for new ways to express their disapproval. Resisting the Fugitive Slave Law constituted one such approach. Another was that taken by anticompromise Whigs, Democrats, and Free-Soil leaders. In state legislatures they arranged political deals that brought powerful "fellow travelers" into the U.S. Senate—Charles Sumner, Benjamin Franklin Wade, Salmon P. Chase, and Henry Wilson. Stowe's readers, opponents of the Fugitive Slave Law and politicians who created Senate seats for "fellow travelers" were all now approaching the two-party system as "passionate outsiders" had always urged, as steeped in corruption and ripe for transformation.[29]

The transformation, if that is what it was, began with the passage of the Kansas-Nebraska Act in 1854. Though antislavery ideology in the North now sustained itself independent of specific legislative enactments, the power to reignite open sectional conflicts remained in the hands of the politicians such as those who repealed the Missouri Compromise. Yet after more than a decade of voting as they prayed, a significant portion of the free-state electorate, its "Bible Belt" evangelicals, had just undergone an election cycle unlike any other—one that had deepened their fears and sent them seeking new outlets for expressing their resentments. Now, with the repeal of the 1820 Missouri Compromise, they looked all the more to politicians who would forcefully oppose slavery. Their defunct Whig Party had always encouraged them to expect this. More basic still, this was what they believed Christian conscience required. This is what their "codependent" relationship with abolitionists had been all about.

Commenting on the Republicans, the abolitionist editor Gamaliel

---

29. Quoted from Michael F. Holt, *The Fate of Their Country: Politicians, Slavery Extension, and the Coming of the Civil War* (New York: Oxford University Press, 2004), 91. For an overview of resistance and compliance to the Fugitive Slave Law, see Stanley Campbell, *The Slave Catchers: The Enforcement of the Fugitive Slave Law* (New York: W. W. Norton, 1970). For the selection of "fellow traveler" senators, see Gerteis, *Morality and Utility*, 99–105, 112–13, 121–24, 126–27.

Bailey observed in the mid-1850s that a "political party is not a church or a philanthropic association." It is not being argued here that the Republican Party came into being as a spontaneous expression of evangelical conscience and abolitionist agency. Far from it. The party of Lincoln was a coalition constructed from a welter of conflicting interests and ideologies that had little to do with the abolitionists.

For example, historians continue to assess the importance of the fleetingly powerful Know-Nothing Party in destroying the Whigs, disarranging the Democrats, and shaping the emerging Republicans. We are, moreover, only now beginning to understand the important roles that Northern Democrats and secular, antievangelical, working-class activists played in antislavery politics. The political impact within the United States of slavery and postemancipation conflicts in the greater Atlantic world also needs further study. So do the political implications of the abolitionists' direct attacks on Southern slavery, documented by Stanley Harrold. The most pressing and least understood questions of all involve the impact on party politics of Northern women, who intervened in free-state political culture so decisively during the 1840s and 1850s through evangelical churches, moral reform organizations, literary productions, and female academies and colleges. But whatever the mix of factors and unanswered questions, it is clear that secular political managers and insiders, not "religious virtuosos," presided over a Republican organization that had no incentive to collaborate with the abolitionists.[30]

Abolitionists quickly realized this. They complained bitterly about how far removed they found themselves from the new Republican mainstream. They lamented over how deeply infected the new party was with

---

30. Bailey quoted in Carwardine, *Evangelicals and Politics*, 253. Differing perspectives on the Know Nothing Party are found in Gienapp, *Origins of the Republican Party*; Holt, *Rise and Fall of the American Whig Party*; and Foner, *Free Soil, Free Labor, Free Men*. On secular and Democratic Party contributions to antislavery, see Earle, *Jacksonian Antislavery*. For direct abolitionist attacks on slavery, see Stanley Harrold, *Subversives: Antislavery Community in Washington, D.C., 1828–1865* (Baton Rouge: Louisiana State University Press, 2003). The literature on female activism and politics can be approached through Lori Ginzberg, *Women and the Work of Benevolence: Morality, Politics, and Class in the Nineteenth-Century United States* (New Haven: Yale University Press, 1990); Nancy Isenberg, *Sex and Citizenship in Antebellum America* (Chapel Hill: University of North Carolina Press, 1998); Susan Zaeske, *Signatures of Citizenship: Petitioning, Antislavery, and Women's Political Identity* (Chapel Hill: University of North Carolina Press, 2003); Michael D. Pierson, *Free Hearts and Free Homes: Gender and American Antislavery Politics* (Chapel Hill: University of North Carolina Press, 2003). Mary Kelley, *"Learning to Stand and Speak": The Making of Learned Women in Nineteenth-Century America* (Chapel Hill: University of North Carolina Press, 2006), offers the most comprehensive explanation to date for the widespread emergence of women into antebellum public life.

white supremacy and antiabolitionism. Republicans made every effort to ensure that this was precisely where the abolitionists would find themselves. Charged by slaveholders and by Northern Democrats that they, the Republicans, were themselves covert abolitionists and race "amalgamators," party leaders defended themselves by condemning the movement as vehemently as possible. Abolitionists suddenly found themselves playing the role of the Republicans' negative "reference group," precisely opposite from the role they had played in the politics of the Northern Whigs. All remaining ties between the abolitionist movement and electoral politics disintegrated, and abolitionist political agency within the two-party system collapsed.[31]

In its absence, as the 1850s wore on, abolitionists pursued scattered and highly individualistic actions. Some, like Garrison, openly yearned to join the Republicans: "If there were no moral barrier to our voting," he remarked in 1856, and "if we had a million votes to bestow, we would gladly give them all to the Republican Candidate." Most, however, condemned the new party. Wendell Phillips and Frederick Douglass gained unique celebrity as abolitionist emissaries to the public at large, filling lecture halls across the free states with audiences that cheered their charismatic calls to resistance. Countersubversion captured abolitionists' imaginations as never before. Vigilance committees styled themselves as latter-day Minutemen and Sons of Liberty. Some "religious virtuosos" contemplated the "righteous violence" of slave insurrection. Still others dreamed of a truly emancipationist political party or explored the efficacy of compensated emancipation. African American abolitionists felt ever more closely drawn to black nationalism, weighed the pros and cons of emigration, and practiced armed resistance against slave catchers.[32]

Times had changed profoundly since the 1840s. Back then, abolitionists involved in "Bible politics" had stimulated the North's two-party system to battle over the future of slavery and to question racial discrimination within the free states. Now, stripped of their electoral pertinence, politics seemed to offer them nothing. So instead, they resisted, yearned,

---

31. Sewell, *Ballots for Freedom*, 321–42.

32. Quotation from *Liberator*, July 11, 1856; Stauffer, *Black Hearts of Men*; Jeffrey Rossbach, *Ambivalent Conspirators: John Brown, the Secret Six, and a Theory of Slave Violence* (Philadelphia: University of Pennsylvania Press, 1982); Pease and Pease, *They Who Would Be Free*, 206–77.

and conspired. Congress meantime lurched from crisis to crisis while fears of the "slave power" continued to deepen and spread. What more empowering an environment could John Brown have asked for? In this respect, the collapse of their political agency, not its exercise, led abolitionists inspired by "righteous violence" to play their most obvious and most disruptive roles in bringing on Civil War.

The contrast between the abolitionists' marginalization in the later 1850s and the political potency of today's right-wing evangelicals could not be more obvious. For all their complaints of "oppression" by "secular society," contemporary conservative activists exercise power in the highest levels of governance. Take, for instance, the U.S. Supreme Court, where the "influence" of Pat Robertson and the rest goes far to determine what justices are to be confirmed and what the court itself is likely to decide. For the abolitionists during the 1850s, the equivalent would have been the historically unimaginable situation of figures like Thaddeus Stevens and Owen Lovejoy, not the likes of Lemuel Shaw and Roger B. Taney, defining federal law in the free states with respect to slavery. The compelling historical connections for right-wing evangelicals are again to slavery's defenders, not to the abolitionists.

In 1860 Wendell Phillips claimed far too much for abolitionist political agency when stating that his movement "gave these [Republicans] a cause to fight for and a platform to stand on. It put them in office. It gave them their votes." The better assessment was Gamaliel Bailey's caution that political parties should never be confused with churches. In no sense were the abolitionists directly responsible for the Republican vote in 1860. But Phillips's claim was not entirely unfounded. During the 1840s, the abolitionist movement had, indeed, given the Northern Whig Party a "cause to fight for and a platform to stand on," and this, in turn, had held important consequences for the Republicans.[33]

In the free-state "Bible Belt," during the 1840s, the "great, silent army of abolitionists" interacted constantly with evangelicals who took their religion to heart, generally voted Whig, and placed opposition to slavery high among their many moral concerns. Always attentive to this crucial group, Northern Whig politicians certainly did take the abolitionists

---

33. Wendell Phillips, *Speeches, Lectures, and Letters* (Boston: Higginson and Lee, 1863), 136–37.

and their religion seriously. In closely contested campaigns against the Democrats, party leaders responded to abolitionist opposition by defining their party as an emphatically antislavery organization. The actions of Whig "fellow travelers" softened distinctions between "abolitionism" and "antislavery." "Codependent" relationships with the abolitionists increased the Whigs' competitiveness. Party leaders responded to abolitionists by assuring evangelicals that voting Whig meant standing up to slavery. When the Whigs abruptly abandoned their guarantees, these evangelicals helped foster a political realignment that made unyielding opposition to slaveholders' claims a leading feature of the Republican Party. And finally, when the abolitionists' political agency ended after 1854, they directly threatened both slavery and the political process by transforming their movement into one that fostered countersubversion, confrontation, and violence.

In all these ways the abolitionists exercised more than enough political agency to justify much fuller index entries than they are currently allotted in books that explain the coming of the Civil War. They did not cause that conflict. They never came close to achieving their postmillennial vision—the godly revolution that would peacefully abolish slavery and inaugurate racial equality. The fate of religious virtuosos is almost always disappointment. Yet in an age when so many "voted as they prayed," abolitionists' activism led evangelicals to confirm that opposing slavery was a prime responsibility of Christian citizenship. That confirmation went far to ensure that as civil war drew closer, so did an ultimate reckoning with the "peculiar institution."

Index

Abdy, Edward, 192
abolitionist movement. *See also*
  Garrisonians; immediatism;
  individual abolitionists: British,
  185–186; continuing influence of,
  55–57; militancy increasing in, 5,
  16–19, 21, 24, 27–28, 85–86, 225;
  origins, 3–4; Republican Party and,
  222–225; respectability movement,
  suppression of, 36, 48; schism in, 17,
  52, 79, 158–161, 211; Whig Party
  codependency, 213–220
abolitionist political agency: collapse of,
  222–223, 225; scholarship on,
  205–207
abolitionists. *See also individual*
  abolitionists: aiding fugitive slaves,
  24–25; idealism of immediatists,
  12–13; interracial imperative of
  white, 47; motivation of white,
  25–26, 63–64, 89, 179
abolitionists, black: 1850s
  marginalization, 223; in immediatist
  movement, 13–14, 19–21;
  motivation, 62–64; political impact,
  215; redirection from uplift to racial
  independence, 54–55, 84–85
activism. *See also specific individuals:*
  female, 47, 211–212, 215, 222;
  interracial, 21–23, 46–47, 54, 61–

62, 84–88, 197–200. *see also* New
  Haven Negro College
Adams, Henry, 87
Adams, John Quincy, 51, 119–120,
  123, 133
African-Americans, freed. *See* free blacks
Alford, Julius, 130
Allen, Richard, 38, 173–174, 187
Allen Ephraim, 98
amalgamationism, 47, 48, 50, 78
America, post-Revolution, 20–21,
  175–181
American and Foreign Anti-Slavery
  Society, 17
American Anti-Slavery Society, 7, 17,
  159–161, 185
American Civil War, 27
American Colonization Movement,
  47
American Colonization Society, 11, 19,
  44, 76, 80, 176, 186, 195
American Missionary Association, 188
American Revolution, 86–88
Anti-Slavery Herald (newspaper), 82,
  195
Appeal to the Colored Citizens of the
  World (Walker), 12, 28, 36, 46, 180
Appleton, Nathaniel, 80
Astabula County Anti-Slavery Society,
  118

INDEX